Understanding Watchman Nee

Understanding Watchman Nee

Spirituality, Knowledge, and Formation

Dongsheng John Wu

WIPF & STOCK · Eugene, Oregon

UNDERSTANDING WATCHMAN NEE
Spirituality, Knowledge, and Formation

Wipf & Stock
An Imprint of Wipf and Stock Publishers
199 W. 8th Ave., Suite 3
Eugene, OR 97401

www.wipfandstock.com

ISBN 13: 978-1-61097-532-2

Manufactured in the U.S.A.

To My Father

and

In Memory of My Mother

Contents

Contents

Contents

Foreword

Watchman Nee (1903–1972) was one of the most important figures in Chinese Christianity during the twentieth century, and his writings continue to inspire evangelical Christians not only in China but also throughout the world. Founder and leader of an extensive "Local Church" movement in China, Nee was a prolific speaker and author who spent the last twenty years of his life in mainland China's prisons and labor camps. Despite his prominence and widespread influence, Nee is still not very well known outside of evangelical circles, and even some within that community have questioned the orthodoxy of his theological views. Dongsheng John Wu's insightful study provides a reliable introduction for those unfamiliar with Nee's spiritual teachings, along with a constructive reassessment of his writings (especially *The Spiritual Man*) that should challenge the critics to take another look at his theological anthropology.

Wu's bibliographical research is extensive, including all the relevant literature published both in Chinese and English. By combining a complex historical perspective with astute theological analysis, Wu situates Nee's spirituality firmly within the broad ecumenical tradition of Christian spirituality. This study begins with a concise presentation of Nee's biography and writings in the context of early twentieth-century Chinese history and culture, especially the development of evangelical Christianity. Then Wu carefully assesses the influence on Nee's theology from the Brethren tradition of Radical Reformation, the Holiness and Keswick revival movements, the Quietist mystics (e.g., Miguel de Molinos, Jeanne Guyon, and François Fénelon), and patristic allegorical interpretation of the Bible. In the following chapters, he offers a critical correlation of Nee and the contemporary Anglican theologian Mark

McIntosh on the critical topics of illumination, knowledge, and spiritual formation. By showing that aspects of Nee's theology that have sometimes been criticized as Gnostic or fideistic are in fact congruent with a broad range of mystical Christian authors as synthesized by McIntosh, Wu convincingly argues for Nee's status not only as an orthodox thinker, but as a significant contributor to Christian spirituality and theology with relevance for contemporary believers across the ecumenical spectrum.

This book will obviously be of interest to many evangelical Christians, regardless of their previous assessment of Nee's life and thought. But Wu's thorough and judicious analysis also has much to offer other scholars of Christian spirituality who will now have to include Watchman Nee in the canon of important spiritual theologians of the modern era. Nee took many of his key concepts from Western missionaries and teachers, but the mystical theology he forged owed just as much to his own creative intuition and pastoral experience, and might have been shaped by the philosophical and cultural traditions of China.

Dongsheng John Wu's work is an excellent example of the best interdisciplinary work now being done in the field of Christian spirituality. As Nee believed and this study demonstrates, there is an urgent need today for both scholars and Christian disciples to integrate intellectual inquiry with existential commitment. In Nee's words:

> If we did not have a mind, it would be impossible for the truth to reach our life. Therefore, an opened mind is very crucial to our spiritual life. If our mind is fully occupied with opinions, whether they are about the truth or about the person who preaches the truth, there will be no way for the truth to enter into our mind or life.[1]

Readers of many different backgrounds and interests who come to this study with an open mind will find themselves invited into a deeper appropriation of the cruciform way of discipleship, the mysterious truth at the heart of the universe, and the abundant life that is God's gift to humankind.

—**Arthur Holder**
Dean and Vice President for Academic Affairs
John Dillenberger Professor of Christian Spirituality
Graduate Theological Union
Berkeley, California

1. Nee, *The Spiritual Man*, 3:565.

Acknowledgments

THIS BOOK IS A revision of my doctoral dissertation. I am therefore especially grateful to my dissertation committee. Throughout the dissertation project, my supervisor Arthur Holder gave me enthusiastic help, support, and encouragement, from guiding me through the initial proposal, to going over every draft chapter promptly with great thoroughness and perceptive advice. Philip Wickeri was very kind to work with my schedule and always offered constructive suggestions. Wan Wei-yiu was so gracious in offering his valuable help and support.

I owe my debt of gratitude to the United Board for Christian Higher Education in Asia, for providing me the opportunity and financial aid of a 2006 IASACT (Institute for Advanced Study in Asian Cultures and Theologies) scholar, which enabled me to spend a concentrated six-week period in writing and research as well as interacting with other participant scholars. I am deeply thankful to my IASACT mentor Kenan Osborne for his insightful comments and generous assistance during the most critical period of my writing.

My profound gratitude goes to my family, friends, and pastors. My father has had great confidence in me and offered considerable understanding and support. The deep affection for and loving hope in me by my mother (1933–2003) have been most precious and invaluable. My sister Doreen has been a wonderful source of inspiration and support. My roommates at different points in my PhD studies have prayed for me consistently: Wang Haihong, Liu Guangtian, Henry Ma, and Cliff Govinden. I deeply appreciate the brothers and sisters in the small group who have prayed for me constantly during the last phase of my writing, including Jenny Lan, Arthur Wang, Caroline Chen, Hsiao Ya-Wen, Forest Yu, Tevin Tseng, and Elisa Liu. Dennis Xie has faithfully prayed with me for the last two to three years of my doctoral program. Pastors Grace Chiang and Rebecca Lu have given me valuable insights into Watchman Nee's life and thought. During this book's composing period, Pastor Joseph Qian's support and encouragement have meant very much to me. I especially need to thank Pastor Ernest Chan for believing in my call for teaching and writing, and for providing me an opportunity and space to fulfill such vocation. I owe my thanks to Pastor Ernest Chan also for suggestion of this book's title. In addition, Deborah Wan has helped to draw the diagram on page 89. And I would like to thank Nancy Shoptaw and Ian Creeger for their expertise and thoroughness during this book's editing and typesetting processes. I can never thank God enough for bringing around me this incredible array of people as well as providing me with all the grace I need to complete this work.

Note on Names and Terms

THE *PINYIN* SPELLING HAS been used for book titles, names of places, and most personal names except when quoting or citing from sources in which other spellings are used. Another exception for personal names is when referring to a writer of a published work, in which case the original spellings are followed.

A glossary of names and terms is listed at the end of this book. For each work in Chinese, the author's Chinese name and the Chinese title are also included in the bibliography.

Introduction

THROUGHOUT MUCH OF MY career as a graduate student in theology and Christian spirituality as well as my more recent vocations of teaching and pastoral ministry, I have often had a twin concern for both the intellectual pursuit and the spiritual quest. One of my underlying questions has been that of epistemology (or theory of knowing), namely, how does one know anything for certain with respect to the spiritual realm? Somewhere in the process I began to have a vague feeling that mere intellectual inquiry would not satisfy my restless seeking for meaning and certainty, and that there must be a kind of "spiritual knowing" (in contrast to rational knowing) that can bring about real meaning and true conviction. This vague feeling later became a clear belief as I was reading a variety of spiritual writings in the history of Christian spirituality as well as participating in a local Chinese church community that integrates different elements from the evangelical, the charismatic, and the contemplative or mystical traditions. Several questions then emerged for me: What does this kind of spiritual knowing look like? What is its place in the spiritual life, especially, what is its relationship with intellectual study or rational investigation? And further, how can one's capacity for such spiritual knowing be cultivated or fostered? With these "self-implicating"[1] questions in heart, I was drawn to the writings of Watchman Nee in twentieth-century China.

---

1. Sandra M. Schneiders's term suggesting that the academic study of spirituality, just like "psychology and art and some other fields," necessarily involves in some way the dimension of personal transformation. See Schneiders, "Hermeneutical Approach," 14.

NATURE, SCOPE, AND THESIS

Watchman Nee (Ni Tuosheng, 1903–1972) founded an indigenous Chinese church (the "Local Church") in the tradition of the Radical Reformation,[2] which by 1949 was estimated to have approximately 70,000 adherents dispersed over many provinces of China.[3] A characteristic feature in Nee's preaching and writings is his emphatic concern for the deeper spiritual life.[4] Nee's particular perspective is regarded as representing one of the three major theological approaches in China for the first half of the twentieth century.[5] Nee's books have also been widely circulated in the English-speaking world, and influential to different extents in America's renewal movements such as the prayer group movement, the Jesus People movement, and the charismatic movement.[6] Indeed, Nee's life, work, and writings have deeply influenced the thought and practice of modern Chinese Christians worldwide.[7] Yet Nee both inspires and confounds his readers. While many find his views helpful for their growth toward God, others see in Nee's teachings questionable ramifications for the theology and practice of the spiritual life. While some of Nee's views have provoked considerable controversy, to date there has not been one single scholarly volume published in English focusing on Nee's teachings of the spiritual life.

Scholars have pointed out that Nee's tripartite anthropology—which holds that the human person consists of three distinct components of body, soul, and spirit—is both the backbone of Nee's whole theology and the source of many perceivable tensions or problems.[8] Particularly noteworthy is Nee's insistence on a clear distinction between the spirit and the soul. Influenced by both the mystical and revivalist traditions, Nee identifies the spirit as corresponding to a person's God-consciousness or that which enables communication and communion with God, while

2. For the Radical Reformation, see George, "Radical Reformation," 334–71; and McClendon, *Witness*, 47–48, 326, 330–31.

3. J. Lee, "Little Flock Movement," 78.

4. Pamudji, "Little Flock Trilogy," 187.

5. Lam, "Huaren shenxue" [Chinese theology], 4–5.

6. Roberts, *Secrets of Watchman Nee*, xv.

7. G. Y. May, "Breaking of Bread," 2.

8. Liao Yuan-wei notes that scholars such as Paul Siu, Dennis Schiefelbein, Dana Roberts, Lam Wing-hung, and Lee Ken Ang all agree that "anthropology is the key to understanding Nee's theology as a whole." See Liao, "Nee's Theology of Victory," 3–4.

the soul represents the seat of one's personality that has the three basic functions of thinking, feeling, and willing. Nee holds that it is via the spirit—a distinct human faculty—that a person can receive divine revelation, by which Nee means a kind of intuitive spiritual knowledge, as opposed to conventional knowledge gained from either sense experiences or rational activities. Nee also equates the soul with the "self" and, referring to the Pauline language in Romans 7:22 and 2 Corinthians 4:16, Nee teaches that the soul and body together constitute the "outer person," while the spirit constitutes the "inner person." Further, Nee emphasizes the necessity of the "breaking" or losing of the outer person in order for the inner spirit to be "released" or liberated to govern the whole of a person's life. Basing this teaching on the New Testament pattern of Jesus's dying and rising, Nee stresses the importance of submitting to "the discipline of the Holy Spirit" in one's life circumstances in order to receive the grace of God. With the sharp divide between the spirit and the soul and with the apparent denigration of the mind's function as well as the self's role in the spiritual life, Nee's teachings have been perceived by different scholars as exhibiting an extreme polarity of the human and the divine, as well as containing strong anti-intellectual and Gnostic implications for both the belief and practice of the spiritual life.[9]

The critiques of Nee's thoughts are complex, yet a pervasive theme in Nee's writings (and in his own life experience) is the issue of divine revelation or illumination,[10] which has a crucial connection with his understanding of what it means to be a spiritual person. Exploring Nee's theology around the theme of divine revelation and illumination, then, can afford a promising perspective for evaluating the strengths and weaknesses in Nee's views. Also, as Nee's concern is with theological teachings for living a deeper spiritual life, an assessment of Nee's thoughts can be pursued in conversation with contemporary critical studies on spirituality and theology. The works of Mark A. McIntosh offer rich avenue for such a dialogue and evaluation.

9. See for example K. L. Leung, "Huaren nuosidi zhuyi" [Chinese Gnosticism], 189, 197, 248–64, esp. 255, and "Sanyuan renlun" [Trichotomistic anthropology], 196; Liao, "Nee's Theology of Victory," 203, and "Sanyuan renlun guan" [Tripartite anthropology], 102; and K. Lee, "Watchman Nee," 180–81.

10. See Henry, "Footnotes," cited in K. Lee, "Watchman Nee," 233. Carl Henry suggests that the term "revelation" used by Nee is more in line with the traditional theological notion of "illumination." Nee, however, uses both terms in similar contexts with some nuanced differences. We will look more at this distinction in chapter 3.

Mark A. McIntosh received a PhD in Theology in 1993 from the University of Chicago, and his dissertation was on the intersection of theology and spirituality in the Christology of Hans Urs von Balthasar. Since then he had been on the faculty of the Theology Department of Loyola University of Chicago until his recent move to the Britain. During that time he also served as a chaplain to the House of Bishops of the Episcopal Church of the USA, and as canon theologian to the twenty-fifth Presiding Bishop and Primate. McIntosh currently is Van Mildert Canon Professor of Divinity at Durham University, and canon residentiary of Durham Cathedral. McIntosh's research focuses on the interaction of theology and spirituality. He has been a contributor for some prominent dictionaries and reference works in theology and Christian spirituality, as well as producing several impressive monographs, including *Divine Teaching: An Introduction to Christian Theology* (2007), *Discernment and Truth: The Spirituality and Theology of Knowledge* (2004), *Mysteries of Faith* (2000), *Mystical Theology: The Integrity of Spirituality and Theology* (1998), and *Christology from Within: Spirituality and the Incarnation in Hans Urs von Balthasar* (1996). McIntosh thus describes the aim of his own inquires: "If I'm focusing on mystical thought per se, or spiritual discernment, or on what it could mean to sense all creation as alive with divine intent and to see all things in God (as with the divine ideas tradition), in all such questions I'm seeking to elucidate how we might understand the beliefs of Christian faith more deeply—precisely by considering them in the light of spiritual traditions and mystical thought."[11] The works of McIntosh are replete with insightful studies of the history of mystical theology as well as penetrating analysis of the relation between spirituality and theology, and so can be employed as a helpful lens toward evaluating the soundness of Nee's teachings as well as examining specific scholarly controversies about Nee's thoughts. This way of studying Nee also leads to new possibilities for assessing the truthfulness and intelligibility of Nee's spirituality and spiritual theology.

In looking into Nee's perspective through the lens of McIntosh, my interest lies in gaining greater clarity toward some ambivalent points regarding the meaning, significance, and practicability of spiritual knowledge in the spiritual life. Centered upon the theme of revelation or illumination, McIntosh and Nee can be brought into a critical and constructive dialogue in three closely related issues and

---

11. See Durham University, "Staff Profile."

concerns. First, McIntosh articulates a view of spiritual knowledge that is situated within a broadly Augustinian tradition of divine illumination theory, which in turn has rapport with significant studies on the Pauline notion of "the mind of Christ." It can be demonstrated that there are enough substantial similarities between McIntosh's understanding of divine illumination and Nee's idea of revelation to suggest that Nee's view is intelligible within this broadly Augustinian tradition. Seen in this light, the Gnostic tendencies in Nee's views perceived by his critics are more apparent than real.

Secondly, McIntosh's analysis of the relationship between spirituality and theology yields rich insights for an assessment of Nee's views on the relation between intellectual and spiritual knowledge, as well as for an evaluation of the criticism of anti-intellectualism in Nee's teachings. For instance, McIntosh expounds on a major strand of the Christian apophatic traditions which sees the infinite reality of God as calling for a renunciation of one's ordinary ways of knowing so that, by means of an abandonment to love, one can come to the only truthful knowledge of God possible. In light of this Christian apophatic tradition, then, Nee's thought can be shown to be not, as some of his critics perceive, anti-intellectual, but rather, in congruence with the Christian mystical tradition.

Thirdly, McIntosh suggests that a more bodily, participatory involvement in the Christian community—after the trinitarian pattern of self-giving love that discloses historically in the life, death, and resurrection of the Incarnate Son—is the great prerequisite for the transformation of the would-be discerners for divine knowledge. Here, analogous to the apophasis of the cross, self-surrender to God results in the only kind of "knowledge" of God possible; such self-loss, paradoxically, is a fulfillment of the true self-in-relation-with God and others. This matrix of Christian spirituality can serve as a framework to explore the perceived tension between the human will and the divine will in Nee's writings.

In sum, this book explores the sometimes-controversial views of Watchman Nee on divine illumination or spiritual knowing, its relation with theological studies, and its connection with spiritual transformation. This project begins by synthesizing strategic aspects of Nee's teachings as well as formative events and sources in the development of Nee's own spirituality and theology. It then utilizes the critical work of contemporary theologian Mark McIntosh to bring Nee's views into conversation with some major voices in the history of Christian spirituality. The thesis of this book is this: By bringing Watchman Nee's views of divine illumination, theological knowledge, and spiritual formation into dialogue with Mark McIntosh's studies on theology and history of spirituality, Nee's crucial theological convictions can be shown to have strong parallels with related themes found in the treasures of the church's spiritual or mystical traditions, and some major weaknesses in Nee's thoughts that his critics perceived can be overcome or substantially ameliorated. Therefore Nee's spiritual teachings are significant and relevant for the spiritual formation of contemporary believers.

METHODOLOGY, STRUCTURE, AND SIGNIFICANCE

I will explore Nee's spirituality and theology and investigate scholarly critiques of Nee's views from the perspective of Christian spirituality, as understood by McIntosh in terms of "a journey in the Spirit into the ever greater freedom, love, and generosity of Jesus's relationship with the one he called Abba."[12] This study draws on the methodology for studying spirituality articulated by Sandra M. Schneiders as the hermeneutical approach, which is inherently interdisciplinary and includes three dimensions: description, critical analysis, and constructive interpretation.[13]

On the dimension of description, I will synthesize available research and studies on Nee in order to have an understanding of the various milieux in which Nee's spirituality emerges. I will take into account the textual witness to Nee's life experiences, the historical setting of early- to mid-twentieth-century China, the missionary and ecclesiological environment before and during Nee's time, and the different theological sources of influence for Nee's spirituality. On the level of critical analysis, I will analyze the works of both Nee and McIntosh with both a "hermeneutics of consent" and a "hermeneutics of suspicion" by letting the strangeness of the texts raise challenges on the one hand and, on the other, by asking critical questions related to their historical, cultural, and theological contexts.[14] On the level of constructive interpretation, I will engage Nee and McIntosh in a critical dialogue in the sense that their

12. McIntosh, "Trinitarian Perspectives," 179.

13. Schneiders, "Hermeneutical Approach," 12–13.

14. Sheldrake, *Spirituality and History*, 180–84; and Principe, "Broadening the Focus," 1, 3–5.

conversation will attempt the task of "mutual illuminations and corrections" and "possible basic reconciliation."[15]

This book is divided into two parts: part 1 is the preliminary part
for description of the background materials, and part 2 is the substantive
part for critical analysis and constructive interpretation. Part 1 consists
of chapters 1 and 2. Chapter 1 first offers a survey of Nee's time in the
contexts of Christianity in China as well as China in its modern era, and
then provides an overview of Nee's life and work, focusing on several key
spiritual experiences of his life. Chapter 2 is a survey of different theological sources of influence on Nee, both identifiable direct influences
and likely, but perhaps indirect, influences on Nee's theology and spirituality. The methodology employed in these two chapters is more in the
descriptive mode, drawing from some studies on the history of China
and the history of Christianity in China, from a number of biographies
and studies on Nee, and from different works on the particular sources
that influence Nee's theological and spiritual outlook.

Part 2 of this book—consisting of chapters 3 to 5—is a sustained
attempt to substantiate this book's thesis, namely, Nee's major theological convictions on spiritual knowledge and spiritual formation can be
shown to have strong parallels with related aspects in the Christian spiritual traditions, and some major perceived tensions in Nee's views can be
overcome or substantially ameliorated. While there have been a number
of dissertations and other studies written on Nee, there has not been an
in-depth analysis of Nee's views of divine revelation and illumination as
related to the spiritual life. Also, as far as I can tell, there has not been
any substantial study written on McIntosh. Thus a major portion of each
of these three chapters is devoted to the expositions of the respective
views of Nee and McIntosh. These three chapters follow a similar structure comprising three distinct sections. Each chapter first begins with
an exposition of Nee's views on relevant issues without engaging in an
evaluation, then continues with a comparable exposition of McIntosh's
thoughts on related concerns, and finally proceeds to a constructive dialogue between Nee and McIntosh in an attempt to assess the soundness
and intelligibility of Nee's theology and spirituality.

The conversation between Nee and McIntosh in these three chapters—chapters 3, 4, and 5—is engaged in three different aspects respectively, each corresponding roughly to the three questions of *what, why,*

15. Tracy, *Blessed Rage for Order,* 32.

and *how* underlining the theme of divine revelation or illumination. Broadly speaking, chapter 3 attempts to answer such questions as "What does divine revelation or illumination look like?" and "What role does it play in the spiritual life?" This chapter deals with some basic issues about the characteristics and functions of revelation and illumination in the context of the spiritual life journey. This chapter also examines the alleged Gnostic tendencies in Nee's views. Chapter 4 explores such issues as "Why is divine illumination or revelation a significant concern for the spiritual life, especially as compared with the conventional way of knowing through intellectual studies?" This chapter considers the differences between spiritual knowledge gained through revelation or illumination and conceptual knowledge acquired via rational inquiry, as well as the various roles that the mind plays in the spiritual journey. This chapter also probes into the charge of anti-intellectualism in Nee's teachings. Chapter 5 tackles such problems as "How can divine revelation and illumination be better received?" or "How can one foster one's discerning capacity for better receiving such revelation and illumination?" This chapter looks into the crucial link between discernment and spiritual maturity, as well as some ways that personal transformation may best be pursued. This chapter also considers the apparent tension between the human will and the divine will in Nee's writings.

In these three substantive chapters, the frequent quotes from both Nee and McIntosh are intended not only to provide evidence from primary sources, but also as an attempt to practice the "theological hermeneutics" as proposed by McIntosh. In McIntosh's view, spiritual writings should be conceived as mystical (or hidden) speeches that contain a "superabundance of meaning" or "apophatic momentum" that cannot simply be abstracted or paraphrased.[16] McIntosh believes that spiritual texts are "not ultimately descriptions of objects but invitations to particular ways of life," thus the theological meaningfulness of such texts lays not "in a 'finished' product of definitions or formulas but in the 'unfinished' activity of orienting the believer towards God."[17] McIntosh therefore suggests that in order to access the "maximum value" of such texts, one needs to pay attention to their "particularities of imagery, structure and language,"[18] and to be ready to allow one's own

---

16. McIntosh, *Mystical Theology*, 123.

17. Ibid., 145, 142.

18. Ibid., 122.

framework of understanding to be altered or transformed: "To enter into the meaning of a mystical text is to allow one's own categories for understanding and experiencing reality to be given over—perhaps broken—certainly to be transformed, by the reality of the other who is always beyond oneself."[19]

For the expositions of McIntosh's thoughts, I rely mainly on his three works on spirituality and theology, namely, *Discernment and Truth*, *Mystical Theology*, and *Mysteries of Faith*. For primary sources by Nee, I choose as my main focus of this study his books *The Spiritual Man*, *The Breaking of the Outer Man and the Release of the Spirit*, and *The Normal Christian Life*, supplemented by several other relevant works. *The Spiritual Man* is the only book Nee wrote—completed during his early years—with the intent to systematically synthesize his theology of the human person (other works in the sixty-six volumes of Nee's *Collected Works* are usually compiled from his sermons and from articles he wrote for newspapers, periodicals, or other special publications).[20] *The Breaking of the Outer Man and the Release of the Spirit* is a shorter work on some similar topics that Nee preached toward the end of his public career. *The Normal Christian Life* is, among Nee's works, the most widely circulated book, which has been translated into more than thirty languages.[21] These three works are also that which have aroused much scholarly attention and discussions.

Nee's spirituality is significant in that it integrates to some extent different elements from both the evangelical and the mystical traditions, and it does so in a contextualized Chinese way. Yet many critiques of Nee come from evangelical or conservative scholars who habitually assume that anything "mystical" is incompatible with authentic Christian faith. On the other hand, some intellectually-minded Protestants tend to look with suspect at Nee's theological outlook, especially because of his anti-denominational stance. In particular, Nee's notions of divine revelation and illumination have been viewed as too

---

19. Ibid., 135.

20. *The Collected Works of Watchman Nee* are available in both Chinese and English, and most of the volumes are also available online. Most of Nee's works were originally written and published in Chinese, but a few of them were first published in English, including *The Normal Christian Life*, *What Shall This Man Do?*, and *Sit, Walk, Stand*.

21. G. Y. May, "Breaking of Bread," 2n4.

enthusiastic or too slippery for any objective control for many believers across different Christian persuasions.

Mark McIntosh's voice is important in the West as part of some mainline theologians' effort to return mystical theology to the heart of the Christian orthodox tradition. By looking at Nee's perspective through the lens of McIntosh's works, this book brings Nee's voice into dialogues with some important figures in the history of Christian spirituality. By doing so, this study situates Nee's views within the rich heritage of the Protestant, Catholic, and Eastern Orthodox spiritual traditions, and thus renders Nee's thoughts more intelligible to Christians of both evangelical and more liberal persuasions. By showing there are strong parallels between Nee's views and those found in the treasures of church history, this book also responds to some unsympathetic critics of Nee's, and rehabilitates the practicality and significance of Nee's teachings for the spiritual life of contemporary believers. Particularly, in the related areas of divine illumination, theological knowledge, discernment, and spiritual transformation, critical interpretations and judgments will be offered that will have explicit or implicit relevance for the spiritual formation of ordinary believers as well as theological students and teachers. This book will therefore be helpful for pastors, students, teachers, scholars, and others who are interested in the theology and practice of Christian spiritual and intellectual formations. This book will also be of value for evangelical believers to reevaluate their attitudes toward the mystical strand of the broad Christian tradition as well as to re-source the spiritual legacy within the evangelical tradition. My hope is that the fruit of this study will also lessen the tension between Nee's Local Church tradition and other Protestant groups, and will facilitate the building of the bonds of love among various Christian communities.

PART ONE

Background

1

Turbulence and Emergence

The Context and Life of Watchman Nee

NEE'S HISTORICAL CONTEXT

WATCHMAN NEE (1903–1972) LIVED through an age of great upheavals. His life span journeyed across four of the five "revolutionary civil wars" (except the Taiping Uprising of 1851–1868) in the last two centuries of China's history. These four wars or revolutions were: (1) the Republic Revolution of 1911, (2) the Northern Expedition of 1926–1927, (3) the Nationalist-Communist civil war of 1945–1949, and (4) Mao's Cultural Revolution of 1966–1976.[1] Furthermore, Nee also lived through other major political and social events such as the May Fourth Movement of 1919 and the anti-Christian movement of the 1920s, as well as the eight-year Sino-Japanese war in 1937–1945. Nee's life in the first half of twentieth-century China also witnessed different Protestant mission developments, and the burgeoning indigenous church movement in which Nee himself played a notable part.

Christianity in China and China in Its Modern Age

Christian mission efforts in China before the mid-nineteenth century were sporadic. It is uncertain as to when Christianity first entered

---

1. The five civil wars are noted in Fairbank, *Great Chinese Revolution*, cited in Liao, "Nee's Theology of Victory," 10. See also Brook, "Toward Independence," 317–19.

China.[2] One tradition maintains that the missionary work in China goes back to St. Thomas the apostle, but Kenneth Scott Latourette notes that no historical evidence exists to corroborate with any suggestions that Christianity was in the empire before the Tang dynasty (618–907).[3] There is reliable information that in 635, Nestorian missionaries from Mesopotamia and Central Asia came to China, but their major propagation lasted only to 845, and it is doubtful that they left "any permanent influence on Chinese life and thought."[4]

Then in 1294 the first Roman Catholic missionary reached the then Mongol-ruled China, beginning the Franciscan mission work, which survived in the Yuan dynasty till the middle of the fourteenth century.[5] The third attempt to evangelize the Middle Kingdom began with the Jesuit Francis Xavier who was nonetheless forbidden to enter mainland China and died near Macau in 1552. Xavier was followed by other Jesuit priests, among them the Italian Matteo Ricci, who was finally allowed to set foot on Chinese soil in 1582. With much labor and prudence, Ricci introduced Western scientific learning to China and found a warm reception among Chinese officials. Subsequently other able Jesuit scientists and philosophers came in and had great influence on the Chinese court. However, the issue of Chinese ancestor worship brought about what is known as the "Rites Controversy," which developed into an intense conflict of authority between the Pope and the Chinese emperor. Eventually, in 1724 an imperial edict was issued to expel from China all Catholic missionaries (except for a few who attached to the Bureau of Astronomy in Beijing), and Chinese believers were commanded to renounce their faith. The number of Catholics in China, in 1800, was estimated to be between two hundred thousand and two hundred fifty thousand.[6] The influence of the Russian Orthodox Church's missionaries in China, according to Latourette, was so small that it can be neglected, although it is

2. Latourette, *History of Christian Missions*, 48; and Z. Wang, *Zhongguo jidujiao* [Christianity in China], 22.

3. Latourette, *History of Christian Missions*, 46–48. Wang Zhixin, however, believes that there was a Christian presence in China as early as 411. See Z. Wang, *Zhongguo jidujiao* [Christianity in China], 25–26.

4. Latourette, *History of Christian Missions*, 55.

5. Z. Wang, *Zhongguo jidujiao* [Christianity in China], 45–49.

6. Cohen, "Missions and their Impact," 543–47; Z. Wang, *Zhongguo jidujiao* [Christianity in China], 54–70; and Chao, *China Mission*, 17–19.

notable that their scholarship contributed to the interpretation of China to the Russian people.[7]

Protestant mission in China began in the nineteenth century, fueled by the Evangelical Revival in Great Britain and the Great Awakening in America. In 1807 the first Protestant missionary, Robert Morrison (1782–1834) of the London Missionary Society, arrived in China. By 1840, there were more than twenty Protestant missionaries in China, but the Chinese who had been baptized were fewer than one hundred. This was a foundation-laying period that produced a sizable Christian literature in Chinese. For instance, Morrison, with the assistance of William Milne, completed a translation of the entire Bible in 1819, and later produced the first Chinese-English dictionary. Another form of literary work was by way of introducing China to the West, including information on the life, conditions, and mission works in China. During this early period, two other important fields of Protestant activity were medicine and education.[8]

Beginning with the two Opium Wars around the mid-1800s, China's door—after many years of self-imposed closure—was forced to open to Western powers that were attracted by the lure of trade in this Oriental "sleeping beauty." Yet along with profit-oriented traders and privilege-minded diplomats and soldiers, also came the missionaries who were "at least ostensibly, to serve the interests of the Chinese."[9] Britain waged the first Opium War against China in 1839, for China's refusal to allow the import of opium. This war ended in 1842 with China's defeat and the signing of the Treaty of Nanjing, through which China ceded Hong Kong to Britain, and opened five seaports for foreign trade: Shanghai, Ningbo, Fuzhou, Xiamen, and Guangzhou. Within these open ports, foreigners were given express permission to erect churches. This new treaty and other edicts issued in following years facilitated considerably both Catholic and Protestant mission operations. Many British and American missionaries, including Hudson Taylor (who founded the China Inland Mission) from England, came to China and began to establish their work there.[10] A few years later in 1858, China lost again in the second Opium War (against Britain and France)—this

7. Latourette, *History of Christian Missions*, 825.

8. Cohen, "Missions and their Impact," 547–48.

9. Ibid., 543.

10. Ibid, 550–52; and Chao, *China Mission*, 19–20.

time signing the Treaty of Tianjin, which further enhanced Europe's trade position and granted foreigners rights to travel throughout the land. Consequently China was flooded with "more ship loads of opium," despite protests among British as well as Chinese citizens.[11] The Sino-French Treaty of Tianjin revolutionized the position of all Christian missions in China. The treaty formally rescinded all previous official announcements against Christianity, guaranteeing the freedom for Catholic priests to propagate their religion anywhere in China as well as the right for the Chinese people to practice Christianity. Because of the most-favored-nation clauses, Protestant missionaries also enjoyed these treaty privileges. As missionaries expanded in their multifold mission of evangelistic, medical, educational, and social work, by 1900 there were more than seven hundred thousand Catholics as well as approximately one hundred thousand Protestants in China.[12]

In 1895 China lost its first war with Japan; this humiliation triggered a short-lived (one-hundred-day) political reform movement in 1898. At the same time mounting pressure from colonial powers to partition China's major cities for more concessions flamed the fire for a national anti-foreign riot. In 1890 the anti-foreign and anti-Christian Boxer Uprising broke out and killed about two hundred missionaries and thousands of Chinese Christians. All this political and cultural disintegration finally led to Sun Zhongshan's (Sun Yat-sen) Republic Revolution in 1911, which announced the demise of the two millennia monarchial rule in China. Yet the dream of national renewal was soon shattered, for the newly born republic was facing both strong warlords competing from inside and the now powerful Japan pressing from outside.[13]

Meanwhile, the traditional civil service examination system that had lasted for over one thousand years was abolished in 1905; consequently there was a growing tendency for the intellectually-minded young to seek education abroad as well as in local schools run by missionaries. As this new generation of Chinese intellectuals was emerging, many of them were searching hard as to what, apart from political revolution, could indeed save China. Some new intellectuals in Beijing, many of whom

---

11. G. Y. May, "Breaking of Bread," 21.

12. Cohen, "Missions and their Impact," 552–59.

13. K. L. Leung, *Fu lin zhonghua* [Blessing upon China], 116, 125; and Chao, *China Mission*, 21.

had returned from studying abroad, concluded that the problem lay in the ignorance and slumber of the people. Thus in 1915 these intellectuals initiated what was later known as the New Culture Movement, which was then extended into the early 1920s. The movement was marked by a critical attitude toward traditional Chinese culture especially the orthodoxy of Confucianism, and a welcoming openness toward all Western ideas and values, especially science and democracy. Christianity, for a period of time, was also entertained as one possible alternative to save China, and enjoyed some development for its missions in literature and evangelization as well as in education, medicine, and other philanthropic works.[14] Many Protestants attempted to combat various kinds of suffering and evils in both the Christian community and the nation at large. As Latourette notes: "Famine relief, the campaign against opium, public health, popular education, the movement against foot-binding, education of the blind and the deaf, anti-gambling and anti-prostitution crusades, and efforts for better labor conditions are only a few of the many activities which were either begun or substantially supported by Protestants."[15] Daniel H. Bays also speaks of a "conspicuous growth in the sheer size of the Protestant church in China" during the first quarter of the twentieth century.[16]

The New Culture Movement both paved the way for and overlapped with the May Fourth Movement. Chow Tse-tsung defined the May Fourth Movement as the 1917 to 1921 period with two phases separated by the 1919 May Fourth Incident (an anti-imperialist and patriotic demonstration of the young intellectuals in Beijing). The first phase was mainly within intellectual circles with some new intellectuals' effort to instill their ideas to the students, and the second phase was principally the students' "all-out attack on tradition and conservatism" which was carried to other sectors of the society.[17] Chow describes the movement as "a complicated phenomenon including the 'new thought tide,' the literary revolution, the student movement, the merchants' and workers' strikes, and the boycott against Japan, as well as other social and political activities of the new intellectuals, all inspired by the patriotic sentiments

14. K. Li et al., *Zhongguo jindai shi* [Modern history of China], 313, 477–86; K. L. Leung, *Fu lin zhonghua* [Blessing upon China], 123–35; and Chao, *China Mission*, 22.

15. Latourette, *History of Christian Missions*, 829.

16. Bays, "Independent Christianity," 307–8.

17. Chow, *May Fourth Movement*, 6.

after the Twenty-one Demands and the Shantung resolution, and by the spirit of Western learning and the desire to reevaluate tradition in the light of science and democracy in order to build a new China."[18]

While the May Fourth Movement contained cross currents of intellectual and socio-political activities, Chow maintains that it was essentially an intellectual revolution because it was led by intellectuals to the precipitation of a nationwide intellectual transformation, which was deemed a prerequisite for the modernization of the nation. Along with a critical spirit toward tradition and authority, individual and independent judgment was highly valued. Especially in the early stage of the May Fourth period, the young intellectuals' minds were infused with a pluralism of ideology, including idealism, realism, rationalism, empiricism, pragmatism, utilitarianism, liberalism, and agnosticism. These individualistic and pluralistic streams, however, were later overwhelmed by the rising tides of nationalism and socialism, which set their aim on building a strong nation-state that could deliver its people from their manifold crisis and suffering.[19] Such vision of national emancipation partly contributed to the founding of the Communist Party of China (CPC) in 1921.

Amidst the waves of nationalism and modernization, an anti-Christian movement broke out in 1922, which, at least partly, led to the subsequent indigenous movement of the Chinese church. These two movements had significant impacts on Chinese Christianity as well as on Nee's life and work, so both movements will be looked at more closely in the next section. Meanwhile, in 1925 China witnessed an anti-imperialist upsurge triggered by the May thirtieth shooting of Shanghai demonstrators by British police. This event, Jessie Gregory Lutz judges, demonstrated the need for political parties with military force, and became the turning point for many activists of nationalism to shift their attention from cultural transformation to political revolution.[20]

As the pluralism and openness of the early May Fourth Movement was gradually replaced by nationalism and the perceived responsibility of the modern state, the Guomindang (the Nationalists) "viewed itself as custodian of the national orthodoxy," and maintained that "citizens

18. Ibid., 5.

19. Ibid., 358–61.

20. Lutz, *Politics and Christian Missions*, 7.

must be nationalized and socialized in the one correct teaching."[21] The Educational Rights Movement (ca. 1924–1925) then targeted the parochial mission schools for purging their "cultural imperialism."[22]

During the years of 1924 and 1927 the Guomindang and the Communists collaborated in an effort to get rid of the warlords and to combat their imperialist supporters, which led to the 1926–1927 Northern Expedition that later declared its success in 1928. The greater part of China was finally united under Jiang Jieshi's (Chiang Kai-shek) Guomindang government.[23] From 1928 to 1937, then, the Guomindang ruled from Nanjing and the government adopted a more cooperative attitude toward Christianity.[24]

From 1937 to 1945, China was under an eight-year period of occupation by the Japanese army. During this interval, the indigenous and independent movement of the church was thrust forward due to different factors including the withdrawal and imprisonment of missionaries, the cutting off of Western financial supports, the forced unification of churches in cities under Japanese rule (church union itself was an act of independence from Western denominationalism), and the development of the church in interior China where many evacuated people and refugees had come. Despite all the turmoil of wartime, church adherents grew from about 560,000 in 1936 to nearly seven hundred thousand in 1945.[25] After Japan's unconditional surrender in 1945, most foreign missionaries went back to their original fields of work, and many churches again relied on foreign (especially American) funding because of the destitute postwar situations in China. About a year after the Japanese defeat, the conflict between the Guomindang and the Communists broke out into full scale civil war, which continued until 1949 when the Guomindang fled to Taiwan and Mao Zedong established the People's Republic of China.[26]

21. Ibid., 279–80.

22. Ibid., 281.

23. Hsu, *Rise of Modern China*, 523–35, esp. 531.

24. Varg, *Missionaries, Chinese and Diplomats*, 211; and Yuan, *Zhongguo jiaohui shi* [Chinese church history], 34–35. Yuan notes that the Guomindang's change of attitude toward Christianity was undoubtedly influenced by the recent marriage of their president Jiang Jieshi (Chiang Kai-shek) to Song Meiling, who was from a Christian family.

25. Brook, "Toward Independence," 317–37.

26. K. L. Leung, *Fu lin zhonghua* [Blessing upon China], 179; Yuan, *Zhongguo jiaohui shi* [Chinese church history], 43; and Chao, *China Mission*, 23.

Meanwhile, a small group of Protestants had concurred with the Marxist critique of society for some years, and after 1949, they began to assume the role of communicating between the Communists and the churches.[27] The Three-Self Movement ("self-governing, self-supporting, and self-propagating") then was organized in the early 1950s, entertaining "the possibility of Christian-Communist cooperation."[28] Under the leadership of Wu Yaozong (Y. T. Wu, 1893–1979), a "Christian Manifesto" was published in July 1950, and was eventually signed by some 417,000 Chinese Protestants.[29] The manifesto calls the churches to sever their links with foreign imperialism as well as to a "deeper understanding" of Christianity in the "New Age." As Philip L. Wickeri notes, the manifesto "combines what was important for resolving the question of religion and patriotism from the CPC viewpoint with an insistence on the necessity of 'Love-Country-Love-Church' in Chinese Christianity."[30]

Then a denunciation movement followed to purge any imperialist and anti-revolutionary taint. As M. Searle Bates notes, with the tremendous nationalist and anti-imperialist appeal, "the Communists and the intermediary Three-Self Committee were able to induce . . . a flood of repudiations of the American and other 'imperialist' connections of Christianity, often personalized in well-known missionaries."[31]

By 1958, many churches were closed or merged with other churches. For instance, the 240 odd Protestant churches in Shanghai were merged into about twenty, the sixty-some churches in Beijing were reduced to four, and Guangzhou's situation was similar to Beijing's.[32] Let us now turn back to the earlier part of the century to look more closely at the anti-Christian movement and the Chinese church's endeavor in indigenization, so as to gain a better understanding of the context of Nee's life and work amidst the struggles of Christianity in China.

---

27. Bates, "China," 216.

28. Wickeri, *Common Ground*, 127.

29. Ibid., 129–31.

30. Ibid., 130–31.

31. Bates, "China," 217.

32. Ibid., 221.

The Anti-Christian Movement and the Chinese Church's Indigenous Effort

The anti-Christian movement in the 1920s and the subsequent indigenous effort of the Chinese church drastically changed the landscape of Christianity in China. Paul A. Cohen notes that anti-Christian attitude in China can be traced back to long before the Opium Wars. At least from the Sung dynasty on, as state power was becoming inseparably tied to Neo-Confucianism orthodoxy, heterodoxy in China was defined as any ideologies that presented presumably considerable cultural, social, and political threat. There was also a tendency to xenophobia—fear of foreigners or anything strange—that always existed (one can think of foreigners being sometimes referred to as *gui*, meaning demons). The propagation of Christianity in the late sixteenth century, with its foreign origin as well as its contradiction with Confucianism, quite naturally became a suspect for heterodoxy. There were literary outbursts against Christianity in the late Ming and early Qing periods (seventeenth century). In 1724, Christianity was officially declared a forbidden sect and evangelism was proscribed. The heterodox and dangerous character of the Christian religion was confirmed in the mind of many Chinese, especially in light of the Taiping movement (1850–1864) that was influenced by certain Christian doctrines.[33] While the Emperor's prohibition against Christian mission was repealed by the post-Opium War treaties (mid-nineteenth century), the anti-Christian hostility continued with the eruption of "hundreds of separate and localized attacks on missions and Chinese converts" between the 1860s and 1880s.[34]

This "long-standing tradition" of anti-foreign and anti-Christian attitude was carried forward into the twentieth century; only it was now "shaped more by anger than fear, more by modern nationalism than by old-style xenophobia."[35] Years of Western unequal treatment and injustice brooded in the Chinese minds a deep resentment toward any sign of foreign presence. May Fourth expressed many educated youth's "totalistic rejection of conventional authority"; thus the initial attacks on Confucianism soon became a condemnation of any religion including

---

33. Cohen, "Missions and their Impact," 560–63; and Lutz, *Politics and Christian Missions*, 1.

34. Lutz, *Politics and Christian Missions*, 2.

35. Cohen, "Missions and their Impact," 560, 590.

Christianity.[36] The anti-Christian movement was germinated in the soil of the era's nationalism. For China had suffered long with wars, poverty, sicknesses, corruption, and humiliation; in the beginning of the twentieth century, the Middle Kingdom became increasingly aware of its own economic, political, and military impotence. There was then an emergence of a tremendous nationwide energy for rebuilding a new and strong nation-state that could suppress internal turmoil as well as for withstanding foreign transgressions. "Salvation of the nation" or "national regeneration" thus became the clarion call with a religious urgency and a unifying power for many divergent groups of people.[37] In the early 1920s, then, amidst the mixed torrents of Chinese nationalism and modernization, Christianity was perceived as irrational, anti-scientific, and imperialistic "opium" from the West for deceiving the people and denationalizing the country.

Consequently an anti-Christian movement broke out in 1922; it was later renewed and became more intense during the years 1924 to 1927.[38] This was the period of collaboration between Guomindang and the Communist Party of China. During their 1926 to 1927 Northern Expedition, missionaries and believers were persecuted by the soldiers as well as the students.[39] By the summer of 1927, nearly all of the eight thousand Protestant missionaries were evacuated from China's interior either to the treaty ports or (about five thousand of them) to Japan and the Philippines.[40] According to Leung Ka-lun, however, the anti-Christian movement for the most part was not carried out through violent means, but rather by means of intellectual debates and through propaganda in literature, public speeches, and demonstrative parades; for this reason its influence persisted in many Chinese minds decades after the 1920s.[41]

As the anti-Christian movement raised serious questions about whether being a Christian and being a Chinese could be compatible,

36. Lutz, *Politics and Christian Missions*, 3.

37. Lam, *Chinese Theology*, 52–53, 119.

38. Latourette, *History of Christian Missions*, 813.

39. Liao, "Nee's Theology of Victory," 15–17; and Chao, *China Mission*, 22–23.

40. Yip, *Religion, Nationalism and Chinese Students*, cited in Liao, "Nee's Theology of Victory," 17; Chao, *China Mission*, 22; and cf. Latourette, *History of Church Missions*, 699.

41. K. L. Leung, *Fu lin zhonghua* [Blessing upon China], 153.

Chinese Christians were groping for responses to three related sets of questions or concerns. First, relevance for society: is Christianity really the "opium" that makes one concerned only with the afterlife and so neglectful of the affairs of this world? Or how can Christianity contribute to the life of the Chinese people here and now? Secondly, relationship with the nation: as China was in a desperate situation politically, economically, and socially, what is Christianity's role, if any, in saving and rebuilding the country? Thirdly, indigenization: as Christianity came into China in recent history with the help of imperial invasions accompanied by unequal or dehumanizing treaties, what sides are Christians to take amidst the current intensive accusation of Christianity's relation with foreign imperialism? And how to develop an indigenized Chinese church that can survive in such a contemporary context?[42]

Seemed to the Chinese church to be the most pressing, the third set of questions, of indigenization, would also have direct implications for the first two sets of concerns. While Leung does not favor a simple "challenge-response" interpretation for this part of the church's history, he nevertheless believes that the anti-Christian movement did probably play the role of raising the urgency of many already existing problems in the minds of Chinese Christians. At any rate, an obvious consequence of the anti-Christian movement was that many churches began to separate themselves from foreign missions, and this also catalyzed different efforts to establish indigenized or independent Chinese churches.[43]

According to Lam Wing-hung, as China in the 1920s was under tremendous political and cultural crisis, internally torn apart by warlordism and externally humiliated and exploited by imperialism and capitalism, many Chinese—after being dislocated by the May Fourth Movement's anti-traditional iconoclasm—placed their hope of salvation in "the political religion of nationalism."[44] The Chinese Christians, then, were overwhelmed by the tasks of coping with the problems raised both by nationalism and by their cultural heritage. Thus their responses were inevitably driven by "a theological tactic of survival," characterized by a "Christo-centric apologetics" to defend the Christian faith.[45] Lam suggests that the indigenous theologies that subsequently arose were to a

42. Ibid., 158.
43. Ibid., 158–59; and Chao, *China Mission*, 23.
44. Lam, *Chinese Theology*, 1–3, 153–58, esp. 156.
45. Ibid., 156, 30.

great extent a reaction to the era's political, social, and intellectual upheavals. Thus such indigenization or contextualization of theology was
governed by a desire to sever any ties with the imperialistic West, as well
as by a practical (not merely theoretical) concern for the pressing demands of the present situation. This kind of theology is inevitably fragmentary at times, as Lam comments: "This 'contextual theology' began
with particular events and specific problems of the time. There was no
systematic theology or metaphysical scheme, for the Chinese experience
was chaotic and unsystematic. Rather, it was a living theology forged on
the anvil of fear and hope, frustration and promise."[46]

Daniel H. Bays notes that the most important feature of the
Chinese Protestant churches in the period 1900 to 1937 was the growth
of the spirit of independence. Bays outlines two different categories of
"independence": one within the foreign mission churches, and the other
outside the existing mission structures. The first category was the so-
called Three-Self Movement which aimed at making Chinese Christians
responsible for "self-government, self-support, and self-propagation" in
the already-existing mission-related churches of the day. Many foreign
missionaries as well as Chinese Christian leaders since the mid-nineteenth century had spoken of this ideal.[47] Lam notes that the National
Christian Conference, with its theme as "The Chinese Church," was a
milestone in the development of the Chinese church. With its longsuf-
fering "from the stigma of being a foreign institution and from the chaos
of denominationalism," the Chinese church in the first decades of the
twentieth century cried out for its "desperate need for unity and coop-
erativeness in establishing an indigenous church."[48]

This goal of indigenization reached a watershed in the 1922 National
Christian Conference. Out of the conference came two organizations.
One was the ecumenical Church of Christ in China (CCC) which favored a significant degree of Chinese leadership coexisting with foreign
guidance, and which eventually comprised a membership of about a
quarter to one-third of the Protestant community. The CCC was joined
by churches of both American and British backgrounds, including many

---

46. Ibid., 157.
47. Bays, "Independent Christianity," 308.
48. Lam, *Chinese Theology*, 51.

Presbyterians and Congregationalists as well as the Methodists who joined later, while the Baptists were usually not joining.[49]

The other organization resulting from the 1922 conference was the National Christian Council (NCC) that acted as a national Protestant coordinating and liaison body. According to Paul A. Varg, in the wave of the anti-Christian and anti-foreign currents of the 1920s, by 1926 the Chinese comprised 75 percent of the NCC and they held the most important offices. The NCC then represented about 70 percent of the Protestant membership. Some more conservative denominations or mission groups, such as the China Inland Mission, either did not join or had withdrawn from the CCC or the NCC, because the biblical interpretation of the CCC and/or the NCC was deemed too liberal. Many of these dissenting groups nonetheless pursued some forms of Sino-foreign unity and some ways for nurturing Chinese Christian leadership.[50] Yet in Bays's judgment, "all things considered, within the mission-related structures there was only slight movement toward an authentically autonomous or indigenous Chinese church before 1937."[51]

Bays notes that the second category of independent effort—also three-self (self-governing, self-supporting, and self-propagating) in its spirit—came from an altogether different sector of Chinese Christianity, "one which was independent of foreign missions, autonomous in operations, and indigenous in ideas and leadership."[52] This category was made up of quite diverse streams, among them the China Christian Independent Church federation (which by 1920 had over one hundred member churches), as well as three new church groups—the True Jesus Church (founded in 1917), the Jesus Family (founded in 1921), and the Assembly Hall (founded in the mid-1920s), all of which had at least several tens of thousands of adherents by 1936, and continued to grow rapidly in the years that followed. Both the True Jesus Church and the Jesus Family drew upon the new Pentecostal current that came to China after 1900: both stressed the use of supernatural spiritual gifts such as speaking in other tongues, healing, and prophetic or similar revelations,

---

49. Varg, *Missionaries, Chinese and Diplomats*, 206; and Bays, "Independent Christianity," 308–9.

50. Varg, *Missionaries, Chinese and Diplomats*, 205–6; and Bays, "Independent Christianity," 308–9.

51. Bays, "Independent Christianity," 309.

52. Ibid.

insisted on strong millennialism (expecting the imminent return of Christ), and flourished mainly in rural or semi-rural areas. In contrast, Watchman Nee first organized the Assembly Hall along the coastal cities. Yet all these three new church groups shared a common denunciation of ordination and denominationalism, and the pursuit for restoring a "New Testament model" of the church. They were all therefore exclusivist or sectarian to different extents, and were resented—by mission church-es—for their proselytizing efforts.[53] Joseph Tse-Hei Lee outlines several reasons why these groups enjoyed rapid growth and popularity during that era. First, these groups' Chinese origins protected them from the anti-foreign campaigns during the late 1920s. Secondly, their nationwide networks and institutional flexibility shielded them from the control of the Nationalist government. And thirdly, their theological beliefs and emphases struck a cord in their contemporary world: "Their millenarian and otherworldly belief systems, their emphasis on individual salvation, their rejection of the sinful world, and their belief in the Second Coming of Jesus Christ spoke to the strong sense of fear and insecurity pervasive in Chinese society during the 1937–45 Sino-Japanese War."[54]

Besides these notable independent bodies, there were also a few nationally recognized independent evangelists, pastors, and teachers who left indelible marks in this period of the Chinese church history— among them Wang Mingdao (1900–1991), Song Shangjie (John Sung, 1901–1944), Jia Yuming (1880–1964), Chen Chonggui (Marcus Cheng, 1884–1964), and Wang Zai (Leland Wang, 1898–1975). A common characteristic of this group of Christian leaders was that they usually did not have regular pay or means of financial support, but rather they lived "by faith." And most of them did not receive formal theological training—most had only a high school education—yet they emphasized discipleship and life application of the gospel, and it is noted that their preaching was much more powerful and their impact far greater than their missionary counterparts of the day.[55]

This category of independent church groups and individuals usu-ally rejected traditions and liturgy in favor of spontaneity and lay partic-ipation. They are often criticized for their heavily literal interpretation of

53. Ibid., 309–12.

54. J. Lee, "Little Flock Movement," 78.

55. Yuan, *Zhongguo jiaohui shi* [Chinese church history], 38–39; and Bays, "Independent Christianity," 313–16.

the Bible, for their emotionalism and anti-intellectualism, and for their focus on personal salvation and otherworldly happiness to the neglect of social welfare and concerns.[56] Bays believes that in the 1940s, this sector of independent Christians may have numbered over two hundred thousand persons, that is, about 20 to 25 percent of all Protestants in China.[57]

While the majority of people in the church did not tackle the problem of indigenization since they were quite comfortable with the lifestyle (and sometimes the social prestige) of the denominational church, Lam notes that those who responded to the urgency of the task included both conservative preachers and (for the most part) theologians of more liberal persuasion.[58] Lam outlines five different perspectives that these indigenous thinkers held toward Chinese culture.[59] First, at the left end of the spectrum were radical thinkers like Wu Leichuan, who sought to maintain double loyalties to Christianity and Confucianism, which were seen as different expressions of the same one truth, the *Dao*. Secondly, close to this position was the effort to harmonize Christianity with Chinese culture. Advocating this approach were Wang Zhixin and Fan Zimei, who attempted to preserve the Chinese heritage by searching out Christian support for Confucian teachings. Thirdly, there was the view represented by Wei Zhuomin and Zhao Zichen, both maintaining a similar distinction between the essence and the expression of Christianity. "Recognizing the finality of Christianity in one way or another," they held that Christianity fulfills Chinese culture while the culture can at the same time contribute to Christianity's fuller or more acceptable expressions.[60] Fourthly, Zhang Yijing spoke for a more conservative approach as he compared Jesus and Confucius with a sun-moon analogy—original light versus reflective illumination. While acknowledging there were "glimmers of truth" in the Chinese culture as general revelation, Zhang insisted that only the special revelation of Christianity could offer "any

---

56. Hunter, "Continuities," 9; Yuan, *Zhongguo jiaohui shi* [Chinese church history], 39–40; and K. L. Leung, *Fu lin zhonghua* [Blessing upon China], 163.

57. Bays, "Independent Christianity," 310. According to Yuan, around 1949 the three church groups—the True Jesus Church, the Assembly Hall, and the Jesus Family—had 250,000 adherents, more than a quarter of the total number of Protestants then in China. See Yuan, *Zhongguo jiaohui shi* [Chinese church history], 38.

58. Lam, *Chinese Theology*, 53.

59. Ibid., 60–81, 154.

60. Ibid., 70–71.

redemptive possibility" for transforming the culture.[61] Lastly, at the far right extreme of the spectrum were conservative preachers like Wang Mingdao, who viewed the church and the world as two opposing forces, and so stressed the doctrine of salvation while largely bypassed the doctrine of creation. Although such anti-cultural dualism "negated any attempt at indigenous thinking," the problem of indigenization was resolved, or rather dissolved, by "returning to the plain sense of Scripture as the timeless and timely word of God."[62] Similar to Wang Mingdao, Nee believed that indigenization would not work by making Western practices such as church ritual and organization "more relevant to Chinese culture"; but rather, it could be accomplished through "allowing Chinese Christians to express themselves freely about the content of the Bible."[63]

NEE'S LIFE AND WORK

Family and Schooling

Watchman Nee was born in 1903 in Fuzhou, the capital city of Fujian Province in Southeast China and one of the five treaty ports opened to foreign trade after the mid-nineteenth century Opium War.[64] While the first three decades of the twentieth century was a tremendously fluid period all over China, Ryan Dunch has demonstrated that Chinese Protestants were deeply and extensively involved in the ebbs and flows of the political and social torrents in the Fuzhou area.[65] Nee was a third-generation Protestant. His paternal grandfather converted to Christianity through the first missionary presence in Fuzhou, the Congregationalists of the American Board, and later became one of the first ordained Chinese pastors among the Congregationalists in the northern Fujian Province.[66] Watchman Nee's father attended a

---

61. Ibid., 79.

62. Ibid., 77.

63. Sumiko, *Protestantism in China*, 111.

64. In this section, I rely mainly on a biography of Nee—Kinnear, *Against the Tide*—as well as two scholarly analyses of Nee's life: Lam, *Shuling shenxue* [Spiritual theology]; and C. Li, "Difang jiaohui yundong" [Local Church movement]. Li's study, according to Liao, is one of the more rigorously researched documents about Nee's life. See Liao, "Ni Tuosheng de zhuanji" [Biographies of Watchman Nee], 289.

65. Dunch, *Fuzhou Protestants*, xvii–xxi.

66. Dana Roberts demonstrates from mission records that he was the second (a month later than the first) Chinese to be ordained in the province. See Roberts, *Secrets*

Christian elementary school, later obtained a traditional Confucian education and earned a customs officer position in the port of Shantou in Guangdong, as well as serving, in the 1910s and 1920s, on the board of the Fuzhou YMCA.[67]

Nee's mother, Lin Heping, a native of Guangdong Province, was adopted early by a merchant couple. When she was six, her adopted father converted to Christianity after a Methodist pastor's prayer healed his strange disease. Lin later was educated in an American-staffed Methodist mission school for girls. Often ranked first in her class, she wanted to go to the United States to study medicine. But her adopted mother opposed the idea, and Lin's dream was dashed at age eighteen when her parents, whom she found impossible to disobey under the cultural pressure of her time, arranged her marriage.

The first two children born in her marriage were both girls, and her mother-in-law feared that Lin would be like her sister-in-law who had given birth to all girls—six in a row. Under great apprehension, Lin remembered the story of Hannah in the Old Testament (1 Sam 1–2), and prayed likewise to God, asking for a boy and, if granted, willing to dedicate the boy back to God. Then the happiest thing happened to her and her family: to them was given the firstborn boy! This was the boy who later became known as Watchman Nee.

Nee grew up in a relatively well-to-do family of nine children—having four younger brothers and two younger sisters after him. While their father was an amicable and decorous gentleman, their mother was stern and strict in disciplining them. Nee received home schooling in traditional Chinese education from age six. He was bright and active in temperament as well as exhibiting leadership ability early among his playmates. Nee was nine when Dr. Sun Yat-sen overthrew China's last dynasty and established the Republic of China. From age thirteen, Nee received a Western-style education, first in an Anglican mission-based vernacular middle school and later in the English-medium high school of Trinity College in Fuzhou, which was run by Anglican missionaries from Trinity College, Dublin. This was one of the best schools in the city and offered many different subjects for study. Nee usually ranked first in his class, excelling in most courses except in physical education, due to his weak constitution. And he quickly acquired fluency in the northern

of Watchman Nee, 45n6.

67. Dunch, *Fuzhou Protestants*, 195.

dialect (known now as *guoyu* or Mandarin) that had just become the official national language of the new republic. He also became proficient in the nascent *baihua wen* (meaning "plain written language")—a reform of written Chinese from the highly compact ancient form to the colloquialized and easily understandable form—which greatly promoted the dissemination of ideas and thoughts, including Christian ones, in modern China. Nee loved novels, movies, and writing for newspapers, and was once the president of the school's student association.[68] Yet at that time he found Christianity unimpressive and resented mandatory chapel and Bible classes, probably due to the discrepancies he saw between Christian ideals and its practices as well as the general antagonism toward foreign rule in the Chinese society.[69] Grace Y. May thus comments: "While indebted to the missionary enterprise for his education and enrolled in the Methodist church, Nee would renounce all denominational affiliations before he graduated from Trinity. Nee's conversion in 1920 marked the beginning of his struggle for identity as a Chinese Christian."[70]

Conversion and Character Formation

At age seventeen, Nee underwent a conversion experience triggered by the revival meetings of Yu Cidu (Dora Yu, 1873–1933). Yu was a leading independent revivalist-evangelist, who had conducted revival meetings during the 1900s and 1910s. In 1920 she came to hold evangelistic meetings in Fuzhou. At one of her meetings Nee's mother Lin experienced a profound conversion. Touched by the change he saw in his mother's life, Nee went with her to Yu's meeting and subsequently was also drastically converted. About fifteen years later, Nee gave an account of his conversion in the form of a testimony, describing his struggles about whether or not to become a Christian, because he felt that he was asked by God not only to accept the grace of salvation but also to dedicate his life wholly for God's service right from the start. Yet in a vision-like experience, he saw not only many of his own sins, but also Jesus on the cross with outstretched arms welcoming him. He finally surrendered to such love, subsequently seeing light in his room and losing consciousness of his surroundings:

68. Cha, "Ni Tuosheng" [Watchman Nee], 310; and Kinnear, *Against the Tide*, 39.

69. G. Y. May, "Breaking of Bread," 14.

70. Ibid., 15.

On the evening of April 29, 1920, I was alone in my room. I had no peace of mind. Whether I sat or reclined, I could find no rest, for within was this problem of whether or not I should believe in the Lord. . . . There was a real struggle within me. Then I knelt down to pray. At first I had no words with which to pray. But eventually many sins came before me, ... I saw the filthiness of sin and I also saw the efficacy of the Lord's precious blood cleansing me and making me white as snow. I saw the Lord's hands nailed to the cross, and at the same time I saw Him stretching forth His arms to welcome me, saying, "I am here waiting to receive you." Overwhelmed by such love, I could not possibly reject it, and I decided to accept Him as my Savior. . . . I wept and confessed my sins, seeking the Lord's forgiveness. After making my confession, the burden of sins was discharged, and I felt buoyant and full of inward joy and peace. . . . Alone in my room that evening, I saw the light and lost all consciousness of my surroundings.[71]

This conversion experience led to Nee's giving up his ambition for further education and worldly success (with his academic records at Trinity, he had a very promising future to pursue further study abroad). This also led to his decision to become a minister of the gospel, a profession that he had deeply despised before. A few months after Nee's conversion, Trinity College was forced to temporarily suspend its operation because of the civil war situation in Southern China. Nee took the opportunity to go up to Shanghai to attend the Bible school led by Dora Yu. There he learned from Yu's life to look solely to God for life's provisions, and to let the word of God dwell in the heart rather than just register in the head. But a year later he was asked to leave the school by Yu because of his lack of discipline as well as his proclivity for good food and nice clothing. Deeply disappointed yet acknowledging his own faults, Nee went back to Trinity College to finish his education.

There he set out passionately to evangelize his classmates on campus, but after a year's busy endeavor, not one single soul was converted. Counseled by an English missionary Miss Groves, Nee began to reflect on his own life and to deal with some uneasy conscience or "hidden sins" in his life. He sought reconciliation with different people by confessing his own wrongs and when applicable, making repayments to them. Then he wrote down a list of seventy schoolmates and prayed for their salvation every day as well as witnessed to them whenever he had a chance.

71. Nee, "First Testimony."

After a few months, all seventy schoolmates except one came to accept Christ as their savior. Some of these new converts and Nee then went out to evangelize on the city's streets, and when the school was on holiday, also went into nearby villages to witness to the gospel.[72]

Soon afterwards Nee again saw a slow result for his evangelistic work and had a great desire to be filled by the Holy Spirit. At this point he got into contact with another English missionary, Margaret E. Barber (1866–1930). Barber had for seven years been a missionary to China sent by the Anglican Church Missionary Society, but later due partly to her disagreement with an Anglican bishop over the issue of infant baptism (as opposed to believer baptism), she came back to China as an independent missionary, accompanied by her niece who was twenty years younger. While in England, she obtained doctrinal and spiritual help from D. M. Panton. After returning to China, Barber also received from Panton spiritual, and sometimes financial, support, while she trusted firmly throughout that all her needs would be provided for by God.[73]

Guided by Barber, Nee believed that there must be some hindrance inside him that was blocking the free flowing of the Holy Spirit's power in his evangelism. After making confession to and seeking reconciliation with many people, one day as he was reading Psalm 73:25—"Whom have I in heaven but you? And there is nothing on earth that I desire other than you"—he realized that he could not honestly say as the psalmist did because of his passionate love for his girlfriend Charity. Charity had been a friend of his since childhood and was very beautiful and intelligent, but at that time she was not showing any interest in Christianity. Nee sensed that Charity had become for him a competition for God and felt that he must give her up in order to be filled by the Spirit. After a period of difficult struggle, Nee finally prayed to God that he was willing to let her go so that he might focus his whole heart on loving God alone. As a result, Nee experienced great joy from the Spirit,[74] and he also wrote a moving poem expressing his total abandonment to God and his passion to carry the cross in order to gain Christ.[75] It so happened that more than ten years later, in 1934, Charity eventually became Nee's wife, after

72. Nee, *Zhuo jianzheng* [Testimonies], 43–45.

73. Reetzke, *M. E. Barber*; and X. Chen, "Paomao yu wuxian" [Anchoring on eternity].

74. Nee, *Zhuo jianzheng* [Testimonies], 46.

75. S. C. T. Chan, *Wo de jiufu Ni Tuosheng* [My uncle, Watchman Nee], 15–16.

she had received a master's degree from Yenching University and finally became a rather devoted Christian. Stephen Chan, Nee's nephew, comments that this was like Abraham who gave his son Isaac up but later got him back from the hand of God.[76]

Barber was formative for Nee's life and spirituality in many ways. Besides introducing Nee to different theological and spiritual writings of the West (which will be looked at in the next chapter), Barber left an indelible stamp on Nee's life and character development. One thing Barber modeled for Nee was a lifestyle of "living by faith," which meant not relying on any conventional methods of fundraising, nor even telling anyone about her financial needs, but simply trusting that God would supply all the needs for her living and ministry—usually through prompting other Christians to give to her at the exact (often the last) moment when her need had to be met. This principle of "living by faith," Chan suggests, had been formative for Nee's later insistence on "self-supporting" of the Local Church he founded as well as for his own attempt to live out a similar lifestyle.[77] Nee also told of several of his own "living by faith" experiences in a testimony he gave.[78]

Another way in which Barber left a deep imprint on Nee was in fostering a character of humility and obedience. For instance, Nee spoke of an eighteen-month period during which he had continual disagreement and argument with a coworker in evangelism who was five years older than he. Each time he sought a just arbitration from Barber, what she would give him was the demand simply to obey someone who was older. After some painful struggles (often accompanied with weeping), Nee finally realized that God was using those incidents to form in him a lamb-like character so that he could later cooperate with many others in team ministry. The following is Nee's own account of what he deemed as "the most precious lesson he learned," and how grateful he was to Barber for instilling in him the conviction that what exactly was right or wrong was not as important as whether one was growing in the Christlike character of meekness and submission:

76. Ibid., 16; J. Chen, *Ni Tuosheng dixiong* [Brother Nee], 48; and Kinnear, *Against the Tide*, 133–34. Witness Lee also comments that it was because of the sovereignty of God that Charity had not gotten married in those ten years. See W. Lee, *Ni Tuosheng* [Watchman Nee], 97.

77. S. C. T. Chan, *Wo de jiufu Ni Tuosheng* [My uncle, Watchman Nee], 14.

78. Nee, "Third Testimony."

In one controversy I had very good arguments. . . . But she said, "Whether that co-worker is wrong or not is another matter. While you are accusing your brother before me, are you like one who is bearing the cross? Are you like a lamb?" . . .

. . . My head was filled with ideas, but God wanted to see me enter into spiritual reality. . . . In those eighteen months I had no opportunity to put forward my proposals. I could only weep and painfully suffer. . . . God wanted to polish me and to remove all my sharp, projecting edges. . . .

. . . It is only the spirit of a lamb that God takes delight in: the gentleness, the humility, and the peace. Your ambition, lofty purpose, and ability are all useless in the sight of God. . . . It is not a question of right or wrong; it is a question of whether or not one is like the bearer of the cross. In the church, right and wrong have no place; all that counts is bearing the cross and accepting its breaking. This produces the overflowing of God's life and accomplishes His will.[79]

On another occasion, Nee referred to that same period as "learning the lessons of the cross":

I was always ranked first in my class as well as in my school. I also wanted to be first in serving the Lord. For this reason, when I was made second, I disobeyed. I told God repeatedly that it was too much for me to bear; I was receiving too little honor and authority, and everyone sided with my elder co-worker. But today I worship God and thank Him from the depths of my heart that this all happened to me. It has been the best training. God wished me to learn obedience, so He arranged for me to encounter many difficulties. Eventually, I told Him I was willing to be placed second. When I became willing to yield, the joy I experienced differed from the joy I experienced at the time of my salvation; it was not a broad joy but a deep one. After another eight or nine months, on many occasions I was willing to be broken and did not do what I wished. On my spiritual path I was filled with joy and peace. . . . The Lord, existing in the form of God, did not consider being equal with God a treasure to be grasped, but emptied Himself (Phil 2:6–7). . . . Eventually, I told God that I would choose the cross, accept its breaking, and put aside my own ideas.[80]

79. Nee, "First Testimony."
80. Nee, "Second Testimony."

Barber functioned like a spiritual mother to Nee, as Nee recalls: "If I did but walk into her room, I was brought immediately to a sense of God. In those days I was very young and had lots of plans, lots of schemes for the Lord to sanction . . . . With all these I came to her to try and persuade her; to tell her that this or that was the thing to do. But before I could open my mouth she would say a few quite ordinary words—and light dawned. It simply put me to shame. My scheming was all so natural, so full of man, whereas here was one who lived for God alone. I had to cry to Him, 'Lord, teach me to walk that way.'"[81] The relation between Barber and Nee later gradually became distant, mainly because Nee disagreed with her belief that women could preach in church. Nonetheless it is said that Barber had such a mature, selfless forbearance that she never argued with Nee on that point, and when sometimes Nee came to visit at her village, she would be happy to let him preach at her pulpit.[82] When she died, she left her much-thumbed Bible, virtually her only legacy, to Nee. And in it Nee found a note: "I want nothing for myself, I want everything for the Lord," which also became Nee's own life motto.[83] Barber's influence on Nee remained deep and long-lasting, and Angus Kinnear notes that Nee in later years repeatedly spoke favorably of her influence in his life and he always thought of her "as a 'lighted' Christian."[84] It is noted that several other older women in his life had shaped Nee's faith formation: his mother Lin Heping, the evangelist Yu Cidu, and Margaret Barber[85] (as well as the writings of Madame Guyon and Jessie Penn-Lewis). May notes that these female mentors had contributed to Nee's "profound appreciation for the church as family," seen in part perhaps in his attraction to the bread-breaking communion as an embodiment of "the familial dimension of life and faith."[86] It is also quite possible that these women's more intuitive as well as more relational approach to the spiritual life had left an indelible mark on Nee's development of his own relationship with God.

81. Kinnear, *Against the Tide*, 62; cf. Nee, *Normal Christian Life*, 161–62.

82. S. C. T. Chan, *Wo de jiufu Ni Tuosheng* [My uncle, Watchman Nee], 14, cited in C. Li, "Difang jiaohui yundong," [Local Church movement], 61.

83. Kinnear, *Against the Tide*, 113; and C. Li, "Difang jiaohui yundong," [Local Church movement], 56.

84. Kinnear, *Against the Tide*, 62.

85. G. Y. May, "Breaking of Bread," 101–2.

86. Ibid., 343, 101.

Early Work, Sickness, Writing The Spiritual Man, *and Healing*

Early after his conversion, with the support of the evangelist Wang Zai, Nee began publishing in Fuzhou the magazine *Fuxin Bao* ("Revival News"), which was aimed at promoting the deeper spiritual life. Both Wang and Nee stressed personal evangelism; their evangelistic efforts on the streets were quite effective, and many were led to their fellowship. But soon Nee and Wang disputed over some hermeneutical or theological issues. Contrary to Wang's convictions, Nee believed, from his reading of the book of Acts, that the emphasis of Christian ministry should be in establishing churches, rather than in holding revival meetings. And Nee also believed that being a pastor is a gift given by God, rather than an office established via human order, thus ordination of the pastorate should not be pursued. As a result of these controversies, Nee was forced to leave Wang's fellowship in 1924.[87]

Nee then traveled and preached in Japan and Southeast Asia for some time; and then went to Shanghai, establishing the Gospel Book House there and beginning to publish another magazine, *Jidutu Bao* ("The Christian"), which was geared toward building up new converts. Yet in the same year (1924), Nee contracted a tubercular disease that lasted for about five years. Thinking that he would die soon, Nee prayed and felt that he should write a book to record all that he had learned and experienced of the things of God. So beginning in the spring of 1927 he set out to write *The Spiritual Man*, and after a sixteen-month period of intermittent writing amidst some serious pains and struggles, he finally finished composing the book in three volumes in 1928, the year he reached twenty-five years of age. In the preface to the book he spoke of a two-month period when he "was living between Satan's jaws"[88]; and in 1936 he recalled:

> I rented a small room in Wusih, Kiangsu province, where I shut myself up and spent my days writing. At that time my disease became so aggravated that I could not even lie down. While writing I sat on a chair with a high back and pressed my chest against the desk to alleviate the pain. Satan said to me, "Since you will

87. Tung, "'Local Church,' I, II," 5; and Lam, *Shuling shenxue* [Spiritual theology], 29–31.

88. Nee, *The Spiritual Man*, 1:xiii. There are four different editions of Nee's *The Spiritual Man* cited in my study: two in Chinese, and two in English. These editions were cited by different writers, and I saw a basic congruence among the editions.

soon be dying, why not die in comparative comfort rather than in pain?" I retorted, "The Lord wants me just like this; get out of here!" It took four months to complete the three volumes of *The Spiritual Man.* The writing of this book was a real labor of blood, sweat, and tears. I despaired of life, yet God's grace brought me through. After completing each time of writing, I would say to myself, "This is my last testimony to the church." Though the writing was done in the midst of all sorts of difficulties and hardships, I felt that God was unusually near to me.[89]

The Spiritual Man was the only book that Nee sat down to write, for the explicit purpose to provide guidance for the spiritual life, with special attention to the area of spiritual warfare (which was understood by Nee—quoting such scriptures as Ephesians 6:12 and 2 Corinthians 10:3–4—as combating against evil spirits).[90] Other works in the sixty-six volumes of Nee's *Collected Works* are mainly his sermons edited as well as some articles and songs written for different occasions. Yet years later, in 1941, Nee ordered the publishing house to stop reprinting *The Spiritual Man,* not because his views now had changed, but because he thought that the way the material was presented in the book was too perfect or so detailed that it led to the over-introspection of some readers (despite the caution he gave in the book's preface).[91] According to Kinnear, Nee thought that the book was too "perfect" in providing answers to all the questions regarding the spiritual life, but then he discovered that this is not the way God does things. Kinnear reported that Nee had said: "For the danger of systematizing divine facts is that a man can understand without the help of the Holy Spirit. It is only the immature Christian who demands always to have intellectually satisfying conclusions. The Word of God itself . . . speaks always and essentially to our spirit and to our life."[92]

---

89. Nee, "Second Testimony."

90. Nee, *Shuling ren* [The spiritual man], 217–20.

91. W. Lee, *Ni Tuosheng* [Watchman Nee], 286–87. Lee also notes that Nee realized after 1939 that spiritual warfare was not mainly an individualistic matter, but rather a corporate matter of the Body of Christ. But in *The Spiritual Man,* he mainly drew from Evan Roberts and Jessie Penn-Lewis, both of whose views on spiritual warfare were chiefly individualistic.

92. Kinnear, *Against the Tide,* 103.

After finishing writing the book, Nee collapsed and remained virtually in bed for over a year.[93] With news of his imminent death spread around, Nee felt that he had given his last testimony for the Church, and once prayed that God would let him pass over to the next life in peace. Yet one day he devoted himself to prayer and fasted from morning till three o'clock in the afternoon, which led to his receiving this series of words from God: "The just shall live by faith" (Rom 1:17); "By faith you stand" (2 Cor 1:24); and "We walk by faith" (2 Cor 5:7). "These words filled me with great joy," Nee said, "for the Bible says, 'All things are possible to him who believes' (Mark 9:23). . . . I believed that God had cured me."[94] Yet the miraculous healing came not without some serious struggle; Nee's own account of the process was quite vivid and deserves to be quoted at length:

> The test came immediately. The Bible says, "By faith you stand," but I was still lying in bed. A conflict arose in my mind: Should I get up and stand or remain lying down? . . . Then the word of God manifested its power, and ignoring all else, I put on my clothing, clothing which I had not worn for a hundred and seventy-six days. As I left the bed to stand, I perspired so profusely that it was as though I had been soaked through with rain. Satan said to me, "Are you trying to stand when you can't even sit up?" I retorted, "God told me to stand," and I rose to my feet. Being again in a cold sweat, I nearly fell down. I kept repeating, "Stand by faith, stand by faith!" I then walked a few steps to get my trousers and socks. After putting on my trousers, I sat down. No sooner was I seated than the word of God came to me that I should not only stand by faith but also walk by faith. I felt that the ability to rise and walk a few steps to get my trousers and socks was already something marvelous. How could I expect to walk further? "Where do You want me to go?" I asked God. He answered, "Go downstairs to Sister Lee's home at number 215." A number of brothers and sisters had been fasting and praying for me there for two or three days.
>
> . . . I tell you honestly that when I stood at the top of the staircase it seemed to me to be the tallest staircase I had ever seen in my life. I said to God, "If You tell me to walk I will do so, even if I die as a result of the effort." But I continued, "Lord, I cannot walk. I pray that You will support me with Your hand while I am

93. J. Chen, *Ni Tuosheng dixiong* [Brother Nee], 39; and Nee, *Zhuo jianzheng* [Testimonies], 35.

94. Nee, "Second Testimony."

walking." With one hand holding onto the rail, I descended step
by step. Again I was in a cold sweat. As I walked down the stairs,
I continued to cry out, "Walk by faith, walk by faith!" With each
step down, I prayed, "O Lord, it is You who enable me to walk."
While descending those twenty-five steps, it seemed I was walking hand in hand with the Lord in faith.[95]

Nee finally landed on the ground floor, and went straight to Sister Lee's
home, where he found seven or eight people there. Nee described what
happened next: "They were speechless and motionless. For about an
hour everyone sat quietly as if God had appeared among men. I also
sat there full of thanksgiving and praise. Then I related all that had happened in the course of my being graciously healed. Exhilarated and ju-
bilant in spirit, we all praised God aloud for His wonderful work. That
same day we hired a car to go to Kiangwan in the suburbs to visit Dora
Yu. . . . When I appeared, I was looked upon as one who had been raised
from the dead. That was another occasion of joyful thanksgiving and
praise before the Lord. On the following Sunday, I spoke on the platform
for three hours."[96]

During this time of sickness, it also became clear to Nee what God
was asking him to do with regard to his life work. Nee was convinced that
it was not God's calling for him to write a hundred-volume Bible commentary as he once ambitiously planned, nor was he to travel around
holding evangelistic and revival meetings like some popular Christian
leaders of his day; rather, he was to focus on helping believers to live a
victorious life in the Spirit, and to build up Local Churches to manifest
the glory of God.[97]

The Local Church Movement

Amidst the turbulent anti-Christian movement and anti-foreign nationalism during the 1920s, there emerged in the Chinese church different indigenous efforts, of which Nee's Local Church (*Difang Jiaohui*)
movement constituted one major stream. What started out in 1921 as a
small group in Fuzhou—studying scriptures and breaking bread together—in 1928 became, under Nee's leadership in Shanghai, the Christian
Assembly (*Jidutu Juhuichu*) or the Assembly Hall (*Juhuisuo*). The term

95. Ibid.
96. Ibid.
97. Ibid.

"assembly" referred to a *place* of gathering rather than a human institution, and the group is also widely known as the "Local Churches" as well as the "Little Flock" (*Xiaoqun*), a term derived from the Gospel of Luke 12:32: "Do not be afraid, little flock, for it is your Father's good pleasure to give you the kingdom."[98]

Historian Joseph Lee notes that influenced by Brethren ideas (to be discussed in next chapter), Nee rejected the division between clergy and laity, for he believed that the office of pastor contradicted biblical teachings on the priesthood of all believers, especially obstructing ordinary believers' communion with God and their participation in service within the church. Joseph Lee also points out that Nee's rejection of the pastoral office was influenced by the historical context of Western imperialism in China. For decades, Chinese pastors were ordained or employed by foreign missionaries and were dependent on mission societies for support. Thus Nee urged Chinese Christians to break away from their dependence on the West for doctrinal, administrative, and financial support. Also aspired by a vision of church unity and by his interpretation of the New Testament, Nee advocated a return to the practices of the apostolic church (with simplicity of worship and weekly communion of the Lord's Table), and maintained that there should be only "one church in one locality."[99] This insistence stemmed from his antagonism toward denominational varieties, and his understanding that the church should be "a spiritual body" in unity.[100] While the missionaries who championed the social gospel "tried desperately to make Christianity relevant to the problems of hunger, disease, floods, famine, illiteracy, and the deplorable working conditions of factory labor,"[101] the Local Church brought a "renewed emphasis on individual piety" that was "explicitly non-political."[102] The unique theological thought of Nee, in Lam's view, can be located within the broader indigenous movement—largely a factor of the nationalistic reaction to the upheavals of warlordism and

---

98. Wickeri, *Common Ground*, 162, noted in J. Lee, "Little Flock Movement," 68n2.

99. Nee read that in the New Testament the churches were called only after the name of a locality, rather than after any personal or denominational names.

100. J. Lee, "Little Flock Movement," 74–75.

101. Varg, *Missionaries, Chinese and Diplomats*, 320.

102. Dunch, *Fuzhou Protestants*, 195.

imperialism—which envisioned for China a Christianity stripped of the Western "dogmatism, ritualism, and credalism."[103]

In an open letter published in 1928, Nee expressed his despair over the institutional church: "God's purpose in this age is being hindered by the church. We firmly believe that within a short period of time, God will surely gather His children into oneness so that His church might cease to be an object of hindrance, but rather would work together with God to accomplish His eternal ordination. We humbly hope that we might have a little part in this glorious work under God's hand."[104] Lam notes that because Nee was exceptionally bright, rich in Bible knowledge, outgoing in temperament, gifted in speech, and powerful in preaching, he was able to deliver messages that brought comfort to many in the turbulent days of China.[105] While the number of people meeting in Nee's gathering was only about twenty or thirty in 1928 when Nee first arrived in Shanghai, four years later in 1932, it grew to around four thousand, spreading in more than twenty Assembly Halls in the coastal areas.[106] It is estimated that by 1949 the Assembly Hall had grown to have as many as seventy thousand adherents.[107] According to another report, there were more than eight hundred thousand Assembly Christians in China in the 1990s.[108]

As the Local Church movement was flourishing in the 1930s, Nee married his childhood sweetheart Charity Zhang (Zhang Pinhui) in 1934. Charity's aunt objected to the marriage for she did not want the girl she once raised, beautiful and now highly educated, married to a poor preacher. She advertised her objections several times—attacking Nee's morals—in Shanghai's largest nationwide newspaper and circulated propaganda tracts among Christian circles, which were readily taken up by those who had resented Nee. Soon after the wedding, Nee became profoundly disturbed and depressed, and exiled himself from his leadership position in Shanghai for some months.[109]

103. Lam, *Chinese Theology*, 2–3, 154.

104. Nee, *Present Testimony (1)*, 2, as quoted in G. Y. May, "Breaking of Bread," 104.

105. Lam, *Shuling shenxue* [Spiritual theology], 37.

106. Tung, "'Local Church,' I, II," 6.

107. J. Lee, "Little Flock Movement," 78.

108. Tung, "'Local Church,' I, II," 2.

109. Kinnear, *Against the Tide*, 135; J. Chen, *Ni Tuosheng dixiong* [Brother Nee], 51; and Tung, "'Local Church,' I, II," 7. Charity proved to be a great help both to Nee's

About a year into his wilderness wandering, in Yantai, Nee participated in the revival meetings of Elizabeth Fischbacher, a Scottish missionary influenced by the contemporary charismatic movement. In the
meetings and during prayers, Nee had new and profound experiences of
being filled by the Spirit; as a result he felt that his then barren spiritual
life was revived by the Spirit's resurrection power. He sent a telegram
back to Shanghai, stating: "I have met the Lord." Indeed, Nee came back
to public ministry again and preached, in both Shanghai and Fuzhou, on
the double themes of Christ's victory and the Spirit's outpouring—stressing the two gates that a Christian needs to pass through: victorious in
life and empowered for service.[110] Yet Nee did not accept the charismatic
movement without reservation. While he did not oppose divine healing,
dreams, or speaking in tongues, Nee himself—as reported by Witness
Lee—"never spoke in tongues" and held that "not all speak in tongues"
(see 1 Cor 12:30).[111] In his view many of the charismatic phenomena
could have come from the human soul as well as from the divine Spirit.[112]

During the 1930s, Nee visited the West twice, staying more than a
year each time. Invited by the Brethren in 1933, Nee visited Europe and
North America. Nee had previously corresponded with the Brethren, and
received eight Brethren visitors (from Britain, Australia, and
America) in Shanghai and broke bread with them there. In Europe,
Nee traveled extensively, enjoying the hospitality and fellowship of the
Exclusive Brethren, as well as preaching, sharing, and breaking bread
with them. Yet without informing his hosts, one week Nee worshipped
and had communion at the Christian Fellowship Center on Honor Oak
Road in South London, a center of Keswick spirituality founded by T.
Austin-Sparks. Also, while he was in the United States on his journey
back home, he visited and broke bread with his friend Dr. Thornton
Sterns, a former missionary to China. These actions of Nee alarmed
the Exclusive Brethren, who refused to have fellowship and break bread

---

work, for her proficiency in both Chinese and English, and to his life, as his caretaker
during his sickness and as the only allowed visitor for him during the last twenty years
of his life in prison (Kinnear, *Against the Tide*, 135; and W. Lee, *Watchman Nee*, chap.
13, "Married and Engaging in Business"). Charity suffered a miscarriage in 1938, and
never conceived again, so the Nees had no children (Kinnear, *Against the Tide*, 151–52).

110. Tung, "'Local Church,' I, II," 7–8; Kinnear, *Against the Tide*, 139; and J. Chen,
Ni Tuosheng dixiong [Brother Nee], 52–57.

111. W. Lee, *Baptism in the Holy Spirit*, cited in Kinnear, *Against the Tide*, 140.

112. Lam, *Shuling shenxue* [Spiritual theology], 42.

outside their recognized assemblies. After Nee returned to China in 1934, the European Brethren and the Shanghai Assembly corresponded over the next two years, debating the issues of prophecy, ecclesiology, and admission to the communion table. Despite the many doctrinal and practical similarities between the two groups, in the end the London Brethren "excommunicated" the Chinese Assembly from their table fellowship, although Nee never actively sought to be affiliated with them in a formal way. This event only reinforced Nee's commitment to an independent and autonomous Chinese church.[113]

In 1938, Nee visited Europe for a second time, during which he mainly stayed in London with Austin-Sparks, with whom he discussed his views on some practical church issues. Nee also participated in the annual Keswick Convention in Cumberland, England, as well as visiting Denmark and giving a series of ten addresses there. This series of sermons—continuous with his views in *The Spiritual Man* and bearing imprints of the Keswick tradition—were recorded by Elizabeth Fischbacher and Angus Kinnear[114] and later published as *The Normal Christian Life*, which was then translated into many languages and became the most popular title among Nee's books.[115]

After the beginning of the Sino-Japanese war in 1937 and as the Japanese were invading deeper and deeper into China's inland, the price of living was soaring and jobs were scarce. By around 1940 the assembly had over two hundred coworkers, and supporting them financially had become an enormous burden. At that time Nee's younger brother Huaizu, a chemistry professor, invited Nee to be a partner in his stagnant bio-chemical pharmaceutical factory. Considering it as a way to provide for the needs of the coworkers and inspired by the example of Paul's tent-making (Acts 18:3, 20:34; 1 Cor 9:18), Nee decided to join the venture in early 1942. Yet unlike Paul's simple manual labor, Nee's involvement in the business turned out to be too consuming for his time and energy, as well as too preoccupying for his mind. While the

113. Ibid., 38–41; and G. Y. May, "Breaking of Bread," 124–27, 132–35, 163.

114. Kinnear, son-in-law of Austin-Sparks, spent some weeks with Nee during Nee's stay in London, was later a medical missionary to Asia, and became the author of Nee's biography and editor of several of Nee's books that appeared first in English (later translated into Chinese). See Kinnear, *Against the Tide*, 150–51; F. Chen, *Ni Tuosheng* [Watchman Nee], 135; and Roberts, *Secrets of Watchman Nee*, 1n*.

115. Kinnear, *Against the Tide*, 150–52; J. Chen, *Ni Tuosheng dixiong* [Brother Nee], 43–46, 61–62; and Lam, *Shuling shenxue* [Spiritual theology], 44–46.

enterprise in Nee's hand was expanding and provided employment to some assembly members, the elders of the Shanghai Assembly regarded Nee's action as that of a renegade or a plowman who had looked back from the furrow. So at the end of 1942 they asked Nee to discontinue preaching at their Local Churches. Even Li Yuanru, a strong supporter of Nee since the beginning, became profoundly disappointed and depressed, and sadly left Shanghai. Many others who had deeply respected Nee also left him or disavowed him, all because of this business incident. While downhearted, Nee did not defend himself, but continued working in the business, making enough money to purchase several properties including a fifteen-building property in Guling Hill near Fuzhou, which was used later for training assembly coworkers.[116]

In 1947 Nee finally set aside his work in the pharmaceutical company and began to offer a small group of Local Church members in Fuzhou an intensive course of study on the message of the cross, which was later published as *The Breaking of the Outer Man and the Release of the Spirit*. In 1948 through the mediation of Witness Lee (Li Changshou) and others, Nee made a full confession of his mistakes in the past few years to the Shanghai Assembly. As a result he was warmly welcomed back, and the implicit "number one" seat during their meetings was unanimously reserved for him. The new messages Nee preached after coming back were "gospel emigration" and "handing over." "Gospel emigration" was the idea of sending out gospel teams and relocating them throughout inland China in the hope to "take all of China in 14 to 15 years,"[117] which was later condemned by the Communist state as a "counter-revolutionary plot."[118] "Handing over" meant surrendering in three aspects: personal property, one's ministry, and one's very self (to be available for different assignments and coordination of the church). To set an example, Nee handed over his pharmaceutical factory to the Local Church. Hundreds followed his example. This brought the assembly unprecedented and incomparable wealth, which led to an expansion

---

116. J. Chen, *Ni Tuosheng dixiong* [Brother Nee], 64–70; S. C. T. Chan, *Wo de jiufu Ni Tuosheng* [My uncle, Watchman Nee], 53–58; Kinnear, *Against the Tide*, 172; and Tung, "'Local Church,' I, II," 8–9.

117. Ren Zhongxiang, "Li Changshou I Know," 106, as quoted in Tung, "'Local Church,' I, II," 10.

118. Tung, "'Local Church,' I, II," 13.

of the Local Church movement, but also to later suspicion of exploitive capitalism by the Communist government.[119]

Publications, Conferences, and Trainings

Throughout the years, besides founding Local Churches, Nee saw himself also called to engage in three other specific kinds of work: publishing literature, holding conferences, and training coworkers (deacons or ministers).[120] Nee published many volumes of books, mainly edited from his own frequent preaching and teaching, but also some translated from such authors as Andrew Murray, Jessie Penn-Lewis, and T. Austin-Sparks. In addition, he edited an eschatological chart and coedited two hymnals—translating some and authoring a few hymns himself. He also published several newspapers or magazines that served different functions. His topics included different themes of the gospel, the edification of new converts, Bible studies and expositions, the deeper spiritual life in Christ, the formation and training of ministers, and various issues regarding the church. However, his main burden or passion was clearly what he perceived to be the central message, that is, the producing of a victorious church—through appropriating the power of Christ's death and resurrection—in order to usher in the perfect eschatological kingdom of God. In other words, his central message was "Christ in His crucifixion, resurrection, ascension, return, and kingdom."[121] Witness Lee writes: "For this reason, he [Nee] considered messages on these matters as the central messages. His burden to hold the overcomer conferences and to publish *The Present Testimony* was to present such central messages. He also translated books in this same category into Chinese. All the books in the other categories . . . were intended by him to prepare the believers to apprehend these central messages. . . ."[122]

Holding conferences was another way Nee adopted to spread his life vision and work. There were four major ones that were called overcomer conferences, while the rest were simply called special conferences. The first two overcomer conferences were held in 1928 and 1931,

119. J. Chen, *Ni Tuosheng dixiong* [Brother Nee], 70–72; S. C. T. Chan, *Wo de jiufu Ni Tuosheng* [My uncle, Watchman Nee], 59–60; Kinnear, *Against the Tide*, 183, 188; and Tung, "'Local Church,' I, II," 9–10.

120. W. Lee, *Watchman Nee*, chap. 23, "The General Means of Nee's Ministry."

121. W. Lee, *Watchman Nee*, chap. 27, "Specific Means of Nee's Ministry (4)."

122. Ibid.

expounding on topics like God's eternal purpose (or God's covenant and wisdom), Satan's opposition, and the victory of Christ and victory in Christ. The third overcomer conference was held in January 1934, stressing what Nee considered to be God's only center, that is, Christ and the cross. Nee wrote in *The Present Testimony* (Oct–Dec 1933) about the nature of this conference:

> God has only one center, which is Christ—Christ and Him crucified. . . .
>
> . . . Many of the gospel messages, interpretations of prophecy, Bible expositions, and answers to questions are not God's center. . . . If a person has not laid hold of God's center, all these truths will only be doctrines to him and will not give him any help. Knowing God in His center, and living in the center is victory, holiness, and glory. Everything else follows afterward.
>
> . . .
>
> . . . Finally, in this conference, our hope is to meet Christ, to receive light and revelation from heaven, and to be filled with the life that is unknown to ordinary people. We do not intend to pay attention to the many minor, outward matters. "To know Him" (Phil 3:10)—this is what we seek.[123]

The fourth conference was held in October of the same year on the subjects of "The Life of Abraham" and "Spiritual Warfare."[124]

In keeping with his accent on fostering spiritual development and character formation, Nee was also devoted to training younger believers for their maturity and ministry in the church. Starting in 1933, for about two years he held informal training sections for some brothers. In 1936 he purchased a property in suburban Shanghai and began building a training center on it, but unfortunately it was destroyed during the Sino-Japanese war before the construction was completed. Finally in 1940 he rented a place in Shanghai and held his first formal training section there, which lasted for about two years, during which time he taught messages on the Body of Christ and on personal dedication to some seventy participants. Later he used the purchased fifteen-building

123. Nee, *Present Testimony (4)*, chap. 1, "A Letter Concerning the Third Overcomer Conference."

124. W. Lee, *Watchman Nee*, chap. 24, "The Specific Means of Watchman Nee's Ministry (1)." The first three of these conferences were all held in Shanghai while the fourth was held in Hangzhou (Hangchow). The first conference had about fifty attendees while the third and the fourth each had about three hundred participants, more than one hundred of whom came from other parts of China.

property in Guling Hill near Fuzhou to conduct two training sections there. The first Guling training was conducted in 1948 and lasted for four months with about eighty participants. The next training began initially in Guling in August 1949 for another one hundred or so coworkers and was later moved, upon the pressing situation of the concluding civil war, to Fuzhou to finish its course. Both of the Guling trainings resulted in several publications and prepared some next generation Local Church leaders.[125]

Arrest, Imprisonment, and Death

Shortly after the conclusion of the second Guling training in 1949, Nee went to Hong Kong to develop the assembly's work in that strategic place. Nee stayed in Hong Kong for some months (except for coming back to Shanghai in-between for over a month), and held special meetings there. In May 1950, against all friendly persuasion from his colleagues not to go back to mainland China, Nee decided to return to Shanghai out of a deep concern for the churches and his spiritual children there, exclaiming: "I do not care for my life. If the house is crashing down, I have children inside and must support it, if need be with my head."[126]

Joseph Lee comments that at that time Nee was still quite optimistic about the future of the Assembly in China, believing that they would be tolerated by the new Communist state. Back in China, Nee worked hard for nearly two years, navigating among the rapidly changing political situations of the new nation. Appealing to Romans 13:1–7, he taught the Local Churches to be submissive to the government in civil matters and to help rebuild the war-torn country. Unlike the renounced fundamentalist preacher Wang Mingdao, Nee did not openly oppose the state-sponsored Three-Self Patriotic Movement. Instead, he attempted to cooperate with it and submitted in support of its Christian Manifesto some thirty-five thousand signatures of his followers (amounted to 17 percent of all the signatures collected among the Protestant churches).[127] Lee states: "As long as there was freedom of worship, freedom of religious instruction, freedom to preach and baptize, and no state intervention into the Little Flock affairs, Watchman Nee was willing to maintain pro-

125. W. Lee, *Watchman Nee*, chap. 24, "The Specific Means of Watchman Nee's Ministry (1)"; and J. Chen, *Ni Tuosheng dixiong* [Brother Nee], 64–65, 72–79, 151–69.

126. Kinnear, *Against the Tide*, 197.

127. J. Lee, "Little Flock Movement," 84, 93.

active and collegial relationships with leaders of the Three-Self Patriotic Movement."[128]

In April 1952 Nee was arrested during the Five-Anti's movement that was directed against bribery, tax evasion, theft of state property, cheating on government contracts, and stealing of state economic information. But Nee was not put to trial until 1956 when he was condemned as the head of a "counter-revolutionary clique." In the presence of more than twenty-five hundred people, Nee was accused of stealing from the nation 17.2 billion dollars (old currency) worth of medicine, property, and information, in addition to charges of gross indecency as well as several charges of a political nature.[129]

For the reason of Nee's arrest, the majority of overseas biographers of Nee have been convinced that Nee was totally innocent and so he was suffering persecution for the sake of Christ and the gospel, but there have been other studies and speculations. For instance, while believing that the campaign to eliminate counter-revolutionaries (which resulted in Nee's imprisonment) "was a disheartening and disappointing political movement," Tung Siu Kwan suggests that the reason that Nee was drowned in the revolutionary "red torrents" was due largely to his own failure to grasp "the relation between politics and reality" which resulted in a series of indiscretionary actions on Nee's part during that turbulent time of China's transitions.[130] Ying Fuk-tsang, however, is persuaded that Nee did violate some state economic statutes.[131] Besides, Leung Ka-lun argues that the charge of gross indecency or adultery was indeed valid.[132] This argument of Leung has provoked some responses such as the collection of articles by James Yu and others.[133] While it is beyond the scope of this book to judge the soundness of either Ying's or Leung's research and judgment, I would like to note the biblical passage to which Wu Zhuguan refers with regard to judging others (especially while evidences are not conclusive): "Therefore do not pronounce judgment before the time, before the Lord comes, who will bring to light the things now hidden in darkness and will disclose the purposes of

---

128. Ibid., 85.

129. Tung, "'Local Church,' I, II," 15, 20.

130. Ibid., 20–21.

131. Ying, *Fandi, aiguo* [Anti-imperialism, patriotism], esp. 94–98.

132. K. L. Leung, *Ni Tuosheng de rongru* [Watchman Nee: his glory], 1–96, 277–323.

133. Yu et al., *Zai pidou* [New censure].

the heart. Then each one will receive commendation from God (1 Cor 4:5)."[134] It is clear from this verse that God does not judge according to mere external acts, but rather, looks at hidden factors and inner motives behind the appearance (see also, for example, 1 Sam 16:7). I would also like to point out that a committed believer's serious failures (if any) in certain areas do not necessarily negate the truthfulness of his or her spirituality and life teaching. Just like such biblical figures as David and Peter, who failed quite miserably at points during their lives,[135] human fallibility only highlights the fact that God usually works through frail human vessels to show forth the divine, rather than human, nature of the power and glory of God (see 2 Cor 4:7). And such failures, when responded with a spirit filled with grace, often produce genuine sorrow and repentance, and subsequently wholehearted reliance on and grateful devotion to God—a wonderful kind of soul perfection that otherwise would seem hard to obtain by those who have not been through similar valleys of death.

At any rate, Nee was sentenced to fifteen years in prison, but when the term was completed in 1967, it was at the peak of the Cultural Revolution, so he had to stay in prison for another five years.[136] In early 1972, Nee's wife died after Nee had been transferred to a farm-camp and had hope of being released soon. At this point Nee was quite frail, suffering, among other things, from his heart condition. Several months after Charity passed away, Nee died on June 1, 1972, in the farm-camp in Anhui.[137] In his last letter dated May 30, 1972, he told his aunt: "In sickness my heart remains joyful—please don't be concerned about me."[138] This note of joy appeared also in another letter dated April 22, 1972,[139] and these are not surprising at all in light of Nee's own preaching series

134. Z. Wu, "Aixin shuo chengshi hua" [Truth in love], 83.

135. Cf. Roberts, *Secrets of Watchman Nee*, 10.

136. Silas Wu, in his book, *Po ke feiteng* [Breaking out and flying], documents some research on the little known history of Nee's years in prison. It is reported that during much of his imprisonment, Nee lived in a small cell with two other inmates, one of which converted to Christianity as a result of Nee's life witness. And Nee was mostly silent yet peaceful, at times humorous. He was also assigned to do some translation of English scientific writings into Chinese (instead of doing manual labor).

137. J. Chen, *Ni Tuosheng dixiong* [Brother Nee], 82–89; Lam, *Shuling shenxue* [Spiritual theology], 51–52; and Tung, "'Local Church,' I, II," 20.

138. Nee, *Ni Tuosheng shuxin ji* [Letters of Watchman Nee], 196 (translation mine).

139. Ibid., 183.

years ago on "Be Joyful Always" (the opening paragraph of which includes a reference to 4:4 of Philippians, Paul's epistle from prison).[140] It is
reported that before Nee died he wrote down these words in big charac-
ters with a shaking hand: "Christ is the Son of God, died for redeeming
humans from sin, resurrected on the third day—this is the greatest fact
in the universe. I die believing in Christ. Watchman Nee."[141]

∼

This chapter has surveyed Nee's historical context as well as his life and
work. We have noted that Nee lived through some major political and
social upheavals in China's modern history, particularly remarkable
were the anti-Christian movement in the 1920s and the subsequent indigenous effort of the Chinese church. We have also looked into some
major phases in Nee's life and ministry, paying special attention to several of his significant spiritual experiences. This chapter is then the first
of the two chapters on background, laying down a preliminary building
block toward the construction of this book's thesis, namely, Nee's major
theological convictions regarding spiritual knowledge and the spiritual
life are in substantial agreement with related aspects of the Christian
spiritual or mystical tradition, and thus some major weaknesses in Nee's
view that his critics perceive can be overcome or substantially ameliorated. Let us now turn to the second preliminary chapter on background,
that is, to Nee's theological and spiritual sources of influence and his
innovated adaptation of these sources.

---

140. See Nee, *Yao changchang xile* [Be joyful always].

141. X. Wan, "Wan Xiaoling de jianzheng" [Testimony of Wan Xiaoling], 59 (translation mine). Wan Xiaoling was the witness of this note, which is the simplest (and so
maybe least redacted) one among slightly different versions passed down. Cf. S. C. T.
Chan, *Wo de jiufu Ni Tuosheng* [My uncle, Watchman Nee], 98; and Nee, *Ni Tuosheng
shuxin ji* [Letters of Watchman Nee], 199.

2

Influence and Adaptation

The Theological Sources of Watchman Nee

NEE'S SOURCES OF INFLUENCE

BESIDES ENGAGING IN DILIGENT study of the Bible, Nee also drank deeply from the well of Christian literature, and spoke and wrote favorably on different figures he had read.[1] Nee was a man of unusual intelligence and exceptional memory. Soon after his conversion, Margaret Barber became Nee's major bridge to the theologies and spiritualities of the West. Around 1923 she introduced him to the autobiography of the Quietist mystic Madame Guyon. Probably from her bookshelves also, Nee had access to the writings of nineteenth-century authors G. H. Pember and Robert Govett as well as the twentieth-century scholar D. M. Panton, and through them Nee acquired a particular perspective on eschatology. In addition, Barber led to Nee's reading of the works on the cross by Jessie Penn-Lewis, and introduced him to T. Austin-Sparks's writings, as well as to the scriptural commentaries of two of the Brethren movement's significant spokesmen, namely C. A. Coates and J. N. Darby. Nee was also an avid reader of such writers in the Holiness movement as Charles Finney (1792–1875), Andrew Murray (1828–1917), F. B. Meyer (1847–1929), and Evan Roberts (1878–1951). Between the ages of twenty-two to twenty-four, while struggling

---

1. It is noted that when he was about twenty years old, Nee read through the New Testament once a week for about a year. See W. Lee, *Ni Tuosheng* [Watchman Nee], 20.

with his tuberculosis and spending much time in the scriptures, Nee read widely, ranging from the exegetical works of H. Alford and B. F. Westcott, to the biographies of Martin Luther, John Knox, Jonathan Edwards, George Whitefield, and David Brainerd. Other literature Nee read included John Bunyan's *The Pilgrim's Progress*, Hudson Taylor's biography, George Muller's writing on faith, and A. B. Simpson's works on Christ. Nee also had knowledge of the works of Miguel de Molinos and François Fénelon as well as the German Pietist Gottfried Arnold (1666–1714). In addition, it is noted that the number of Christian hymns Nee was acquainted with was over ten thousand, and that during his early years of ministry he spent one-third of his income for books (with one-third for personal expenses, and one-third for helping others), and his personal library had some three thousand Christian titles.[2] In short, besides noting that some deep layers of the Chinese culture (especially certain Confucianist and Daoist orientations) had perhaps helped shape Nee's theological and spiritual contour,[3] scholars have identified that Nee stepped deeply into several Western theological and spiritual streams: the Brethren movement and dispensationalism, the Holiness and Keswick revival movements, the mysticism of Jessie Penn-Lewis, and the Quietist mysticism of Madame Guyon and others.[4] Let us now look at each of these streams in more details.

Brethren Theology: Apostolic Ecclesiology and Dispensational Eschatology

Scholars have traced the beginning of the Plymouth (Christian) Brethren movement to the 1820s (in Dublin, Ireland, and Plymouth, England), starting with random meetings of discontented evangelicals who were lamenting the doctrinal infidelity, spiritual dryness, and moral laxness, as well as the formalism and clericalism, in many British churches. The Brethren did not join other contemporary dissenting or reform endeavors such as the Oxford movement that appealed for renewal within

2. Kinnear, *Against the Tide*, 56, 62–63, 65, 81, 85, 104; Lam, *Shuling shenxue* [Spiritual theology], 23–29; W. Lee, *Ni Tuosheng* [Watchman Nee], 18–23; and F. Chen, *Ni Tuosheng* [Watchman Nee], 117–18.

3. See for example G. Y. May, "Breaking of Bread," 207; K. Lee, "Watchman Nee," 178, 182–92, 45–46; and Pamudji, "Little Flock Trilogy," 180–81.

4. K. Lee, "Watchman Nee," 45–53; Liao, "Nee's Theology of Victory," 37–45; Lam, *Shuling shenxue* [Spiritual theology], 23–29; and G. Y. May, "Breaking of Bread," 237–39.

Anglicanism through the revival of Nicene Christianity. Instead, they favored a direct appeal to the New Testament apostolic church as the basis of their authority. Determining that the established church had departed from biblical fidelity in ecclesial doctrine and practice, the Brethren rejected sectarian denominational existence as well as ecclesiastical claims to authority. J. N. Darby (1800–1882), the most influential British leader of the movement, distinguished the signs of a true church as spiritual unity and fellowship as well as obedience to scripture and guidance of the Holy Spirit. In contrast, the established church was deemed to have only a visible unity and worldly, human-made systems of church government. The Brethren movement split in the 1840s over church discipline, and later gave rise to the formation of the Open Brethren as opposed to the Exclusive Brethren. The Exclusive group or Darbyites were centralized assemblies who welcomed to Holy Communion only members of their own assembly and those bearing recommendations from recognized assemblies. In contrast, the larger, Open group consisted of autonomous assemblies who continued to "break bread" together with a variety of Christians.[5]

James Patrick Callahan argues that though it was a radical dissenting group, the early Brethren were more than a negative reactionary movement of ecclesial discontent. They are best understood as part of a recurrent phenomenon in Christianity known as primitivist movements that aim at re-appropriating pure, "New Testament" Christianity. The Brethren were characterized by a particular ecclesial piety, and—like some other dissenting Revivalism in the late eighteenth and early nineteenth century—exhibited an intense concern for prophecy and eschatology. Nonetheless, Callahan affirms that an ecclesial negativism and separatism dominated the movement, perhaps related to the Brethren's idealism and their ahistorical perspectives on church history.[6]

According to C. Blaising, the Brethren theologian J. N. Darby was also the founding thinker of classical dispensationalism, which was popularized later partly by the *Scofield Reference Bible*. Dispensationalism is a form of biblical interpretation that has been very influential in late nineteenth- and twentieth-century evangelical thought. Rejecting

5. Callahan, *Primitivist Piety*, xv; G. Y. May, "Breaking of Bread," 106–13, 117–20; Stackhouse "Plymouth (Christian) Brethren," 914; and Hoffecker, "Darby, John Nelson," 317–18.

6. Callahan, *Primitivist Piety*, xi–xix, esp. xiv, xvii.

the belief that the Old Testament Israel is replaced and fulfilled by the New Testament church, dispensationalism reads Israel and the church as two separate dispensations in biblical history. Sometimes, Israel and the church are viewed—in the perspective of the more radicalized classical dispensationalism—as two utterly separate divine programs: earthly, political, and legalistic blessings to ethnic descendants of Israel in contrast to heavenly, spiritual, and gracious blessings to all who are in Christ. The word dispensation here is a translation of the Greek word *oikonomia* which connotes arrangement, administration, management, or stewardship.[7] Dispensational eschatology emphasizes premillennialism and pretribulational rapture—maintaining that the second advent of Christ will happen before the saints' thousand-year millennial reign on earth, and a rapture of believers will occur before the great end-time tribulation (which will then lead to Christ's second coming).[8] Generally speaking, dispensationalists hold a rather pessimistic view of both humanity and the historic church: they highlight the failure of each, and underscore the divine judgment on the world and the apostate Christendom.[9] Nee came into contact with dispensationalism through his reading of Darby's works and his translating into Chinese, in 1926, the Scofield Correspondence Course.[10] And in the 1930s Nee visited as well as corresponded extensively with the Brethren in London.

Revivalism: Holiness and Keswick Movements

M. E. Dieter suggests that Revivalism can be understood as a "movement within the Christian tradition that emphasizes the appeal of religion to the emotional and affectional nature of individuals as well as to their intellectual and rational nature. It believes that vital Christianity begins with a response of the whole being to the gospel's call for repentance and spiritual rebirth by faith in Jesus Christ. This experience results in a personal relationship with God."[11] Scholars note that revivals have occurred in every era of the church history and possibly in all sections of Christianity, including the Roman Catholic and Eastern Orthodox

7. Blaising, "Dispensation, Dispensationalism," 343–45.

8. Usually citing Revelation 19–20 and 1 Thessalonians 4:16–17.

9. Scofield, *Rightly Dividing the Word*, 19; and Bass, *Dispensationalism*, 18; both cited in Liao, "Nee's Theology of Victory," 43.

10. Nee, *Finest of the Wheat*, 17, cited in Liao, "Nee's Theology of Victory," 44.

11. Dieter, "Revivalism," 1028.

churches. Most frequently, however, they have taken place in the Protestant churches, especially since the eighteenth century. The roots of modern Protestant revivals go back to the Puritan (in Britain and the American colonies) and pietistic (in Germany and the Netherlands) reactions against the rationalism of the Enlightenment and the sterile scholastic orthodoxy of Protestantism in the seventeenth century.[12] W. G. Travis notes that Protestant Revivalism is characterized by "the Protestant emphasis on preaching, the Puritan emphasis on a noticeable conversion experience and the pietistic emphasis on warmhearted faith. To these may be added Solomon Stoddard's belief that the Spirit works in 'seasons of harvest.'"[13]

According to R. E. Davies, J. Edwin Orr (1912–1987)—the noted historian of revivals—suggested that there had been at least four major revivals within Protestantism over the past three hundred years.[14] The first of these was the First Great Awakening or Evangelical Revival, from around 1725 to the 1770s, touching every area where Protestantism had spread—central and western Europe, Great Britain, and North America. This revival was led partly by such prominent personalities as Count Nikolaus von Zinzendorf, George Whitefield, John Wesley and Charles Wesley, and Jonathan Edwards. Hundreds of missionaries grew out of this revival, and went out to many countries where the gospel had not been preached. Then came the Second Great Awakening, from roughly 1790 to the mid-1840s, widespread again throughout the United States and Canada, in the British Isles, and in many countries of continental Europe. Characteristic features of this revival included camp meetings as well as college revivals, which provided personnel and impetus for the modern missionary movement that started around 1810. This revival also saw some influential itinerant evangelists such as Charles Finney, who preached for immediate conversion because of his conviction on the crucial role of the will at conversion (for making the right moral choice).[15] The third major revival was the Mid-Century Prayer Revival

---

12. Davies, "Revival, Spiritual," 1026; and Dieter, "Revivalism," 1028.

13. Travis, "Revivalism, Protestant," 1012.

14. Davies, "Revival, Spiritual," 1026.

15. Such decision, Finney emphasized nonetheless, was aided by the grace of God through both prayer and the agency of the Holy Spirit, which helped to mute Calvinist concerns such as possible undermining of the sovereign movement of God (Dieter, "Revivalism," 1029).

from 1858 to the late 1880s, again with impact in many parts of the Protestant world. Noontime prayer meetings and an increasing number of itinerant evangelists such as D. L. Moody, William and Catherine Booth, and Walter and Phoebe Palmer characterized this revival. During this revival, the Palmers as well as Finney were instrumental in leading the Holiness movement, which then spread to England and gave rise to the Salvation Army and the Keswick movement. The Holiness movement also led to a worldwide missionary movement that was fueled by so-called faith work, in which unsalaried missionaries went to the field without formal financial support or advanced pledges. Various other movements (with significant student involvement) also developed out of this period of major revival, such as the YMCA, YWCA, Sunday School movement, and different foreign missions. The fourth major revival movement was the Worldwide Revival of 1900 to 1910, affecting many areas of the world: Asia (Japan, Korea, China, India), Africa (Southern Africa, Madagascar, Uganda, West Africa), Latin America, Australia, and the South Seas, as well as various parts of continental Europe, Britain (such as the Welsh Revival of 1904–1905), and North America (with the beginning of Pentecostalism in Los Angeles in 1906).[16] Among these four major revival movements, Nee was most deeply influenced by the third one, especially the Holiness and the Keswick movements.

The Holiness revival movement had its roots in the teaching of John Wesley (1703–1791) on Christian perfection, which maintained that believers can reach a point in this life where "love controls every thought, word and deed" although such a perfection does not exclude ignorance, mistake, or "backsliding."[17] Scholars note that the Holiness movement began initially in the 1840s and 1850s, when some Methodists in the United States envisioned that the way to spiritual life renewal lay essentially in resurrecting the neglected Wesleyan teaching on Christian perfection. With such a conviction, the movement summoned believers beyond their first crisis of conversion or justification to a second crisis of faith and total commitment, commonly called by the Methodists "entire sanctification," "perfection in love," or "the second blessing"; or among more Reformed-minded believers a "rest of faith," a "deeper" or "higher life," or a "second conversion." This second conversion or blessing was

16. Davies, "Revival, Spiritual," 1026; Dieter, "Revivalism," 1030; Travis, "Revivalism, Protestant," 1013–14; and Jones, "Holiness Movement," 726–28.

17. Watson, "Methodist Spirituality," 224–25.

taught as an experience of the "deeper work" of divine grace that gave one the ability to resist temptation and to avoid committing any sins knowingly as well as to live a life governed by a perfect intention to love God and neighbor. Two influential Wesleyan strands of the Holiness revival were one led by the Methodist laywoman Phoebe Palmer (1807– 1874) and her physician husband Walter Palmer, and the other led by the Oberlin College perfectionists Charles Finney and Asa Mahan. Both strands exhorted adherents to preach the gospel, help the poor, and promote general social welfare. Phoebe Palmer also played a pioneering role in modeling and defending women's right to public ministry in the church.[18] Regarding women's role in church and home around this period, May notes: "In the earlier days of revivalism, the subordination of women was seen as a sinful consequence of the Fall and a situation to be rectified, which was viewed not only as possible but part of God's mandate for redemption. By contrast, a more literalist reading of the Scriptures tended to prohibit women in leadership positions both in the church and in the home."[19] In this regard Nee apparently adhered to the more literalist interpretation of scripture.

S. Barabas notes that the Holiness revival spread to England and gave rise to the Keswick movement that originated with the Keswick Convention for the Promotion of Practical Holiness,[20] which held an-

18. Kostlevy, Introduction, 1–5; Jones, "Holiness Movement," 726–28; Raser, "Holiness Movement," 543–46; Pierard, "Holiness Movement, American," 564–65; and Dieter, "Revivalism," 1028–31.

Scholars note that Holiness orientations have been identified as somewhat parallel to some strong social and cultural forces of the times. On the one hand, the pervading optimism in the social, political, and economic life in the immediate post-Civil War America had contributed to a climate of a new "age of the Spirit"—with great expectation for seeing the power and active presence of God in personal lives and in the world. On the other hand, the depression of 1890s in the United States had encouraged many Holiness churches—who were already convinced that Jesus's return was imminent—to embrace increasingly radical practices of communal ownership of property (Dieter, "Development of Holiness Theology," 66; Raser, "Holiness Movement," 543; and Kostlevy, Introduction, 4).

19. G. Y. May, "Breaking of Bread," 192.

20. The Holiness movement spread to England mainly through the writing and speaking ministry of three Americans: William E. Boardman, Hannah Whitall Smith and her husband Robert Pearsall Smith (Shelley, "Keswick Movement," 612). David Bundy, however, argues against the common scholarly assumption that the Keswick tradition was an American Wesleyan/Holiness export to England *ex nihilo*; he attempts to show that Keswick must be seen as arisen in the context of other evangelical or revivalist movements in both Britain and the Continent. See Bundy, "Experience of

nually from 1875 in the scenic Lake District of northwest England and became a mother of similar conventions in different countries of the world. Rather than merely imparting Bible knowledge, the convention aimed to be a spiritual clinic for restoring believers' spiritual health. Keswick leaders suspected that preaching the total eradication of sin would engender mistrust in the self and undermine the doctrine of human depravity; thus they avoided teaching Wesleyan perfectionism. Yet while attempting to harmonize Revivalism with Calvinism, Keswick teachers, like their Wesleyan counterparts, refused to accept mediocrity in the Christian life. Instead of "holiness," they emphasized the "deeper life," making much from chapters 6 through 8 in the book of Romans— insisting that since believers are identified with Christ on the cross in their death, they are then set free from their slavery to sin. Yet Keswick preachers not only rejected the Wesleyan doctrine of instantaneous sanctification, but also denied the traditional teaching that sanctification must proceed by inward struggle and strife. In keeping with their Reformed accent, they taught that deliverance from the power of sin was available through faith in Christ the Victor, and that believers did not need to succumb to the tyranny of sin if they experienced the Spirit's work in an ongoing series of emptyings and fillings. Thus Keswick teachers stressed on such themes as consecration or complete abandonment to the rule of Christ, and the victorious Spirit-filled life that led naturally to service and mission. Keswick speakers, among others, included Andrew Murray, F. B. Meyer, and R. A. Torrey.[21]

D. D. Bundy notes that A. B. Simpson (1843–1919)—Presbyterian founder of the Christian and Missionary Alliance—who never accepted the Wesleyan doctrine of eradication of sin, accepted the Keswickian understanding of sanctification. And Simpson was attracted to the Pentecostal understanding of baptism of the Holy Spirit but apparently did not ever speak in tongues. His *The Four-Fold Gospel*, organized around the four themes of Christ as Savior, Sanctifier, Healer, and

---

Evangelical Piety," 118–44.

21. Barabas, "Keswick Convention," 654; and Marsden, *Fundamentalism and American Culture*, 77–78, cited in G. Y. May, "Breaking of Bread," 194–95. While distancing themselves from the Wesleyan doctrine of purity of intention, Keswick's insistence on a subsequent religious experience of empowerment (for service to God and fellow humans) remained quite similar to Holiness formulations of the second blessing experience (Kostlevy, Introduction, 4).

Coming King, became a North American paradigm for early Pentecostal theological formulations.[22]

Dieter suggests that there were two distinct periods of theological development in the Holiness movement. The first, represented by Finney, was a theology of traditional Wesleyan perfectionism underlining the growth side of the growth-crisis dialectics of holiness, namely, highlighting that sanctification was a gradual process. The second, represented by Phoebe Palmer who appealed more to Wesley's later writings, was leaning toward the crisis polarity and so accentuated the instantaneous aspect of entire sanctification, which made the second blessing the beginning of a life of growth rather than the culmination point of maturity. This second emphasis on the crisis pole also paved the way later for the transition from a Holiness accent to the Pentecostal ethos. Dieter observes that Wesley's allowance for the possibility of perfection of love in this life eventually led him to move his tension-balance point between the realizable "now" and the eschatological "not yet" to what Karl Rahner later called the "moment of temporal eternity." As he was leaning toward the present moment of the growth-crisis continuum, Wesley applauded the Spirit baptism and Spirit fullness language of John Fletcher, a close friend of Wesley's and the first systematic theologian of the Wesleyan movement. Dieter thus suggests that there was a parallel between the theological progression in Wesley's own mind and the actual transition in history—in the late nineteenth to the early twentieth century—from Holiness to Pentecostal movements.[23]

Dieter argues that the pneumatology of Fetcher—and that of Wesley inherently—breaks with traditional Reformation (Lutheran and Calvinistic) understanding of history and eschatology, which holds that there are only two ages—that of nature and of grace—in history before the arrival of the eternal kingdom of glory. Dieter notes that there is a tradition—beginning with biblical accounts such as Joel, the Gospel of John, and Acts—of emphasizing a last great revelation of the Spirit in history before the final eschatological kingdom. He points out especially Jurgen Moltmann's retrieval of Joachim of Fiore's concept of "the age of the Spirit" that integrates Augustine's concept of history—as seven ages after the pattern of the seven days of creation—with the Cappadocians' trinitarian understanding of history as three successive dispensations

22. Bundy, "Keswick Higher Life Movement," 820–21.
23. Dieter, "Development of Holiness Theology," 61–77.

of the age of the Father, the Son, and the Spirit. In other words, this tradition sees the kingdom of the Spirit as the last great period in time before the ushering in of the perfect eschatological kingdom, whereas for orthodox Protestantism, the activity of the Spirit is subsumed either in the age of grace (of the Son) or in the eternal kingdom of glory. Dieter also notes that Luther himself complained that in the messages of his preachers, there was too much preaching on the cross, but not enough preaching on Pentecost.[24]

Scholars note that in the 1890s both Wesleyan and Keswick Holiness advocates increasingly identified the second crisis with the baptism of (or with) the Holy Spirit, referring to the gift of the Spirit on the Day of Pentecost as reported in the book of Acts. This gave rise, in the early twentieth century, to the Pentecostal movement, which taught that speaking in other tongues (*glossolalia*) was the outward sign of baptism with the Holy Ghost. The two-crisis paradigm (initial conversion and entire sanctification) of the Holiness movement remained for the Pentecostals until later Holiness-Pentecostal denominations developed a three-stage theory of Christian experience, namely, conversion, entire sanctification, and baptism of the Holy Spirit. Still there emerged some "Baptistic-Pentecostal" bodies who taught again a two-stage theory, but with only conversion and baptism of the Holy Spirit—without reference to the Holiness experience of entire sanctification. Differences aside, experience-centeredness and reliance on Spirit guidance are prominent in all Pentecostal thought.[25]

It is noted that both Holiness and Pentecostal adherents comprised an important addition to Protestant conservatism in the period when the Fundamentalist movement was gathering steam. From the late nineteenth century to the mid-twentieth century, a Fundamentalist movement arose within various Protestant churches—especially in the United States after World War I (1914–1918)—reacting against evolutionary theories, biblical criticism, and liberal theology. In the late 1940s, Billy Graham came on the national scene, initially representing a resurgence in Revivalism as well as the growing Fundamentalist movement. And since the end of World War II, the United States has seen different local scale revivals including several college revivals, an awakening among the

24. Ibid.

25. Pierard, "Holiness Movement, American," 564–65; Jones, "Holiness Movement," 726–28; and Mead and Hill, *Handbook of Denominations*, 307n.

Jesus People in California (during the 1960s), the birth of the charismatic movement, and the revival in Brownsville, Florida. Fundamentalism went through some changes in the 1950s with the rise of the more culturally affirming (neo-)evangelicalism, with which Graham and many churches in the revivalist tradition eventually aligned themselves. Revivalism and evangelicalism share some common theological presuppositions such as commitment to the reliability and authority of scripture, belief in the universal human need for spiritual rebirth, and acceptance of Christ's final commission to his disciples (the "Great Commission" of Matthew 28:19–20) as a mandate for personal evangelism and world mission.[26] It is observed that evangelicalism, "with its emphasis on the individual's direct relationship with God," has nurtured revival movements throughout modern history, and that unlike Roman Catholicism and the high church traditions—which stress on God's grace being communicated through the sacraments constantly—evangelical and revivalist spirituality leans toward the momentary, and sometimes is "decidedly energetic and enthusiastic rather than contemplative."[27]

Opposition to Revivalism has come from both the conservative and the liberal sides of the theological spectrum.[28] Dieter summarizes the criticism as follows:

> The strongly emotional nature of the revivalist's appeal, the critics charge, leads to spiritual instability or even to irrational behavior. They also claim that the revivalist's emphasis on crisis experience tends to deprecate the place of growth and process in Christian living. Opponents also charge that the importance revivalism attaches to a warmhearted, spiritual ministry results in a general anti-intellectualism throughout the tradition; they claim as well that the strong appeal to individualized religion leads to a subjectivism that obscures or even denies the social and cultural implications of Christianity. The direct praying and preaching, the tendency to popularize and excite interest by use of promotional psychology, and inclination to judgmentalism and separatism are also common accusations brought against revivalists.[29]

---

26. Davies, "Revival, Spiritual," 1024–28; Dieter, "Revivalism," 1028–31; Travis, "Revivalism, Protestant," 1012–15; and Livingstone, "Fundamentalism."

27. Blumhofer and Balmer, *Modern Christian Revivals*, xi, xiii.

28. Travis, "Revivalism, Protestant," 1014.

29. Dieter, "Revivalism," 1031.

The major response of revival proponents, Dieter notes, has been to point to the positive results in church and society that have been accompanying special periods of religious revivals, such as the dramatic growth of the churches; the significant moral, social, and cultural changes; the ecumenical spirit that has produced cooperation among churches at a level not achieved in any other way; and the expansion of Christian benevolent services as well as the development of organizations promoting Christian causes and social concerns (including many mission bodies and most of America's Christian colleges and seminaries).[30]

From Revivalism to Mysticism: Jessie Penn-Lewis

As early as 1923 or 1924, Nee read *The Word of the Cross* and *The Cross of Calvary and Its Message* by Jessie Penn-Lewis (1861–1927), who was instrumental in the early Keswick movement and the Welsh revival of 1904–1905. Nee became an avid reader of Penn-Lewis's works; and by the mid-1920s he was in regular correspondence with her and was a chief person responsible for translating, interpreting, and disseminating her thought to the Chinese audience.[31] Nee himself apparently also carried the profound faith lessons he learned from Penn-Lewis's works into his own life and ministry.[32]

Leung Ka-lun suggests that within modern Protestantism, Penn-Lewis is an important thinker in spiritual theology and a rare adherent of mysticism, and that her spiritual theology has been influential for the Chinese church (particularly through the work of Nee). Leung notes that following the tradition of Finney, the early Penn-Lewis sought and obtained the gifts and power of the Holy Ghost through the experience of being filled by the Spirit; but she soon became dissatisfied with having the mere experience of Spirit infilling. Influenced by Andrew Murray and other Holiness preachers—who regarded Spirit baptism as the beginning of a spiritual journey that was characterized by continual Spirit indwelling and Spirit guidance—Penn-Lewis believed that Christians should earnestly seek the indwelling of the Holy Spirit, which would

---

30. Ibid.

31. Leung Ka-lun has done some research on Penn-Lewis's thought including her tripartite anthropology, and judged that she was one of Nee's major sources for *The Spiritual Man*. See K. L. Leung, "Sanyuan renlun" [Trichotomistic anthropology], 188–89, and "Fenxing yundong dao shenmi zhuyi" [From revivalism to mysticism], 2–56.

32. G. Y. May, "Breaking of Bread," 203, 206.

eventually lead them into mystical union with God. Thus Leung detects in her thought a transition from Revivalism to mysticism as well as a departure from "mainstream" Protestantism, for she had parted with the usual Reformed path of simply obeying the revealed God; instead she treaded on the mystical way of seeking union with the hidden God.[33]

According to Leung, the way to life in union with God, for Penn-Lewis, was through death to the self, which was none other than the way of the cross. She believed that Jesus's dying on the cross was not limited to such meanings as expiation and propitiation, but rather it was a representative act of revelation—showing forth that all human persons must die to their old natural life, in order to gain the new resurrected life. To her, the true meaning of the cross was "refusing the self"; anything less than this would be putting a limit to the significance of the cross.[34] Grace May also notes that Penn-Lewis felt called by God to be a messenger of the cross, and so strived to apply the principles of the death and resurrection of Christ in both her preaching and her own daily living.[35]

Citing well-respected voices within the Holiness movement such as Andrew Murray and G. H. Pember, Penn-Lewis also adapted a tripartite anthropology that distinguishes between the functions of the body, soul, and spirit as corresponding respectively to *sense*-consciousness, *self*-consciousness, and *God*-consciousness. This tripartite nature of human beings later became the subject of Nee's three-volume book *The Spiritual Man*. Like Penn-Lewis who was convinced of the dire consequence of confusing the soul with the spirit and so devoted many pages to elucidating the differences, Nee also stressed the supreme importance of the contrast between the soul and the spirit, between the natural person and the spiritual person, between what is human and what is divine.[36]

Leung notes that the later Penn-Lewis revised some of her teachings due to her reaction against the Pentecostal movement. She was adamant in her rejection of speaking in tongues as the evidence of being filled by the Spirit, for she feared that such insistence would lead to division of the church. She was also against blindly seeking signs and wonders, for she believed that the way to prove whether certain signs and wonders

---

33. K. L. Leung, "Fenxing yundong dao shenmi zhuyi" [From revivalism to mysticism], 2–14, 56.

34. Ibid., 15–19.

35. G. Y. May, "Breaking of Bread," 205.

36. Ibid., 208–13.

are from God or not lies not in the *fact* or the dramatic nature of the signs and wonders, but rather in the subsequent *effect* of such signs and wonders—especially, whether they are contributing to the promotion of Christian unity. She was also skeptical about certain propagated means to obtain the gifts of the Spirit, and believed that many of the fanatic, unbridled, or rivalistic phenomena in Pentecostal meetings came from either the flesh or the soul, rather than from the Spirit. Since she held that the Holy Spirit works only in the human spirit whereas evil spirits can work only via the human body and mind, she believed that many emotional or compulsive reactions were results of evil spirits' influences. Thus she changed her earlier Quietist orientation, and cautioned the danger of letting the mind go blank or letting the will remain passive, lest one be susceptible to the influence of evil spirits. She now insisted on the importance of the will, and reinstated the significance of the mind (*nous*)—in this case the renewed mind—as the instrumental means for the divine Spirit's working on the human spirit. Also, like many revivalists of her day who did not accept the Pentecostal orientation, she adapted, as a defense for her position, the dispensational hermeneutic that regards the Pentecost phenomena as meant only for the early apostolic dispensation and so no longer to be repeated for the current era.[37]

Quietist Mysticism: Miguel de Molinos, Jeanne Guyon, and François Fénelon

Quietism was a mystical movement, with identifiable precedents in Spain, France, and Italy that gathered strength in seventeenth-century Europe. Louis Dupré, a noted scholar on mysticism, has addressed several significant points regarding the history and interpretation of Quietism. He observes that the attempt to understand this mystical movement has suffered from much "misrepresentation and unfair polemics . . . under the general, derogatory term 'Quietism.'"[38] While the controversy about Quietism usually stemmed from its stress of passivity and contemplative quiet over active virtue and discursive meditation, Dupré points out that the Quietist emphasis was heavily indebted to the "devout humanism" of Francis de Sales (1567–1622), who had merely

37. K. L. Leung, "Fenxing yundong dao shenmi zhuyi" [From revivalism to mysticism], 41–50.

38. Dupré and Wiseman, *Light from Light*, 324.

given fresh articulation to ideas of "a long and venerable lineage."[39] Such lineage, notes Dupré, went back to the desert fathers and mothers of the fourth century, and appeared in the Rhineland mystics (including John Tauler who influenced both Martin Luther and John Arndt) and the Spanish Carmelites (John of the Cross and Teresa of Avila). According to Dupré, Quietists can be understood in contrast with the Jansenists who were their contemporaries. While Jansenists emphasized personal effort and moral seriousness, Quietists distrusted human initiative and stressed passivity and nonresistance. Both assumed a pessimistic concept of human nature; while Jansenists advocated that believers must work out their salvation in fear and trembling "in earnest cooperation with grace," Quietists concluded that only total abandonment of one's corrupt nature could lead to total efficacy of grace. Yet unlike the Reformation which revolted against the immediate past, the inspired representatives of Quietism—namely Miguel de Molinos, Madame Jeanne Guyon, and François Fénelon—attempted to retrieve certain fundamental spiritual principles "from centuries of neglect," and regarded themselves as "solidly anchored in Catholic orthodoxy." And Dupré notes that it is usually "difficult to distinguish the so-called Quietists from their great predecessors" (132, 121).

Miguel de Molinos (b. 1628) was a doctor of theology of the University of Coimbra. His most famous book, *Spiritual Guide*, asserted that spiritual perfection can only be brought about by contemplative, or purely passive, prayer, which can be attained by avoiding "all strenuous ascetic efforts" and concentrating "entirely on inner quiet and abandon" (133). The Jesuits were the first to attack this teaching because their own practice of meditation seemed to be threatened, but several cardinals came to Molinos's rescue immediately. Dupré notes that Molinos did explicitly state, in his *Letters to a Spaniard* (1676), that his intention was never to attack meditation, but merely to provide *another* way to spiritual perfection. For Molinos, however, "there is only *one* form of perfection: the union with God through infused contemplation"—which, Dupré suggests, is a thesis that is not unlike what is "implied in John of the Cross and a number of other orthodox writers" (134–35). Yet eventually the same Pope Innocent XI, who had first protected Molinos, had him arrested; and the reason for this arrest remains uncertain even today. Molinos was then sentenced to lifelong imprisonment for being "guilty

39. Dupré, "Jansenism and Quietism," 132.

of immoral conduct as well as of doctrinal errors," an accusation that historians find puzzling since he "was known for his exemplary life and venerated by his own household" (133–34). Dupré notes that the fact that Molinos admitted all the sixty-eight charges against him "proves only his willingness to practice the nonresistance he preached," and that he died a saintly death after staying in jail for nine years, all the while remaining "a model of goodness and piety" to all those around him (134).

Madame Jeanne Guyon (1648–1717), a relatively uneducated woman, suffered much (including frequent illnesses) during her lifetime. At age sixteen, she was given against her will in an unhappy marriage to a wealthy, invalid, and morose cousin who was twenty-two years her senior. She was then also under the supervision of a hostile mother-in-law, and was denied permission to remove her children during a smallpox epidemic, which resulted in her loss of two children and the deformation of a third one. At around age twenty she had a remarkable conversion experience encountering the wonderful favor and goodness of "Divine Love."[40] After her husband's death in 1676 (when she was about age twenty-eight), she resolved not to remarry and to devote herself to the love of Christ. At about age thirty-seven, she wrote her *Short and Very Easy Method of Prayer* (1685), which popularized a form of contemplative prayer—previously known chiefly to the religious—among the laity.[41] Partly due to this book, she was accused of Quietism and was imprisoned in 1688, and again from 1698–1702.[42]

In this book, Guyon maintained that the easiest and best way to find God is to turn one's gaze inward, because the kingdom of God and all its beauty and glory are within (referring to Luke 17:21 and Ps 45:13).[43] She also appealed to Augustine who lost much time during his early years in searching outwardly for a God who was later found inwardly.[44] Thus Guyon's advice was to turn one's attention within and to wait *upon* the graced presence of God already there. She taught that the fallen nature

40. Guyon, *Autobiography*, 312, quoted in Tyson, *Invitation to Christian Spirituality*, 306.

41. Another English translation of this book was issued as Guyon, *Experiencing the Depths of Jesus Christ*.

42. Cf. Tyson, *Invitation to Christian Spirituality*, 306–7; and Dupré, "Jansenism and Quietism," 135–36.

43. Guyon, *Experiencing the Depths*, 91, 45.

44. Ibid., 11.

is not to be overcome by might or power on the human part, but its transformation occurs only when God's Spirit is at work within a person. She believed that true communion with God happens purely "in spirit," without any mixture of human elements: "All true worship is 'in spirit.' To be 'in spirit,' the soul is annihilated. 'In spirit' you enter into the purity of that Spirit that prays within you; you are drawn away from your own soulish and human methods of prayer. You are 'in reality' because you are placed in the reality of the *all* of God and the *nothing* of man."[45]

While discouraging asceticism, Guyon did not say that one should not act at all, but one should not get ahead of the movement of grace, or should only act in *re*-action to the Spirit. In this book she also taught that all Christians are called to this form of quiet prayer, but in her later work *Spiritual Torrents*, she reserved her message only for the initiated. Regarding this, Dupré thus comments: "This combination of hazardous generalization and spiritual elitism seems characteristic of the entire Quietist movement. Impatience with different approaches easily mixes with a kind of spiritual *gnosis*."[46]

Yet Dupré points out that one looks in vain in her book for "a rash judgment or a questionable principle," though her one-sided emphasis on passive or quiet methods of prayer "tends to oversimplify the course of spiritual development" (ibid.). Struck by the basic concordance between Guyon's teaching and that of less controversial mystics, Dupré discerns that it is "in the expression more than in the content that Jeanne Guyon's theory becomes occasionally questionable"—especially with her tendency to equate her own particular experiences with general spiritual doctrines, and "her naïve way of treating her own single idea as if no history had preceded it and no complications could obscure it" (138). Nonetheless, Dupré judges that "her highly reputed spiritual powers were real," and that "the salient points of her doctrine seem to be sound and entirely compatible with the Christian tradition"—particularly in her teaching that spiritual life is a teleological process moving from lower to higher stages, "a process of disappropriation, a growing detachment that allows God gradually to take possession of the soul" (135–36, 138).

While Guyon had a readiness to commit to writing unrelated feelings or experiences of her own, Dupré points out that some modern

45. Ibid., 91.
46. Dupré, "Jansenism and Quietism," 136.

critics' ridiculing of her hysterical disposition fails to account for the profound influence she had on "some of the most discerning masters of her time"; among them François Fénelon (1651–1715) who had a reputation as "a seriously religious priest gifted with a brilliant mind and connected with the highest circles" (136, 139). Fénelon was reserved and reticent when he first met Guyon, but later his "conversion" or surrender became total: he became a truly devoted disciple of Guyon as well as her theological teacher, providing her and the Quietist movement with some much-needed theological support and articulation (139). Fénelon explained that the higher or ideal state of passivity consists not in the lack of work or active virtue, but in the absence of the soul's impatient inclination to run ahead of the movement of grace. Distinguishing between the lower and higher parts of the soul, Fénelon insisted that sense and imagination (functions of the lower portion of the soul) play no more part in the graced state of simple peace and pure love (of union with God). What Fénelon asserted, notes Dupré, "belongs to the mainstream of the Christian mystical tradition, which has always taught that God's direct communication occurs . . . beyond reflective intelligence and deliberate will" (140). Thus if there was a "heresy" of Quietism, in Dupré's view, it consisted perhaps in "nothing more than the all-too-deliberate decision to leave the ordinary" which barely granted a right for the existence of "the imperfect but commonly attainable" (141). Dupré concludes that "Quietism should be seen as attempts to perpetuate the Christian spiritual tradition in a culture that was breaking away from the basis of that tradition," and their intolerance to mediocrity may have stemmed more from the new culture's "conceptual matrices . . . which they both accepted and resisted—than from personal pride and deliberate elitism" (ibid.).

Nee was appreciative of all three Quietist mystical writers: Molinos, Guyon, and Fénelon,[47] and was most impressed with Guyon's work *Short and Very Easy Method of Prayer*, which was translated by one of Nee's closest associates into Chinese and made available to every new convert of the Local Churches.[48] It is noted that in Guyon's writings Nee

47. F. Chen, *Ni Tuosheng* [Watchman Nee], 117–18.

48. Foster and Smith, *Devotional Classics*, 320. Foster notes that both John Wesley and Hudson Taylor also recommended this book of Guyon's to believers of their day.

This close associate of Nee was the medical doctor C. H. Yu (Yu Chenghua) who also translated Guyon's autobiography as well as Brother Lawrence's *Practice of the Presence of God*. See Y. Li, *Renwu Cidian* [Biographical dictionary].

discovered the significance of complete submission and conformity to God's will, and that the mystical spirit of Guyon found echoes in many of Nee's statements on crucifixion of self and loss of life in Christ.[49] Guyon's stress that contemplative prayer should be the ground and source for any active service also finds echoes in Nee, as he states: "no Christian experience begins with walking, but always with a definite sitting down."[50] Nee's receptivity to this orientation might have been reinforced by the Daoist as well as the Confucianist culture he inherited, as May observes: "Guyon's emphasis on quietude and submission to God resonated powerfully with the Chinese contemplative tradition."[51]

NEE'S ADAPTATION OF SOURCES

The various streams of the Brethren movement, dispensationalism, the Holiness movement, the Keswick revival, and Fundamentalism as well as different mystical doctrines all in their diverse ways informed and shaped Nee's theology and spirituality. Scholars have also pointed out some more specific and unique ways Nee adapted to these and other sources of influence.

Holiness and Brethren Outlook

In her recent dissertation, May identifies some significant influences on Nee, particularly in his Holiness and Brethren outlook. May notes that Penn-Lewis, and through her Holiness and Keswick theology, exerted a pronounced influence on Nee:

> Nee relied on the same Pauline texts as Penn-Lewis in describing the work of the Cross. Nee echoed Penn-Lewis' understanding of the crucifixion of the old self, which they both regarded as essential for Christian maturity and effective service. Nee even adopted her tripartite doctrine of humanity, which viewed human beings as a composite of body, soul, and spirit. Nee was also drawn to Madame Guyon, the mystic that Penn-Lewis and Nee's own mentor, Barber, found so compelling. . . . Nee freely cited from works by Andrew Murray, F. B. Meyer, and Evan Roberts,

49. Wetmore, "Doctrine of Dying and Rising," 12, cited in Liao, "Nee's Theology of Victory," 39.

50. Nee, *Sit, Walk, Stand*, 22, cited in Covell, *Confucius, The Buddha, and Christ*, 198.

51. G. Y. May, "Breaking of Bread," 207.

holiness authors whom Penn-Lewis often referred to in her own
writings. Not surprisingly, the same themes which featured
prominently in Keswick circles found their way into Nee's own
writing and preaching.[52]

Thus while Nee was a biblicist in his insistence that his ideas and practices
were derived directly from the Bible and so not appealing to any tradition
for authority, May points out that Nee's theology clearly fell in line with
the Holiness tradition of the late nineteenth and early twentieth century.
In addition to a strong theology of the cross which resembled that of
Penn-Lewis's, Nee also followed the Holiness tradition in stressing the
believers' break from the world and underscoring "the incompatibility
of faithful living and worldliness, the cosmic battle between good and
evil, the spiritual opposition between God's forces and Satan's, and the
irreconcilability of living for the now and the hereafter."[53] Undoubtedly
influenced by his attendance at the 1938 annual Keswick Convention
and his extensive conversations with T. Austin-Sparks in London, Nee's
theological teaching "could not have coincided more with the standard
teaching of the Keswick Conventions"—particularly in his prioritizing
of the scriptures, his belief in the necessity of a definite conversion experience, his emphasis of dependence on God over and against human
ability, his insistence on the higher or deeper life, his stress on intuitive
spiritual experience over mere rational knowledge, his enjoinment on
prayerfully waiting on God for direction, and his call to surrender all for
Christ.[54] It should be noted that one of Nee's most popular works—*The
Normal Christian Life*—was based on a study of Romans chapters 6 to 8,
which were among the favorite passages of Keswick preachers.

May also points out that many Fundamentalist elements were
also present in Nee's outlook, albeit with important qualifications. As
Western imperialists were exerting their powers in China, Nee looked
beyond his immediate context to the New Testament period. Like the
American Fundamentalists of the 1920s, Nee needed an authority that
could not be affected by social historical forces or outward circumstances, and upheld the undisputed authority of the Bible. He thus repeatedly
sought instruction directly from the pages of scripture. But he differed

52. Ibid., 206–7. In this passage, May references Nee, *Spiritual Man*, 11, and *Shuling
ren* [Spiritual man], 10.

53. G. Y. May, "Breaking of Bread," 183.

54. Ibid., 237–39, 195.

significantly from Western Fundamentalists by asserting the sovereign role of the Holy Spirit in interpreting the scriptures. Nee also kept the practice of weekly breaking of bread which most Fundamentalists did not observe. In addition, while virulently attacking modernism, Nee also departed from Western Fundamentalism in another significant way: his adaptation of dispensationalism did not spare believers from end-time tribulation, which, May believes, probably owed more to China's political turmoil and social instability in the 1930s than to any theological camp. Yet with a similar partisan spirit that characterized Fundamentalists of the day, Nee also withdrew from social and political engagements.[55] May notes: "Nee's insistence on the Local Church as the most biblical expression of the church, his own dogmatic personality, and his anti-denominational stance would earn the Assembly the repu-tation of being a separatist Christian group, not unlike the most zealous Western Fundamentalists or Exclusive Brethren."[56]

The Brethren movement had a long-lasting influence on many as-pects of Nee's theological thinking. From a passage Nee wrote in his *The Orthodoxy of the Church*, Lam notes that even twenty-some years after his initial contact with the Brethren, Nee was still highly respectful of many doctrines that the Brethren had "recovered"—including different topics in salvation, sin, the church, prophecies, and the end time.[57] In particular, similar to the Brethren, Nee challenged the division between clergy and laity, and took an antagonistic stand toward denominational affiliation.[58] May notes that like the Brethren and other primitivists or reconstructionists, Nee rejected the intervening historical periods, and appropriated selected parts of church history, asserting particularly the authority of the apostolic church and its pristine practices. Refusing to concede any historical, social, or political forces in the life of the church, both Nee and the Brethren viewed themselves as direct successors of the apostolic church. Yet unlike the Exclusive Brethren who prized ortho-doxy above all else and broke bread only with those who shared the same definition of orthodoxy, Nee's Assembly—appealing to the priority of the Spirit in matters of discernment—welcomed a much broader range

55. Ibid., 165, 237, 242, 247, 266.

56. Ibid., 239.

57. Lam, *Shuling shenxue* [Spiritual theology], 28. Lam quotes from Nee, *Jiaohui de zhengtong* [Orthodoxy of the church].

58. J. Lee, "Little Flock Movement," 74.

of Christians to their Table although they discouraged their own members from participating in the communion services of other churches.[59]

Theology of Suffering

The great social and political upheavals in China throughout Nee's youth
and adult years probably had encouraged Nee's accent on a theology of
suffering, echoing Penn-Lewis's messages on the cross and Christ's victory over suffering and evil. May notes that the hymns Nee authored
or edited (most likely in the 1930s and 1940s) provided a "far more
poignant outlet" for his view of the costly nature of discipleship. In the
hymn "Let Me Love and Not Be Respected," he wrote:

> It's the pouring, not the drinking;
> It's the breaking, not the keeping.
> A life suff'ring to seek other's blessing,
> A life loving and true comfort giving;
> Not expecting pity and concern,
> Not accepting solace and applause;
> Even lonely, even forgotten, even wordless,
> even forsaken,
> Tears and blood my price for the righteous crown
> shall be.[60]

May comments that the suffering of sacrifice and isolation in this hymn
recalled the image of the grain of wheat that Penn-Lewis wrote about:
"At last the grain of wheat is willing to be hidden away from the eyes of
men. Willing to be trampled upon and lie in silence in some lonely cor-
ner chosen of God. Willing to appear what others would call a 'failure.'
Willing to live in the will of God apart from glorious experiences. Willing
to dwell in solitude and isolation, away from happy fellowship with the
other grains of wheat."[61] Nee learned similar lessons from Barber, who
lived in a poor village near Fujian "by faith" (without recourse to any
financial support), had prayed for ten years before a small band of young
men came to her for discipleship, mentored Nee and several of his peers
for seven years, and lived a fairly lonely and unrecognized existence during her last years in China.[62]

59. G. Y. May, "Breaking of Bread," 149, 162–64, 237.

60. Nee et al., Hymnary, 253, as quoted in G. Y. May, "Breaking of Bread," 233.

61. Penn-Lewis, Much Fruit, 89, as quoted in G. Y. May, "Breaking of Bread," 234.

62. G. Y. May, "Breaking of Bread," 234.

Another hymn, "Olives that Have Known No Pressure," declared:

> If the grapes escape the wine press
> cheering wine can never flow;
> Spikenard only through the crushing,
> Fragrance can diffuse.[63]

In another hymn adapted by Nee, "The Life of the Grape Vine," Nee used sixteen stanzas to contemplate the grape vine, especially its suffering-laden process of growth. Stanza 5 sang:

> But the master of the vineyard
> Not in lenience doth abide,
> But with knife and pruning scissors
> Then would strip it of its pride.
> Caring not the vine is tender,
> But with deep, precision stroke
> All the pretty, excess branches
> From the vine are neatly broke.[64]

A speaker at a recent conference on Nee believed that Stanzas 14 to 16 of this hymn—with the vine's cycle of life, death, and resurrection—best characterize Nee's own life journey.[65] Similarly, Witness Lee notes that for Nee, "life is measured not by gain but by loss and that the one who has suffered the most has the most to share with others. For this reason, he never spared himself, but bore the cross and the fellowship of Christ's suffering, being conformed to His death, in order to live Christ out that others might be nourished and enriched with Him."[66] Despite the rough journey, Nee enjoined believers to persevere and remain faithful as well as to be joyful and thankful under all circumstances, by setting before themselves the goal of union with Christ and the heavenly reward of the glorious crown. Like Penn-Lewis, Nee's ultimate goal was for believers to experience victory; a victory that is intimately connected with fellowship with Christ in both his death and resurrection.[67]

---

63. Nee et al., *Hymnary*, 268, as quoted in G. Y. May, "Breaking of Bread," 234.

64. Nee et al., *Hymnary*, 257, as quoted in G. Y. May, "Breaking of Bread," 235.

65. *Ni Tuosheng shengping* [Life of Watchman Nee], CD no. 3.

66. W. Lee, *Watchman Nee*, chap. 21, "The Sufferings of Nee's Ministry."

67. G. Y. May, "Breaking of Bread," 235–36. May notes that both Penn-Lewis's and Nee's strong emphasis on the cross helped temper what might otherwise be interpreted as a variety of triumphalism.

Patristic Sources and Allegorical Interpretation of Scripture

Did Nee have knowledge of some patristic writings? The answer is yes. While upholding the supremacy of the Bible and generally avoiding reliance on Christian tradition to support his position,[68] Nee nonetheless appealed to writings of some early church fathers in his teaching on observing the Lord's day. The writings he referred to included those of the Didaché, Ignatius of Antioch (ca. 35–107), Justin Martyr (ca. 100–165), Clement of Alexandria (ca. 150–215), Tertullian (ca. 160–225), and Origen (ca. 185–254), as well as the edicts of Constantine in the fourth century.[69] It would not be surprising, then, if Nee's approach to biblical interpretation also bears significant likeness to some of these patristic sources.

Nee's approach to interpreting the Bible has provoked some discussions among scholars, especially with regard to his focus on the texts' spiritual meanings, a focus characteristic of the ancient allegorical method of scriptural interpretation. Lee Ken Ang identifies Nee's hermeneutical method as "that of allegorization," and suggests that Nee's approach contains a "conspicuous taint of spiritualization" as well as being susceptible to the danger of reducing biblical interpretation to "sheer subjectivism."[70] Katheryn Leung also notes several pitfalls in Nee's way of interpreting the Song of Songs, and hints that such an allegorical method has become outdated and unnecessary in light of twentieth-century developments in critical biblical studies.[71] Yet such a privileging of the modern "objective" or critical approaches to the Bible needs to be questioned; as Sandra M. Schneiders points out, there is an emerging post-critical appreciation of patristic and medieval biblical exegesis, due largely to the realization of the "serious limitations of scientific method," the rediscovery of the power of symbolic and metaphorical languages,

68. Ibid., 294.

69. Nee, "Appendix—Ancient Writings."

70. K. Lee, "Watchman Nee," 196–202, esp. 199, 201–2. See also Pamudji, "Little Flock Trilogy," 182.

71. K. Leung, "Yuyifa jiejing" [Allegorical interpretation of scripture], 21–48, esp. 21–25, 34–39, 46–48. For further research, it would be interesting to compare Nee's interpretation of the Song of Songs with Madame Guyon's commentary (available online). There are also numerous Puritan commentaries on the Song of Songs; see the study by Hessel-Robinson, "Be Thou My Onely."

and the new understanding of the function of human imagination, as well as the complexity involved in the process of interpretation.[72]

Schneiders notes that the early church developed two basic approaches to the scripture: "the 'literal' approach and the 'more than literal,' or 'allegorical,' approach," although these terms meant different things to the ancients than what they mean today.[73] Origen developed the theory of the threefold sense of scripture, corresponding to "the tripartite composition of the human person (body, soul, spirit) as this was understood by the Greek fathers."[74] John Cassian (ca. 360–435) later introduced to Western monasticism a similar fourfold sense of scripture that became standard in the Middle Ages.[75] According to Bernard McGinn, in one of Cassian's major works known as the *Conferences*, he distinguished two proper modes of understanding scripture—historical interpretation and spiritual understanding—and three types of spiritual understanding: allegorical, tropological, and anagogical. Cassian illustrates these four senses of scripture by Paul's interpretation of Abraham's two wives in Galatians 4:22–23. As McGinn notes: "The *historia* is the past historical fact, the *allegoria* is the way in which the two women prefigure the two covenants," and tropology is the moral explanation and knowledge "that instruct the Jerusalem of the soul," while anagogy is the message that the heavenly Jerusalem "is our true mother (see Gal 4:26–27)."[76] Thus in this classic example, the four senses of Jerusalem are: "the Jewish city (literal), the church (allegorical), the soul (tropological), and the heavenly city (anagogical)."[77] The three nonliteral senses are sometimes referred generally to as the allegorical sense or the spiritual sense.[78]

Schneiders summarizes these four senses as follows: "the literal sense refers to the events and realities of Jewish history. The other three are spiritual senses: the allegorical, which reveals the Christian or theological meaning of the text; the moral or tropological, which applies the text to the individual Christian's practice; and the anagogical, which

72. Schneiders, "Scripture and Spirituality," 19.

73. Ibid., 9.

74. Ibid., 11, 15.

75. Ibid.

76. McGinn, *Foundations of Mysticism*, 220–21.

77. Schneiders, "Scripture and Spirituality," 15.

78. For an explanation of Bede's use of the term "allegorical" to refer to all the three nonliteral senses, see Bede, *Bede*, 25n5.

points toward eschatological fulfillment."[79] These four senses were captured aptly by an anonymous medieval author in this way: "The letter
teaches what happened; the allegorical sense what to believe; the moral
sense what to do; the anagogical sense whither we go."[80] Proponents of
this type of fourfold approach to the Bible included Augustine (354–
430) and the Venerable Bede (673–735)—both influential for medieval
scholarship. Bede quoted with approval this saying of Augustine: "in all
the holy books it is necessary to consider what eternal things are announced, what deeds are narrated, what future things are foretold, and
what things are enjoined or admonished to be done."[81]

This "fourfold interpretation" also governed the monastics' prayer-
ful practice of spiritual reading (of the scriptures and the church fathers),
known as *lectio divina*.[82] Schneiders notes that the ancient readers believed that every word of scripture was "the bearer, in some way, of divine revelation"; thus a kind of "divine assistance (usually understood as
interior illumination)" was required to properly understand the text.[83]
Besides, one's capacity to receive such illumination was deemed largely
determined by one's moral or spiritual formation: "This led Origen, the
early church's greatest biblical scholar, to insist that the students at his
catechetical school in Alexandria lead a quasi-monastic life since the
purity of their consciences and the intensity of their prayer were sub-
stantively determinative of the quality of their scholarship."[84] Similarly,
McGinn also comments that Cassian "insists that the proper grasp of
the Bible is dependent on moral effort rather than mere study: purity of
heart rather than knowledge of the commentators is the key (see *Instit.*
5.34). *Conference* 14.10 uses the image of constant meditation on the
scripture eventually forming the ark of the covenant within the soul; that
is, the meaning of the Bible becomes connatural."[85]

Schneiders points out that the difference between the pre-modern
and the post-Renaissance approaches to scripture is often caricatured
"as the opposition between 'spiritual' and 'literal' interpretation," which

---

79. Schneiders, "Scripture and Spirituality," 15.

80. Ibid.

81. Augustine, *Gen. ad litt.* 1.1.1, as quoted in Bede, *Bede*, 25.

82. Schneiders, "Scripture and Spirituality," 15.

83. Ibid., 6.

84. Ibid.

85. McGinn, *Foundations of Mysticism*, 221.

does not take into account that each of these two terms has meant different things for the ancient and the modern exegetes.[86] First, in our modern usage, the literal sense is the message determined by the author's intention. In contrast, in ancient usage, the "literal sense" was the letter of the text as opposed to its religious meaning, or the text's "body" versus its "spirit," regardless of whether or not this latter spiritual meaning was intended by the biblical writer. Schneiders gives an example to illustrate what the literal sense means in the ancient minds: "if this theory were applied to the New Testament, the literal meaning of the account of the crucifixion of Jesus would be restricted to the physical and political facts of the story. Its salvific significance (which is obviously the primary meaning the evangelists were trying to convey) would belong to the spiritual meaning" (16). Thus for the ancient exegetes, the "literal meaning" was primarily a door to enter into the true meaning of the text. Yet modern exegetes are usually convinced that the human author determines the text's true meaning, or the text's true meaning is considered identical with its (authorial) literal meaning (16–17).

Secondly, for the ancients, the spiritual sense referred to the text's true meaning, which was "the message God wished to convey through Scripture to the believer," although such message might be "obscure and never more than tentatively discerned" (17). Yet such obscurity in human understanding could be overcome, in Origen's view, by a "divine influence" on the reader with "the same charism of inspiration" that influenced the sacred writer. As Schneiders notes: "The theory of the necessity of divine illumination for the proper understanding of the Scriptures was a constant in the tradition of spiritual exegesis" (ibid.). Schneiders observes several underlying assumptions of the ancients that modern scholars might not share, such as: scripture is inspired by God, scripture (both Testaments) is "concerned uniquely with God's revelation in Christ," and scripture has multiple meanings "corresponding to the richness of the mystery of the Word made flesh" (17–18). In contrast to such "rich and theologically well-founded" understanding, post-Renaissance critical scholars were equipped with historical, philological, and other tools, and were persuaded that the ideal of hermeneutics was the literal sense "that seemed within realistic reach of the careful scholar" (18).

86. Schneiders, "Scripture and Spirituality," 16.

Finally, Schneiders points out a difference between the ancient and modern exegetes in regard to their relationship with tradition. While the faith tradition "provided the universally accepted context for all biblical interpretation" for the ancients, the modern individuals' "quest for objectivity" as well as their "profound suspicion of authority" led to the prizing of scientific or mathematical exactitude over the incertitude of allegorical or spiritual exegesis: "The immediacy of participation in an interpretive tradition was shattered. Scientific method became the sole guide of scholarly investigation, and mathematical exactitude and certitude the ideals of all knowledge worthy of the name. In such an intellectual climate the spiritual exegesis of the patristic and medieval scholars could only appear accidentally insightful at best and frivolously imaginative at worst" (19). Thus while not advocating "a simple return" to the ancient way of reading scripture, Schneiders envisions a kind of post-critical reading—"characterized by what Paul Ricoeur has called 'the second naiveté'"—which "will no doubt involve an aesthetic appreciation and spiritual sensitivity that have long been almost absent from the world of biblical scholarship" (ibid.).

In the atmosphere of modern biblical scholarship, it is not surprising that Nee's method of biblical interpretation has not been appreciated by some of his critics. Fortunately, some scholars have recognized the value of Nee's exposition of scripture. Lam Wing-hung affirms that Nee's reading of the scriptures opens up—beyond litero-grammatical and historical methods of biblical interpretation—a "higher dimension" related to the spiritual life, although Lam also notes the problem, in such an approach, of confusing "illumination" and "personal opinion"[87] as well as depreciating the value of the "objective truth" in scripture by the elevation of "subjective revelation."[88] Liao Yuan-wei also sees that "Nee's insightful exposition of the Bible . . . have proved to be far-reaching."[89] At any rate, even if Nee might not have been influenced directly by the ancient and medieval writers in his allegorical approach to the Bible, his orientation was shaped at least partly by the Pietist and Puritan

---

87. Lam, *Shuling shenxue* [Spiritual theology], 287–89, and "Huaren shenxue" [Chinese theology], 73–74.

88. Lam, *Shuling shenxue* [Spiritual theology], 286–87; see also K. Lee, "Watchman Nee," 234.

89. Liao, "Nee's Theology of Victory," 205.

currents[90] as well as the mystical streams that he imbibed deeply from Guyon, Wesley, Edwards, Penn-Lewis, and others.

A Question about Plagiarism

Liao suggests that one of Nee's major sources for his tripartite anthropology might well be J. B. Heard's *The Tripartite Nature of Man: Spirit, Soul, and Body*, which Nee "failed to give credit to."[91] Leung also surmises that Nee perhaps had copied much from some of his sources.[92] I believe, however, that such allusions to possible plagiarism are not doing justice to Nee. For one thing, Nee himself in the preface to *The Spiritual Man* acknowledged that he was not the originator of the teaching (on the difference between the spirit and the soul), as well as noting that "I have freely quoted" the writings of certain authors and "because there are so many places where I have referenced them, I have not made specific reference to the sources."[93] For another thing, the notions about plagiarism and presumption to originality are very much products of contemporary Western culture, which are probably not commensurable in many Asian contexts, especially not in the first half of twentieth-century China and particularly not for nonacademic writings. As the Plagiarism Policy of Graduate Theological Union states: "The multi-cultural context of the academy reveals certain Western culturally determined presumptions about originality in one's work. In Asian cultures, there may be a tendency to view words in writing as public property that is open, indeed auspicious for one's use. Particularly with regard to religious subjects, one's work may be considered better for belonging to the tradition . . . for scholarly work is both one's own thinking and the result of one's engagement in a particular history of discourse."[94]

Besides, while Nee might have borrowed freely from many books he read, it does appear that he had engaged with those ideas deeply to the extent that he was able to selectively accept or reject some of them as well as coming to form his own convictions. As Peterus Pamudji notes: "But Watchman Nee is too complex to be labeled as an importer

90. Cf. K. Leung, "Yuyifa jiejing" [Allegorical interpretation of scripture], 36.
91. Liao, "Nee's Theology of Victory," 207.
92. K. L. Leung, "Sanyuan renlun" [Trichotomistic anthropology], 228.
93. Nee, *The Spiritual Man*, 1:xvi.
94. *GTU Doctoral Program Handbook*, 53.

or plagiarizer. . . . Nee himself was critical of the Brethren and labeled them 'Laodicea' according to Revelation 3. At the same time he implied that his movement was a movement of Philadelphia, approved and praised by God."[95] Further, Nee's translations of many English terms into Chinese were very original and led to the widespread adoption, among Chinese believers, of those concepts and ideas regarding the spiritual life. Thus it seems safe to assume that Nee was not succumbed to the temptation to appear smart or original as he preached or wrote; rather, he was concerned with passing along the valuable lessons that he had learned (from both his studies and his experiences) to the church, which was also the primary motive for him to write *The Spiritual Man* when he was threatened with a terminal disease.

~

This chapter has surveyed some important sources of Nee, and has identified several specific influences that these sources had exerted upon Nee's theology and spirituality. Particularly noteworthy were Nee's Holiness and Brethren outlook, his theology of suffering, and his allegorical approach to interpreting the Bible. This chapter then forms the second of the two chapters on background, laying down another preliminary building block toward the construction of this book's thesis, namely, Nee's major theological convictions regarding spiritual knowledge and the spiritual life are in substantial agreement with related aspects of the Christian spiritual or mystical tradition, and thus some major weaknesses in Nee's view that his critics perceive can be overcome or substantially ameliorated. Let us now turn to the second and substantive part of this book, that of critical analysis and interpretation. The next chapter will be the first of the three consecutive chapters constituting this book's arguments.

---

95. Pamudji, "Little Flock Trilogy," 181. Pamudji here references Nee, *Orthodoxy of the Church*, 82–102.

PART TWO

Analysis and Interpretation

3

Revelation and Illumination
The Mystery of Hearing God

WHAT IS REVELATION OR divine illumination? How is it received by the human person? How is it related to conventional knowing, and what is the significance of such spiritual knowing? Especially, what role does revelation or illumination play in different junctures of the faith journey? These and related questions will be explored in the writings of Nee and McIntosh respectively in this chapter's first two sections, which will be mainly an exposition of their views without proceeding to an evaluation. In the third section then, we will attempt to evaluate some controversial issues in Nee's views by bringing them into dialogue with the perspectives of McIntosh as well as other contemporary writers who are concerned with similar issues. We will note both their similarities and differences, exploring particularly the question about whether Nee's view of revelation falls within a species of Gnosticism as some of Nee's critics perceive.

NEE ON REVELATION AND ILLUMINATION

After extensive study of Nee's writings, Lam Wing-hung suggests that Nee's theological view can be regarded as a unique form of Chinese indigenous theology, and this theology is characterized by its distinctive overtone of a "spiritual theology." For Nee thinks that the essence of Christianity consists not in creeds, rites, or institutions, but rather, in what he calls "spiritual reality" or "spiritual substance."[1] Nee points out that believers should worship in spirit and truth because God is Spirit (John 4:24). Spiritual reality for Nee has to do with the divine Spirit; it is about being in the Spirit or filled by the Spirit. Once spiritual reality is encountered, one's life is inevitably transformed. Nee uses two examples from the Gospels to illustrate how such spiritual reality can be conceived. One is the story of Jesus asking his disciples who they think he is, and Peter answering, "You are Christ, Son of the living God" (Matt 16:16). Nee points out that Peter's answer here was a result of divine revelation and so Peter in this instance experienced and knew the spiritual reality of Christ. The other example Nee notes is the instance of Jesus's healing of the bleeding woman. When she touched Jesus's cloak, Jesus felt that there was power coming out of him. Nee maintains that the power here was just the manifestation of the hidden spiritual reality. For Nee such spiritual reality can emerge in a person's spirit with the Holy Spirit's revelation, through which the person gets into direct contact with God and obtains life exchange and transformation.[2]

Nee holds that spiritual reality is not something merely objective "out there," but it can and should be experienced subjectively by ordinary believers. Further, such encounter with spiritual reality will result in a change in believers' lives as they increasingly become "spiritual persons"—"spiritual" here for Nee means belonging to the (Holy) Spirit or having a right relationship with the Spirit, according to Paul's usage in 1 Corinthians 2:15.[3] Nee's *The Spiritual Man* is just aiming at showing believers how to become spiritual persons. Lam therefore sees that Nee's spiritual theology can also be understood as a theology of the spiritual person.[4] Thus to explore Nee's spiritual theology, we can start with his theological anthropology, the basic points of which, according to Leung Ka-lun, had remained quite stable for Nee from his completion of *The Spiritual Man* in 1928 to his 1948 publication *The Breaking of the Outer*

1. The Chinese terms Nee uses are either *shuling shiji* [屬靈實際], which can be translated as "spiritual reality," or *shuling shizhi* [屬靈實質], which is better translated as "spiritual substance." Nee sometimes uses one of the terms for either or both senses.

2. Lam "Huaren shenxue" [Chinese theology], 45–48.

3. Nee, *Shuling ren* [The spiritual man], 48, 191, and *The Spiritual Man*, 2:233.

4. Lam, "Huaren shenxue" [Chinese theology], 45–46.

Man and the Release of the Spirit, which is a shorter work on similar topics that he preached on toward the end of his public career.[5]

In this section, we will first look at Nee's tripartite theological anthropology and how it relates to his view of revelation or illumination.
We will then analyze various aspects of his understanding as they are
related to interpreting the scriptures as well as different issues in the
faith journey, such as liberation from the power of sin and walking after
(or in) the Spirit.

Tripartite Theological Anthropology: Spirit, Soul, Body

Probably influenced by Jessie Penn-Lewis, and relying on a survey of
some biblical anthropological words in the original languages,[6] Nee sets
out to explain a tripartite view of theological anthropology, which regards the human person as consisting of the three parts of body, soul,
and spirit. Here Nee bases himself mainly on two scriptural passages:
"May the God of peace himself sanctify you entirely; and may your spirit
and soul and body be kept sound and blameless at the coming of our
Lord Jesus Christ" (1 Thess 5:23) and "Indeed, the word of God is living
and active, sharper than any two-edged sword, piercing until it divides
soul from spirit, joints from marrow; it is able to judge the thoughts
and intentions of the heart" (Heb 4:12). This latter passage in Hebrews,
for Nee, clearly shows the division of soul and spirit. In addition, with
regard to the creation story in Genesis 2, Nee comments that the dust of
the earth and the breath of God correspond respectively to the body and
the spirit of the created person, and the coming together of these two
elements gives birth to a third element, namely the soul.[7] Nee notes that
these three parts in the human person correspond to three kinds of life
that the Bible refers to; he uses some biblical studies of his day to explain
these different kinds of life:

> Some who have studied the Bible have pointed out that there are
> three words for *life* in Greek: (1) *bios*, (2) *psuche*, and (3) *zoe*.

5. K. L. Leung, "Huaren nuosidi zhuyi" [Chinese Gnosticism], 186–89.

6. Nee's *The Spiritual Man* in the Chinese publication begins with a quite extensive
summary of these terms in the Bible, grouped according to different translations (in the
Union Version of the Chinese Bible) of the same word in the original language (both
Hebrew and Greek). These detailed listings are omitted in the English translation of *The
Spiritual Man*.

7. Nee, *The Spiritual Man*, 1:3–7.

> Although all three words denote life, the life which they denote is different. *Bios* refers to the physical life. When the Lord Jesus said that the widow had cast in all the "living" that she had, He was using this word (Luke 21:4). *Zoe* is the highest life, the spiritual life. Whenever the Bible mentions "eternal life," the word *zoe* is used for "life." *Psuche* is the life which makes a man living; it is man's natural life, that is, the life of the soul. When the Bible speaks of man's life, it uses this word. (23–24)

Similar to Penn-Lewis, Nee identifies body, soul, and spirit as corresponding respectively to a person's world-consciousness, self-consciousness, and God-consciousness (8). He regards the soul as having the three "natural" functions of feeling, thinking, and willing. And echoing Madame Guyon, Nee holds that all communications between God and human beings occur, not within the soul, but within the spirit: "Man worships God and communicates with God directly through the spirit, that is, through the 'inner man,' and not through the soul or the outward man" (16). Nee emphasizes that the activity of the spirit is independent of that of the soul; like Penn-Lewis, he also lays paramount importance on distinguishing the spirit from the soul, lest believers "substitute the work of the spirit with soulish activities such as that of the mind and the emotion"(15). Referring to the contrast between "a soulish body" and "a spiritual body" in 1 Corinthians 15:44, Nee especially underscores the difference between a soulish Christian and a spiritual Christian (25).

For Nee, then, the spirit is a distinct part in human beings that enables communication and communion with God. Nee maintains that the spirit has three major functions or faculties, namely that of conscience, intuition, and fellowship.[8] Conscience is for discernment between right and wrong, a function of judgment that is not relying on knowledge of the mind, but rather is "mostly independent and direct."[9] Intuition corresponds to the function for consciousness or knowledge within a person's spirit, and again, it is "direct and is not dependent on anything else" (ibid.). Fellowship, then, is for the function of worshipping God.

---

8. Nee bases this view that the spirit has three faculties on "the experience of the believers" as well as his interpretations of biblical verses (Nee, *The Spiritual Man*, 1:15–19). In his same volume on page 15, I believe that here "faculty" is a more accurate rendering than "organ" for the translation from the Chinese term *jiguan* [機關]; the translator does render the same term in a parallel context on page 25 as "faculties" of the mind, the emotion, and the will.

9. Nee, *The Spiritual Man*, 1:16.

Nee underlines that these three functions of the spirit are deeply integrated and related to one another, but they are independent of the functions of the body and the soul, and especially different from the soul's willing, thinking, and feeling. For he observes that most believers are so accustomed to the mere activities of their soul that they are very weak in functioning in the realm of the spirit:

> The reason we study the main features of the spirit is to show that man has a spirit which is independent of his other parts. This spirit is not man's mind, will, or emotion. It includes the function of the conscience, the intuition, and the fellowship. God regenerates us and instructs us and leads us into His rest. Because the believers have long been controlled by the soul, they have become very weak in their knowledge of the spirit. We should come before God in fear and trembling and should ask Him to show us in our experience what is of the spirit and what is of the soul. (18)

Basing himself again on scriptural verses, Nee holds that the soul includes the function of the will, the intellect, the emotions; and it is the seat of one's personality or what "makes up the person as a human being" (27). He believes that the soul includes all "natural" capacities that human beings are born with. He notes that the Hebrew *nephesh* or the Greek *psuche* in the Bible cannot be translated consistently as soul in many instances, but instead need to be translated as life or "soul-life," denoting both the person's soul and her very life itself. The soul and the soul-life in a person, Nee believes, are distinguishable but inseparable (24). Thus he maintains that the soul in the Bible often denotes a person's life, the self, or (the consciousness of) the "I." Nee thus summarizes:

> We conclude that man's soul is just man's life, man himself, his personality, and the will, mind, and emotion that are included in his personality. From this study we draw the conclusion that the human soul encompasses everything that makes up the person as a human being. . . . The soul is the life which all men of flesh share in common. . . . In other words, the life of the soul is the life which a man acquires from his mother's womb. . . . If we know clearly what is of the soul, it will be easy for us to know what is of the spirit, and we will be able to differentiate between the spiritual things and the soulish things. (27)

God created the body from dust, in Nee's view, as the vessel for receiving the breath of life. Through its five senses it comes into contact with the physical things of the world. Although the body is the outmost dimension of the human being, through its interaction with and effect on the soul, the body can also affect the spirit. While Nee believes that the body is not comparable in its dignity to the spirit, he nonetheless affirms the importance of the body because of the incarnation of Jesus, and because during his earthly life, Jesus did care about the human body's needs and healings. Besides, Nee holds that the consequence of the Fall affected not only the spirit and the soul, but the body as well, and he believes that sickness is a consequence of sin as well as the work of Satan. Seeing that the redemptive work of Jesus includes both forgiveness of sin and healing of sickness, Nee maintains that full salvation includes the salvation of spirit, soul, and body.[10]

Commenting on Genesis 2 and 3, Nee believes that God's original design is for the three parts in human beings to function in the descending order of spirit, soul, and body—the spirit governing the soul, and the soul governing the body. Nee illustrates that the relationships of the spirit, soul, and body are analogous to that of the lady (owner), the steward, and the servant in a house: the lady (owner) is to give charges to the steward, who then is to direct the servant. In this original order, says Nee, outwardly the steward (or the soul) seems to be the master, but in fact "the real master is the lady of the house" (or the spirit).[11] But this original order has been completely reversed by the Fall; after the Fall, the body's desires and lusts control the soul, and the soul in turn suppresses the spirit (or the spirit is now merged with the soul).[12]

Nee's view is sometimes presented as three concentric circles representing respectively, from the inside out, spirit, soul, and body[13]:

10. Lam, *Shuling shenxue* [Spiritual theology], 71–72.

11. Nee, *The Spiritual Man*, 1:29.

12. Lam, "Huaren shenxue" [Chinese theology], 49–51.

13. This popular diagram is recorded in K. Lee, "Watchman Nee," 62; and K. L. Leung, "Huaren nuosidi zhuyi" [Chinese Gnosticism], 211.

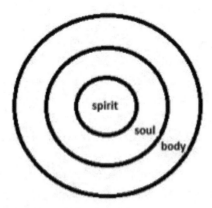

Nee holds that the devil's work is always from the outside to the inside, while God's work is always from the inside to the outside (reminiscent of Penn-Lewis's view):

> He [the devil] beguiled man's soul to sin through the things of the flesh (the eating of the fruit). Once the soul has sinned, the spirit falls into darkness and degradation. This is the order of all his works—from the outside to the inside. Either he works from man's body or he works from his mind or his emotion for the purpose of gaining his will. . . . God's work is always from the inside to the outside. He first works from man's spirit, then enlightens man's mind, touches man's emotion, finally causes man to exercise his will to activate his body to carry out God's will.[14]

Especially noteworthy is Nee's understanding of spiritual intuition. We have seen that for Nee human communication with God occurs within a person's spirit, consisting of the three major faculties of conscience, fellowship, and intuition. The term intuition here is used by Nee to refer to a kind of knowing on the spiritual level, which is analogous to the common psychological notion of intuition in that such intuitive knowing seems to come from nowhere, or seems to just happen without any identifiable causes.[15] Yet Nee's use of the term intuition is meant to denote exclusively to *spiritual* consciousness or sense of knowing, as well as to the faculty in the spirit that makes such knowing possible: "We may say that the intuition is the 'brain' of the spirit."[16] And it is through this

14. Nee, *The Spiritual Man*, 1:34.
15. Nee, *Shuling ren* [The spiritual man], 229.
16. Nee, *The Spiritual Man*, 2:304.

faculty that divine communication enters into the human spirit: "The intuition is the consciousness [sense of knowing] within man's spirit. This consciousness [sense of knowing] is absolutely different from the body-consciousness and the soul-consciousness. . . . Through his intuition, man can truly 'know' something, while his mind can only make him understand it. All God's revelations and all the moving of the Holy Spirit are known by the believers through the intuition."[17] Nee underscores how such spiritual knowing is different from intellectual understanding: "The normal Christian life must begin with a very definite 'knowing,' which is not just knowing something about the truth nor understanding some important doctrine. It is not an intellectual knowledge at all, but an opening of the eyes of the heart to see what we have in Christ."[18]

Thus for Nee there is the distinction between two kinds of knowledge: intellectual knowledge acquired by the thinking faculty in the soul, and spiritual knowledge received by the intuitive faculty in the spirit. For Nee, to have a revelation is to have one's inner eyes opened, and to have an experiential sense of conviction or certainty that is usually lacking in the case of a mere intellectual knowing of doctrine: "We need to have our eyes opened to the fact of our union with Christ, and that is something more than knowing it as a doctrine. Such revelation is no vague indefinite thing. . . . It should be nothing hazy, but very definite, for it is with this as basis that we shall go on."[19]

Revelation: Key for the Faith Journey

Nee is concerned with experiencing or making real in one's life the truths that the Bible teaches. He holds that inspiration was an event for writing the scriptures in the past, whereas revelations occur repeatedly every time the Spirit enlightens readers of the Bible in the present. For Nee the objective revelation of the Spirit-inspired scripture needs further revelations of the Spirit to become subjectively real to believers. In this latter subjective sense, revelation takes place whenever the Holy Spirit again breathes upon the scriptures, imparting light into believers who can then perceive divine truth and receive divine life from the word of God. Carl Henry suggests that the term "revelation" used by Nee in this

17. Ibid., 1:16 (brackets my translation from the Chinese term *zhi jue* [知覺]).

18. Nee, *Normal Christian Life*, 37.

19. Ibid., 44.

subjective sense is in fact more in line with the theological notion of "illumination."[20] However, Nee's use of the term revelation seems to be more in line with biblical usage in similar situations (such as Matthew 11:25, Luke 2:35, Galatians 2:2, Ephesians 1:17, and Philippians 3:15).[21] Nee does also speak of illumination (or enlightening or "shining") in similar contexts, and Nee's different uses can be explained in terms of a difference of emphasis in the divine-human event of revelation-illumination: when the term revelation is used, the stress is more on the divine pole of the event or more on the *fact* of what happens, whereas when illumination (or enlightening or "shining") is used, the accent falls more on the human pole of that same event or on the *effect* of what happens.

Nee maintains that revelation is what makes the otherwise hidden spiritual reality behind the word of God manifest or alive to the believers. Translating part of Ephesians 1:17 as "a spirit of wisdom and revelation in the knowledge of him," Nee believes that knowing the truths in scripture requires the Spirit's revelation or illumination—the shining of divine light into believers' hearts so that their inner eyes are opened to see the truth of reality. Citing Hebrews 4:12, Nee underlines that only with revelation can the Bible become a living word for its readers: "The first thing we have to realize is that the Bible tells us that God's word is living. If we really touch God's word, it will be living to us. If we do not sense the livingness of God's word, it proves that we have not touched God's word. Some people have read through all the words of the Bible, but they have not touched God's word. Only to the extent that we have touched something living can we claim that we have touched God's word."[22] Nee underlines that to be a minister of the word one especially needs to receive such revelation. Yet while Nee insists on the need for continual revelations from the Spirit for today, he is also adamant in holding the Bible as the essential medium for God's speaking. In other words, for Nee the word of God for today must necessarily come out of the Bible; otherwise, it would be heretical. Thus in this sense Nee remains faithful as an heir of the Reformation, for like Calvin, Nee upholds the necessary bond between the Spirit and the scriptures.

Nee repeatedly emphasizes the importance and the priority of revelation or illumination in the whole faith journey. In speaking of the

20. Henry, "Footnotes," 31.

21. See Vine et al., *Expository Dictionary*, 531–32.

22. Nee, *Breaking of the Outer Man*, 83.

various steps in different phases of the spiritual journey, Nee says: "What are these steps? First there is revelation. As we have seen, this always precedes faith and experience. Through His Word God opens our eyes to the truth of some fact concerning His Son, and then only, as in faith we accept that fact for ourselves, does it become actual as experience in our lives."[23] Nee maintains that this initial revelation usually leads to the sequential experience of a one-time crisis (an entrance) followed by a continual process (a path). Nee suggests that different phases in the faith journey would more or less have these steps (cf. ibid.):

1. Revelation
2. Faith: A wicket gate (Crisis)
3. Experience: A narrow path (Process)

Nee thus teaches:

> One thing is certain, that revelation will always precede faith. . . . When we see something that God has done in Christ our natural response is: "Thank you, Lord!" and faith follows spontaneously. Revelation is always the work of the Holy Spirit, who is given in order that, by coming alongside and opening to us the Scriptures He may guide us into all the truth (John 16:13). . . . when such difficulties as lack of understanding or lack of faith confront you, address those difficulties directly to the Lord: "Lord, open my eyes. Lord, make this new thing clear to me. Lord, help Thou my unbelief!" He will not let such prayers go unheeded. (138–39)

Nee often highlights revelations about Christ that are related to various truthful self-knowledge for the believers, such as identity as children of God, union with Christ (already co-crucified and risen with Christ), freedom from the law, the corruption and deceitfulness of the self, the need for separating the soul from the spirit, identity as members of the corporate Body of Christ, and indwelling of the Holy Spirit (already being filled by the Spirit). The priority of revelation, in Nee's view, applies to different processes in the faith journey, including justification and spiritual rebirth, deliverance from the power of sin, and walking after the Spirit.

---

23. Nee, *Normal Christian Life*, 137.

Revelation and Faith: Liberation from the Power of Sin

Regarding Christ's redemptive act in history, Nee distinguishes between the blood and the cross in the work of Christ. Nee notes that the blood of Christ has to do with justification or forgiveness of sinful acts or *sins* (plural), while the cross of Christ has to do with sanctification or salvation from sinful nature or *sin* (singular). In other words, the blood deals with sinners' conscience or *what* they have done (outwardly), while the cross deals with sinners' life or *who* they are (inside): the first, says Nee, is objective or positional, while the second is subjective or experiential (9–10, 22–23).

From his reflection on Romans chapter 6, Nee sees that merely becoming "saved" or justified by the blood of Christ is only half of the gospel. The fuller gospel encompasses the work of the cross for sanctification, which includes deliverance from the power of sin. To be liberated from the power of sin, Nee maintains, believers need to go through three steps: (1) receiving revelation that results in a knowing that their sinful nature has been crucified with Christ on the cross; (2) entering the narrow gate of faith that keeps reckoning the already accomplished divine "fact" of their co-crucifixion with Christ; and (3) walking the narrow path of continual dedication that eventually leads to the experience of freedom from sin's dominion.[24] Nee is quick to add that these steps (of knowing, reckoning, and dedicating) do not always proceed in a precise order and one should be careful not to put the work of the Holy Spirit under any rigid framework.[25]

Nee speaks of his own experience of receiving the revelation of knowing that he had indeed been crucified with Christ as he was wrestling with Romans chapter 6. Verses 6 and 11 in this chapter say that the old person of believers has been crucified with Christ and they are no longer slaves to sin, so they should count themselves already dead with Christ on the cross. Nee says that he was puzzled by these verses for a long time because despite his constant counting of himself dead with Christ during the years of 1920–1927, his old person seemed to be more alive and well than ever. He then prayed (and at times fasted) for

24. Nee, *Shuling ren* [The spiritual man], 126–30, and *Normal Christian Life*, 137–38, 23, 33–72. Nee speaks of a fourth step of "walking after the Spirit," which will be discussed later in this chapter.

25. Nee, *Normal Christian Life*, 137–38.

revelation to understand this dilemma for some months in 1927, until one day a revelation came upon him in such a sudden and illuminating way:

> I remember one morning—that morning was a real morning and one I can never forget—I was upstairs sitting at my desk reading the Word and praying, and I said, "Lord, open my eyes!" And then in a flash I saw it. I saw my oneness with Christ. I saw that I was in Him, and that when He died I died. I saw that the question of my death was a matter of the past and not of the future, and that I was just as truly dead as He was because I was in Him when He died. The whole thing had dawned upon me. I was carried away with such joy at this great discovery that I jumped from my chair and cried, "Praise the Lord, I am dead!" . . . Oh it was so real to me! I longed to go through the streets of Shanghai shouting the news of my discovery. From that day to this I have never for one moment doubted the finality of that word: "I have been crucified with Christ." (43–44)

Thus Nee sees that the first step to deliverance from sin's dominion power is to receive the revelation to know—or to have the inner eyes opened to see—the truth that believers' old sinful nature has already died with Christ on the cross and their new nature has risen with him at their new birth, as baptism symbolizes. Nee especially stresses that believers' being in Christ—or their union with Christ in his death and resurrection—is a historical fact already accomplished by God and secured for the believers at baptism. In other words, believers do not need to strive for union with Christ, but only need to know (by revelation) the truth that they are already in Christ, and to live from such realization (137–38). Nee says: "So our first step is to seek from God a knowledge that comes by revelation—a revelation, that is to say, not of ourselves but of the finished work of the Lord Jesus Christ on the Cross" (38).

This gift of revelation then leads to the second step for deliverance from sin: the "narrow gate" of counting or believing, which refers more to human appropriation of, or cooperation with, the divine revelation just received. In other words, after receiving the revelation that Christ on the cross has finished all the work for them, believers need only to keep on believing such revealed truth in order to receive all that Christ has secured for them. Nee underscores that such ability to count or believe can happen only if one already knows by revelation: "What, then, is the

secret of reckoning? To put it in one word, it is revelation. We need revelation from God Himself (Matt 16:17; Eph 1:17, 18)" (44).

To keep believing by faith this divine revelation (of believers' co-
crucifixion with Christ) is then the process toward making liberation
from sin's power an experiential reality. Convinced that the word "faith"
(*pistis* in Greek) in Hebrews 11:1 includes the sense of an action, and
finding J. N. Darby's translation of this verse as "Faith is the substantiating of things hoped for" to be helpful, Nee regards faith as what sub-
stantiates, or what makes objective reality real in personal experience.
For Nee, God's word signifies objective reality, while believers' personal
experience signifies subjective reality—yet faith is the key element that
makes objective reality subjective as well: "Faith in the objective facts
makes those facts true subjectively" (57). Thus Nee accentuates that after
receiving a particular divine revelation, believers need to exercise their
faith to believe such truth before they can subjectively experience the
reality of such truth or "fact."

Nee uses an illustration to demonstrate the interrelationships between what he calls Fact, Faith, and Experience: "You probably know
the illustration of Fact, Faith, and Experience walking along the top of a
wall. Fact walked steadily on, turning neither to right nor left and never
looking behind. Faith followed, and all went well so long as he kept his
eyes focused upon Fact; but as soon as he became concerned about
Experience and turned to see how *he* was getting on, he lost his balance and tumbled off the wall, and poor old Experience fell down after
him" (52). Nee holds that scripture is the sufficient ground for knowing
divine "facts" or divine reality, regardless of one's feeling or experience.
Thus believers are not to pay attention to, or seek after, experience (inner or outer). But rather they should simply believe the word of God.
Moreover, Nee suggests that in Romans 6:11 the word "reckoning" (or
counting; *logizomai* in Greek) practically has the same meaning as faith
(or believing), and such faith is based on what God has accomplished
in the past. For he especially emphasizes that reckoning or counting,
just like bookkeeping, is about keeping accurate records of the already
existent fact, which, in this case, is what God has accomplished in history: "What is faith? Faith is my acceptance of God's fact. It always has
its foundations in the past. What relates to the future is hope rather
than faith, although faith often has its object or goal in the future, as in
Hebrews 11:1. Perhaps for this reason the word chosen here is 'reckon.' It

is a word that relates *only* to the past—to what we look back to as settled, and not forward to as yet to be" (46).

Why do believers who already know and accept such divine truth still need to keep reckoning or believing? First Nee says that it is because God commands them to do so in Romans 6:11: "Reckon ye . . ." Then it is also because the devil—the father of lies—is constantly tempting believers to doubt God's truth. Nee distinguishes between two kinds of experience: a false experience caused by Satan's deception, and a true experience resulting from believing the word of God. The temptation lies in that what Satan presents is often very real or true to the senses, so Nee points out that a lesser truth is often the enemy of a greater truth: "Whatever contradicts the truth of God's Word we are to regard as the Devil's lie, not because it may not be in itself a very real fact to our senses, but because God has stated a greater fact before which the other must eventually yield" (50). Nee emphasizes that it is crucial not to succumb to tangible or scientifically proven facts: "The crucial test is just here. Are we going to believe the tangible facts of the natural realm which are clearly before our eyes, or the intangible facts of the spiritual realm which are neither seen nor scientifically proved?" (47).

Further, the devil's scheme of lying includes not only verbal lies, but also feelings and experiences that seem very much real to believers. Thus believers have to choose which—Satan's lie or God's truth—to believe:

> The Devil is a skillful liar, and we cannot expect him to stop at words in his lying. He will resort to lying signs and feelings and experiences in his attempts to shake us from our faith in God's Word. . . . As soon as we have accepted our death with Christ as a fact, Satan will do his best to demonstrate convincingly by the evidence of our day-to-day experience that we are not dead at all but very much alive. So we must choose. Will we believe Satan's lie or God's truth? Are we going to be governed by appearances or by what God says? (51)

For Nee, the way to salvation or deliverance is through obedience, especially through believing the word of God and through resisting the tempting question that the adversary put to the first couple: "Does God really say . . . ?" To stand in faith, then, believers must keep on reckoning, which includes keeping records of, declaring, and holding on to God's words. Such believing is possible only if one keeps looking to Christ in faith, rather than looking at the mountain of evidence to the contrary—either within or outside oneself; and such faith will eventually lead one to experience the truth of God's words:

> All temptation is primarily to look within [look at oneself]; to take our eyes off the Lord and to take account of appearances. Faith is always meeting a mountain, a mountain of evidence that seems to contradict God's Word, a mountain of apparent contradiction in the realm of tangible fact—of failures in deed, as well as in the realm of feeling and suggestion—and either faith or the mountain has to go. They cannot both stand. . . . if we refuse to accept as binding anything that contradicts God's Word and maintain an attitude of faith in Him alone, we shall find instead that Satan's lies begin to dissolve and that *our experience is coming progressively to tally with that Word.* (52–53, brackets my translation)

After the two steps of receiving the divine revelation and continuing to reckon that one has been dead with Christ on the cross, Nee sees that the third step for liberation from sin is to go down the narrow path of dedicating oneself totally to God as commanded in Romans 6:13. To dedicate or present oneself to God means to offer or sanctify one's bodily members for God's use: "Let us observe that this 'presenting' relates to the members of my body—that body which, as we saw earlier, is now unemployed in respect of sin. 'Present yourselves . . . and your members,' says Paul, and again: 'Present your members' (Rom 6:13, 19). God requires of me that I now regard all my members, all my faculties, as belonging wholly to Him" (68). The key here, notes Nee, is that one needs to die to one's own will in order to live out the divine will. Believers with such dedication are therefore no longer *servants* who are still masters of themselves outside the job, but *slaves* who in love willingly subject themselves wholly to the Master. As bond-slaves of love, believers should keep on dedicating themselves to the Lord; and they can rest assure that their circumstances are ordained by God for their very best benefit. Thus they should not only accept, but also praise God for everything that happens to them: "[There must be once an initial fundamental act of giving myself to the Lord.] Then, day by day, I must go on giving to Him, not finding fault with His use of me, but accepting with praise even what the flesh finds hard. That way lies true enrichment" (72, brackets my translation). Nee insists: "I am the Lord's, and now no longer reckon myself to be my own but acknowledge in everything His ownership and authority. . . . Whatever He ordains for me is sure to be the very best, for nothing but good can come to those who are wholly His" (ibid.).

Denial of Self: Dying to the Natural Life of the Soul

The steps of liberation from the power of sin are only the initial steps of sanctification; in fact, they constitute only a "gate" or entrance to the lifelong journey of sanctification. Nee maintains that sanctification is dealing with the corrupted nature that the Bible calls "the flesh," which is always in opposition to the Spirit. And he sees that in scripture the flesh can mean one of two things: sin (unrighteousness) or self (self-righteousness). Sin exerts its influence on the nature (or disposition) of the *old person*, which in turn directs the body to commit sins. By contrast, self for Nee here refers to the life of the *natural person* (or *natural life*), which manifests as the soul's independence or self-reliance. Commenting on 1 Corinthians 3:1, Nee maintains that the "spiritual person" is one "who has the Holy Spirit dwelling in his spirit and ruling over his whole being," and the fleshly person is one "who follows his soul and body to sin, act, and behave."[26] Nee would probably have appreciated these remarks by Philip Sheldrake:

> At the risk of simplification, it is important to grasp that, in Pauline theology, "Spirit" and "spiritual" are not contrasted with "physical" or "material" (for which the Greek *soma*, in Latin *corpus*, is the root) but rather with *all that is opposed to the Spirit of God* (for which the word *sarx*, in Latin *caro*, is used). What is opposed to the Spirit may as well be the mind or the will as the body or material reality. The contrast that emerges is therefore between two ways of life or attitudes to life. The "spiritual" is what is under the influence of, or is a manifestation of, the Spirit of God. . . . The "spiritual person" (e.g., 1 Cor 2, 14–15) is *not* someone who turns away from material reality but rather someone in whom the Spirit of God dwells.[27]

Nee notes that in Galatians 5, the flesh has been co-crucified with Christ on the cross (v. 24) on the one hand, yet on the other it is still alive and contending with the Spirit (vv. 16–17). Thus Nee suggests that there are two meanings for the term "flesh" in scripture: in the first instance

26. Nee, *The Spiritual Man*, 1:54, 2:233, and *Shuling ren* [The spiritual man], 81, 48.

27. Sheldrake, *Spirituality and History*, 42–43, part of which is quoted in McIntosh, *Mystical Theology*, 6.

here it refers to the sinful nature or sin, while in the second instance it refers to the natural life or self.[28] In his own teachings also, Nee uses the term flesh (and its cognates) sometimes referring to either sin or self, and sometimes referring to both sin and self, depending on the contexts.[29] And he maintains that the whole flesh (both sin and self) needs to be put to death constantly and to stay in that position of death.[30] In other words, for Nee sanctification is dealing with a twofold problem: sin and self—the old person and the natural person—corresponding respectively to the (negative) power of sin (such as sinful habits or inclinations) and the (positive) reliance on one's own natural power (such as intelligence, affection, or will power). For Nee both problems are dealt with by the cross of Christ: one by the cross's bearing of the old person (the believers' death to sin by their co-crucifixion with Christ), and the other by the natural person's bearing of the cross (the disciples' denial of self by picking up their cross daily to follow Christ).[31]

The term "old person" is similarly used by Nee in both a broad and a narrow sense. It is used in the broad sense to refer to the "old creation" that human beings inherited from Adam—including both their sinful nature and their natural abilities.[32] Yet "old person" is most often used by Nee to refer exclusively to the first meaning of the flesh—the sinful nature that is crucified as Romans 6:6 indicates.[33] For clarity purposes, in my discussion, the term "old person" is used in its narrow sense corresponding to the first meaning of the flesh (the sinful nature).[34] And for referring to the second sense of the flesh (the self), the terms "natural life" or "natural person" is used interchangeably.[35]

28. Nee, *Shuling ren* [The spiritual man], 89.

29. For example, while Nee sometimes equates "of the flesh" with "of the soul (self)" or of the natural life (Nee, *Shuling ren* [The spiritual man], 136–37), at other times he contrasts the natural life with the old person or the flesh (Nee, *Normal Christian Life*, 169). At yet other times he uses the term flesh in a broader sense to include both sin and self (Nee, *Shuling ren* [The spiritual man], 110–11).

30. Nee, *Shuling ren* [The spiritual man], 123.

31. Ibid., 89, 110–11, 134, and *Normal Christian Life*, 137–40.

32. Nee, *Shuling ren* [The spiritual man], 127, and *Normal Christian Life*, 67.

33. Nee, *Shuling ren* [The spiritual man], 126, 135; see also Nee, *Normal Christian Life*, 169.

34. "Old person" is a better translation than "old man" for the neutral Chinese term *jiuren* [舊人].

35. While Nee usually calls this natural life *tianran shengming* [天然生命], he

The second problem (of self), as well as the first (of sin), concerns the Fall's effects. Nee sees that the result of eating from the tree of knowledge of good and evil was that the human soul became too "wise": overdeveloped and seemingly self-sufficient, which inclined the soul to live a self-reliant life—soul-reliant as opposed to spirit-reliant—in independence from, or disobedience to, God.[36] For Nee the death of the old person only means that one's old sinful nature (or disposition) has been changed to a new godly nature (or disposition). Yet beyond the issue of nature or inclination, there is still an issue of life or the source of one's executive power. Seeing that believers can carry out godly desires with un-spiritual means or soulish powers, Nee notes that "we think too little of the source of our energy and too much of the end to which it is directed, forgetting that with God the end never justifies the means."[37] In other words, even after the old person has been dead, there is a further problem because the natural person—the soul-life, instead of the spirit-life—is still the source of one's power:

> Although all sins issue from the sinful nature and the soul merely follows its direction to execute its command, nevertheless the soul is, after all, inherited from Adam. Although the soul is not altogether defiled, it cannot avoid being affected by the fall of Adam. It is natural and quite different from the life of God. The defiled old man within the believer has become dead indeed . . . Although the old man no longer directs the soul, the soul is still the strength of his living. Since God's nature has replaced the sinful nature, spontaneously all the inclinations, desires, and ideas are good, unlike their former filthy state. However, the execution of the ideas, directions, and desires of his new nature continues to be by the same soul-life.[38]

Nee especially notes that while the natural person (the "soul" part of the flesh) is not as evil or defiling as the old person (the "body" part of the flesh), it nonetheless belongs to the flesh and is opposed to the Spirit even while it is trying to serve God:

---

does at times also refer to it as natural person *tianran de ren* [天然的人]. See Nee, *Zhengchang de jidutu shenghuo* [Normal Christian life], chap. 12, "Shizijia yu hun shengming" [Cross and the soul life].

36. Nee, *Normal Christian Life*, 152–54.

37. Ibid., 156.

38. Nee, *The Spiritual Man*, 1:142–43.

The opposition of the flesh to the spirit and the Holy Spirit is of two sides. When the flesh commits sins, rebels against God, and breaks the law of God, it is clearly opposed to the spirit. When the flesh performs good deeds, obeys God, and does the will of God, it is also at enmity with the spirit. Since the "body" part of the flesh is naturally filled with sin and lust, . . . the "soul" part of the flesh is not as defiling as the body. . . . The soul focuses only on one's own ideas, thoughts, preferences, and feelings. . . . Independence and self-support are the characteristics of the works of the soul. . . . self-will rises above the will of God. . . . The deceitfulness and the strength of this self are beyond man's expectation. The flesh is at enmity with the Holy Spirit not only in the matter of sinning against God but even in the matter of serving God and pleasing God, for it is done out of its own strength, not by being led simply by the Spirit and depending entirely on the grace of God. Thus it is at enmity against the Holy Spirit and quenches the Holy Spirit.[39]

On the need to deny the natural life, Nee appeals to Jesus's saying in the Gospels that "those who want to save their life will lose it, and those who lose their life for my sake, and for the sake of the gospel, will save it" (Mark 8:35; see also Matt 10:39, Luke 17:33, and John 12:25). Nee believes that since the Greek word for life here means "soul," it is the soul or the natural person that needs to be denied by bearing the cross daily. In contrast to the old person that has already died by co-crucifixion with Christ, which is a gate to enter once and for all, the denial of the natural person is a lifelong journey that takes daily steps: "the soul life or natural life that is here in view is something further than what we have in those passages which are concerned with the old man of the flesh. We have sought to make [clear] that, in respect of our old man, God emphasizes the thing He has done *once for all* in crucifying us with Christ on the Cross."[40] Nee continues: "But there is a further aspect of the Cross, namely that implied in the expression 'bearing his cross daily' . . . The Cross has borne me; now I must bear it . . . it is a continuous process, a step by step following after Him" (ibid.).

Besides freedom from sin, Nee reads in Romans 7 that believers are to obtain freedom from the law, which means freedom from efforts of the self (the natural life), and reliance solely on the grace of God: "Grace

39. Ibid., 1:104.
40. Nee, *Normal Christian Life*, 169.

means that God does something for me; law means that I do something for God. God has certain holy and righteous demands which He places upon me: that is law. . . . The trouble in Romans 7 is that man in the flesh tried to do something for God. As soon as you try to please God in that way, then you place yourself under law, and the experience of Romans 7 begins to be yours" (105).

Nee views that so long as believers are still trying to live the spiritual life by their own strength, they are subject to the law of death. And in order to be free from the law, believers need to die to the law—so that they can "remarry" the Lord of grace (Rom 7:1–6). Dying to the law means coming to the realization that one cannot do anything to please God with one's own resources, and Nee says that "our end is God's beginning": "When you are reduced to utter weakness and are persuaded that you can do nothing whatever, then God will do everything" (112). Nee stresses that freedom from law does not mean lawlessness, but rather, it means simply trusting oneself to God's grace for living a life over the power of death:

> Deliverance from law does not mean that we are free from doing the will of God. It certainly does not mean that we are going to be lawless. Very much the reverse! What it does mean however is that we are free from doing that will *as of ourselves.* Being fully persuaded that we cannot do it, we cease trying to please God *from the ground of the old man.* Having at last reached the point of utter despair in ourselves so that we cease even to try, we put our trust in the Lord to manifest His resurrection life in us.[41]

Lest some suspect that he is proposing the Christian life to be just "sitting still and waiting for something to happen" (or what we might call Quietism), Nee points out that dying to the law (or to self-effort) is only part of the picture of this sanctification process—the negative aspect of it; the other part, the positive aspect, is to live according to "the law of the Spirit of life" (117). In other words, Nee sees that there are two dimensions to the lifelong sanctification journey: the negative aspect of "not trying" or denial of self, and the positive aspect of "trusting" or walking after the Spirit. These are two sides of the same coin, and the key is to bring the natural person to the position of being submissive

---

41. Ibid., 111. Nee apparently uses the term "old man" here to refer to the flesh in its broad sense, including both the sinful nature and the natural life.

to the Holy Spirit so that the life of Christ within can be manifest (124, 150, 118–35).

Nee sees that there are four different things that the book of Romans is dealing with: the former two are related to "in Adam" and "in Christ" (Rom 5:12—6:23), while the latter two are related to "in the flesh" and "in the spirit" (Rom 7:1—8:39). Nee states: "The former two are 'objective' and set forth our *position*, firstly as we were by nature and secondly, as we now are by faith in the redemptive work of Christ. The latter two are 'subjective' and relate to our *walk* as a matter of practical experience. . . . We think it enough to be 'in Christ,' but we learn now that we must also walk 'in the spirit' (Rom 8:9)" (118). Nee says that walking in (or after) the Spirit means both a burden-less walk (God's work as opposed to human work) and a yielding submission to the Spirit:

> What does it mean to walk after the Spirit? It means two things. Firstly, it is not a work; it is a walk. Praise God, the burdensome and fruitless effort I involved myself in when I sought "in the flesh" to please God gives place to a quiet and restful dependence on "his working, which worketh in me mightily" (Col 1:29). That is why Paul contrasts the "works" of the flesh with the "fruit" of the Spirit (Gal 5:19, 20).
>
> Then secondly, to "walk after" implies subjection. . . . To walk after the Spirit is to be subject to the Spirit. There is one thing that the man who walks after the Spirit cannot do, and that is be independent of Him. . . . Only as I yield myself to obey Him shall I find the "law of the Spirit of life" in full operation and the "ordinance of the law" (all that I have been trying to do to please God) being fulfilled—no longer *by* me but *in* me. (132–33)

Thus for Nee God has already done everything; just as salvation is grace, sanctification is also grace. Believers only need to accept and follow, as well as surrender their own will and relinquish their own effort so as not to get into the way of receiving grace.

In his work *The Breaking of the Outer Man and the Release of the Spirit* (1948), Nee cites Pauline support—from Romans 7:22, 2 Corinthians 4:16, and Ephesians 3:16—to teach that the soul and body together constitute the "outer person," while the spirit constitutes the "inner person."[42] Further, he sees that the inner person or spirit is where the Spirit of God dwells in human beings, and that within a person the

42. Nee, *Ling de chulai* [Release of the Spirit], 10–11.

human spirit and the divine Spirit are distinct but not separate. Holding that God's work is done only in the spiritual realm, he underlines the necessity of the "breaking" or losing of the outer person in order for the inner spirit to be "released" or liberated to govern a person's whole life—so that one can better receive edification (or divine grace) as well as better "touch" (or minister to) the spirits of other people. Nee also draws support for his view from the pattern of Christ's dying and rising as well as Jesus's saying that like a grain of wheat, a person must lose his or her life in order to gain the abundant or eternal life (cf. John 12:23–25).[43]

In Nee's view, all circumstances of a believer's life are actually arranged by the Holy Spirit to bring about the believer's best spiritual benefit. But since circumstances in life are often difficult or painful, they usually are not recognized as *grace* coming from the Holy Spirit. Yet such circumstances are precisely "the discipline of the Holy Spirit" which, for Nee, is the greatest means of (conveying) grace. Nee notes that the Holy Spirit alone can see from God's perspective and so knows what would be best for the believer, whereas the believer's own perspective is often limited, and so their own efforts for spiritual growth would not be as effective as circumstances orchestrated by the Holy Spirit. But in order for the discipline of the Holy Spirit to be freely at work in one's life, one needs to consecrate oneself absolutely and be submissive to whatever circumstances that one finds oneself in. And upon seeing (not necessarily understanding) God's hand of grace in one's life, one's response— rather than complaining, blaming, or feeling depressed—should be praise and worship.[44] Such proper response will enable one to receive divine grace for the outer person to be broken and for the inner spirit to be released. Moreover, Nee insists that even when one's outer person is broken and the spirit can be released, such a release of the spirit can still be impure or mixed with the soul. Thus there needs to be a further process of separating or dividing the soul from the spirit—a process that cannot be accomplished by self-introspection, but can only come from the revelation of the Spirit.

43. Ibid., 10–41.

44. Ibid., 102–6; Nee, "Zanmei" [Praise], 285–304; and Y. D. Lin, *Shizijia* [Cross], 9, 17.

Dividing the Soul from the Spirit: Walking after the Spirit

Besides deliverance from the power of sin, in Nee's view, an even more significant goal of sanctification is to walk after the Spirit. In order to walk after the Spirit, believers need to be able to discern in their inner movements what is truly coming from the Spirit and what is merely coming from the thoughts or aspirations of their own soul. Here revelation figures prominently in Nee's thinking for this sanctification process: from the initial opening of the eyes to see the need to deny the soul life and so the need for separating the soul from the spirit, to the very operation of separating the soul from the spirit so that the pure spirit can come out to govern one's whole life and to minister to others. In the beginning of this journey illumination is needed to see that one's self or the soul-life is precisely what is hindering one's walk after the Spirit, and thus to recognize the need to deny the self by bearing one's cross daily. Especially important for Nee is for the self to truly desire to walk after the Spirit as well as to cease its striving to live the spiritual life by its own work (by the law). Since the believer's spirit is often controlled by their soul, or their spirit and soul is usually comingled together, Nee teaches that a dividing or separating of soul and spirit is necessary so that the spiritual will not be contaminated or confused by the soulish.[45]

How can one tell what is of the soul and what is of the spirit? Nee stresses that this distinction is possible only through revelations, while human analysis or teaching will have no avail. He says this separation happens only when the light of God reveals our hidden motives, for our apparently spiritual thoughts and actions are often masked with our self-centered, or soulish, motivations: "The dividing of the soul and the spirit is not a division in knowledge. It occurs when God's word comes to us and reveals the thoughts and intentions of our heart. The dividing of the soul and the spirit happens when, under God's shining, we see that our thoughts, our mind, and our actions are all of the flesh and that our motives are all for the self."[46] Further, Nee teaches that one cannot discern this by self-examination or by the soul's efforts of looking into itself: "We are never told in the Word of God to examine our inward condition. That way leads only to uncertainty, vacillation and despair."[47] Nee clearly

45. Nee, *The Spiritual Man*, 1:18–19.

46. Nee, *Breaking of the Outer Man*, 85.

47. Nee, *Normal Christian Life*, 159. Nee notes that there are two instances in the scriptures regarding self-examination but he sees these as exceptions that do not pertain

warns against the danger of engaging in such acts of self-introspection: "what . . . we all need to seek from God, is a real revelation of ourselves. I repeat that I do not mean we should be forever looking within and asking: 'Now, is this soul or is it spirit?' That will never get us anywhere; it is darkness. No, Scripture shows us how the saints were brought to self-knowledge. It was always by light from God, and that light *is* God Himself. Isaiah, Ezekiel, Daniel, Peter, Paul, John, all came to a knowledge of themselves because the Lord flashed *Himself* upon them, and that flash brought revelation and conviction."[48]

Nee refers to Hebrews 4:12–13 as the ground for the necessity of dividing the soul from the spirit, and for the absolute need of the Spirit's revelation (through scripture) for such a separation. He underscores that God's word is both living and operative—*living* so its effect is to revive, making alive the human spirit, and *operative* so one can know one's own inner thoughts and intentions. Thus rather than turning to self-introspection, Nee teaches that revelation or illumination is most needed for seeing the truth of oneself as the Psalmist says: "In thy light shall we see light" (Ps 36:9).[49] Nee preaches: "The dividing of the soul and the spirit comes from the shining. What is the shining? May the Lord be merciful to us to show us what the shining is. Shining is seeing what God sees. What does God see? He sees what we do not see. What do we not see? We do not see the things that are of ourselves, the things that we think are of God but which are not. Light shows us how much of what we thought was of God is actually of ourselves. . . . I am a blind man."[50]

So for Nee revelation is seeing what God sees, especially about the inner conditions of one's self. It is a shining light of judgment upon the outer person, so that believers are illumined to see that their thoughts and motives are of and for themselves—seeing their own real self-centeredness. Upon such seeing, they can then deny their own soulish thoughts and aspirations; in this way their soul and spirit can be separated. Not

---

to Christians' daily walk in the Spirit (Nee reads 1 Corinthians 11:28–31 as calling for a special examination of the self to discern the Lord's body, and 2 Corinthians 13:5 as a command to examine whether one has the fundamental saving faith or not). See Nee, *Normal Christian Life*, 159n.

48. Ibid., 163.

49. Ibid., 160.

50. Nee, *Breaking of the Outer Man*, 91.

only is this light operative in separating mixed soulish elements from the spirit, but this divine light itself also brings instantaneous "dealing" of the self or immediate dying of (aspects of) the outer person. In other words, seeing or coming to awareness brings with it effective healing or transformation: "This seeing will take away what we have. Our seeing is the dealing. . . . God's word is operative. Once His word shines on us, our outer man is gone. . . . The shining is the removing; both happen at the same time. As soon as the light shines, the flesh dies. No flesh survives when it is exposed to the light. When a man sees light, he does not have to humble himself; he will fall on his face immediately."[51] While holding that the light of revelation often comes in a flash, Nee also notes that such revelation or illumination does not always come in a sudden manner, but can come as a gradually deepening process, and again, when such light comes, it brings with it the simultaneous effect of purifying and healing: "Such illumination may not come to us all at once, but gradually; but it will be more and more clear and searching, until we see ourselves in the light of God and all our self-confidence is gone. For light is the purest thing in the world. It cleanses. It sterilizes. It kills what should not be there."[52] With this understanding of Nee's views of revelation and illumination, let us turn to McIntosh's exploration of some similar issues that concern Nee.

MCINTOSH ON DIVINE ILLUMINATION

McIntosh's views on divine illumination derive from what he calls a broadly Augustinian tradition of divine illumination. In this section, we will first analyze some key notions in this illumination theory, such as the contrast between wisdom and knowledge, and between the uncreated light of divine illumination and the created light of human reason. We will then explore McIntosh's understanding of divine illumination in both the trinitarian and christological matrices that are significant for explicating his views. Finally we will look at what this particular understanding of illumination—namely, illumination as knowing truth through loving communion with others—might mean for believers.

51. Ibid.
52. Nee, *Normal Christian Life*, 163–64.

Wisdom and Knowledge: Contemplation and Conceptualization

McIntosh uses the work of contemporary philosopher Robert Pasnau as reference in his discussion of divine illumination theory. According to Pasnau, divine illumination theory is the "oldest and most influential alternative to naturalism in the areas of mind and knowledge"; this theory holds that some part of a human's ordinary (not merely mystical) cognitive activity regularly (not just occasionally) requires some kind of "special supernatural assistance."[53] Such postulation of a divine role in the human cognitive function can be thought of as analogous to the idea of grace as applied to human volitional function. Just as divine grace is conceived for explaining certain human acts of willing and choosing (while not intended as an explanation for all human desires and motivations, nor even for all virtuous desires and motivations), the theory of divine illumination holds that there are certain kinds of knowledge that humans can achieve only with special divine assistance. As an ancient assumption broadly shared by most pre-modern philosophers, the theory has been invoked to explain the puzzling phenomenon of rational insight or *a priori* knowledge—to explain our "unhesitating trust to the deliverances of pure reason" and our "confidence that others can come to share our insights."[54]

McIntosh expounds his views on the divine illumination theory of knowledge based on an analysis of Augustine—"the great progenitor of Western illumination theory"[55]—as well as several other notable Christian thinkers. It thus seems helpful to first look briefly at certain ideas in Augustine's theory of illumination. McIntosh draws upon the work of Ronald Nash in interpreting Augustine's views of illumination.[56] Augustine's ontology, according to Nash, consists of a hierarchical structure of three descending levels: God, souls, and bodies. Human beings exist on the second level of reality, and their rational soul has two distinct functions: the higher reason and the lower reason. The higher reason looks upward toward the eternal and invisible reality, while the

---

53. Pasnau, "Divine Illumination."

54. Ibid.

55. McIntosh, *Discernment and Truth*, 232.

56. Nash, *Light of the Mind*, 7–8. This book of Nash's, notes McIntosh, while somewhat aging, provides "temperate and insightful discussions" of Augustine's illumination theory and "a good sense of the debates over the years." See McIntosh, *Discernment and Truth*, 271.

lower reason looks downward toward the temporal and corporeal reality. For Augustine the higher and lower reasons are simply two different functions of the same mind. The lower and higher functions of reason result in two kinds of "knowledge": knowledge (*scientia*) and wisdom (*sapientia*), which differ in many respects. Nash notes that for Augustine: "While science is a knowledge of true things, *i.e.*, a rational cognizance of the temporal, wisdom is a knowledge of truth, *i.e.*, an intellectual cognizance of the eternal. . . . *Scientia* uses the method of investigation, but wisdom uses intuition. *Scientia* has as its object the temporal and mutable, and *sapientia* is knowledge of the eternal and immutable. . . . The end of *scientia* is action or accomplishment. . . . the end of *sapientia* is contemplation."[57]

Corresponding to the three levels of being in his ontology, Augustine's epistemology has three levels of knowing or perception. First, intellection—via higher reason—that is related to *sapientia* or "contemplation of eternal truths by the mind"; second, rational cognition—via lower reason—that is related to *scientia* or "the judgment of sense objects by rational and eternal standards"; and third, sensation—via the senses—that has direct contact with the material world.[58] Theologian Andrew Louth notes that for Augustine, after the Fall the human soul knows only *scientia*, while before the Fall the soul knew *sapientia*, because the Fall has caused the soul to turn from eternal truths to temporal realities. This focus in the senses also turns the soul's attention to private involvement and a corresponding self-centered perception of everything around, which eventually leads to pride, that is, the enthronement of self and the root of all sin. According to Louth: "Augustine therefore interprets the account of the Fall in Genesis by saying that the serpent's achievement was to persuade the woman to grasp a personal and private good, rather than the common and public good which is unchangeable."[59]

For Augustine knowledge of any kind is to be sought not for its own sake, but to be pursued pragmatically for the sake of happiness: "Man has no reason to philosophize except with a view to happiness."[60]

57. Nash, *Light of the Mind*, 8.

58. Ibid., 9.

59. Louth, *Christian Mystical Tradition*, 153.

60. Augustine, *De civitate Dei* XIX, 1, 3, VIII, as quoted in Nash, *Light of the Mind*, 8.

Augustine regards wisdom (for the contemplative life) as superior to knowledge (for the active life) because wisdom is concerned with the ultimate happiness of human existence. McIntosh also notes that for Augustine (and Aquinas and Bonaventure agree), as the mind moves from knowledge (*scientia*) to wisdom (*sapientia*)—from analytical knowing to pure-minded contemplating or "wisdom resting in the divine ideas of things"—it opens to greater illumination.[61] Yet this does not make *scientia* unimportant because knowledge of the created world is necessary for human survival and practical living, so in this sense it is more basic and is indispensable for the pursuit of wisdom and true blessedness.[62] For Augustine, notes Louth, *scientia* or knowledge "has both a good and a bad use: it is not something to be relinquished, but rather rightly used."[63]

Illumination and Reason: Uncreated Light and Created Light

Nash analyzes different major interpretations on Augustine's teaching of illumination, and argues that the Augustinian texts best support a kind of ontologist interpretation. According to this ontologist interpretation, Augustine holds that human beings can, in some way, have direct knowledge of the eternal forms or divine ideas. Nash shows that for Augustine there are two lights that make knowledge possible: the uncreated light of God and the created light of human's intellect—analogous to the original light of the sun and the derivative light of the moon. Similarly, the forms exist first in the mind of God and then in a derived way in the rational structure of the human mind. Thus the eternal forms also exist in a secondary sense in the human mind. This means that human beings, by virtue of their creation in the image of God, possess the forms of thought or rational capacities in a "natural" (as opposed to supernatural) way in so far as they possess such forms when they are born.[64] Since the same Creator also created the world after the pattern of the divine ideas, everything in creation then can be intelligible for human creatures who are endowed with the divine forms: human knowledge of the creation is therefore possible. Augustine, however, further teaches that rational

---

61. McIntosh, *Discernment and Truth*, 235.

62. Nash, *Light of the Mind*, 8–9.

63. Louth, *Christian Mystical Tradition*, 154.

64. Nash, *Light of the Mind*, 108–9, 111, 123.

capacity itself is necessary, but not sufficient, to know truth, because the created light of the human intellect needs the uncreated light for its constant sustenance and assistance. Nash comments that for Augustine, "knowledge is possible because God has created man after his own image as a rational soul and because God continually sustains and aids the soul in its quest for knowledge."[65] Thus Augustine holds—unlike Thomas later who understands illumination "as an infusion all at once at the start"—that divine illumination comes to us "in an ongoing way throughout our lives."[66] Nash states: "Augustine is clear in stating that the soul never ceases to be dependent upon God for its knowledge."[67]

Augustine maintains that instead of looking "out there" to find truth, one must look within, for human beings can know this world "only because they first know the eternal, incorporeal, intelligible world of ideas that exists in the mind of God."[68] These divine ideas or forms in the human mind are *a priori* in the Kantian sense in that they are not derived from experience; rather, they are preconditions of *scientia*.[69] Thus Augustine's understanding of the mind is different from Thomas's view that the intellect can produce truth "by abstracting it in some way from sensation."[70] Pasnau notes that divine illumination theory—in its peculiarly Christian varieties formulated by Augustine and some medieval theologians—envisions at least two ways in which God might influence the human mind. First, God might simply give us certain information or knowledge. Secondly, rather than (or besides) giving the information itself, God provides the insight into the truthfulness of the information we are considering—in other words, God provides the justification of knowledge. In this second model, the ideas we have received from other people remain mere beliefs until we grasp their truth by the aid of divine illumination; only then do they become true knowledge for us. Both these ways are maintained in Augustine's writing, and Augustine preaches that only God can teach us.[71] In exhorting believers to meditate on the humility of Christ, Augustine writes: "Meditate, then, on the

65. Ibid., 111.

66. Pasnau, "Divine Illumination."

67. Nash, *Light of the Mind*, 111.

68. Ibid., viii.

69. Ibid., 107–9.

70. Ibid., 122.

71. Pasnau, "Divine Illumination."

humility of Christ. But, you may say, 'Who will explain it to us, if you do not speak?' Christ himself speaks, interiorly. He who dwells within will speak better of the mystery than he who raises his voice outside you. May he show you the grace of his humility, now that he has begun to dwell in your hearts."[72]

Trinitarian Structure of Truth: Reality as Word-Like and Relational

McIntosh notes that "a large range of Christian thinkers in many eras," similar to Augustine, have understood that all things exist as ideas or thoughts in God's mind even before they are created in time.[73] While this line of thinking may have been shaped by Neoplatonic influence, it is also grounded in the Christian scriptures and tradition. Drawing from Origen (ca. 185–254), Augustine (ca. 354–430), Maximus the Confessor (ca. 580–662), Bonaventure (ca. 1217–1274), and Thomas Aquinas (ca. 1225–1274), McIntosh suggests that the truth of all things originates in the communal sharing (of love and truth) within the Trinity.[74] McIntosh notes that for Augustine, God knows Godself by the Wisdom that is God's eternal begotten Word—the incarnation of which is Jesus Christ. This can be seen in Augustine's homilies on John's gospel, in which Augustine identifies the eternally begotten Word not only with the Son, but also with the Wisdom of God—by which all things are made, and which contains the design of everything before it is made. In other words, God's knowledge of the creation exists eternally as the archetypal ideas of God (in God) *before* their historical existence in time. Thus God's knowledge of every created thing is simply God's knowing of Godself, of God's own ideas subsisting in the Son. McIntosh notes that this divine self-knowledge, in Thomas's view, is also none other than the Word of God.

McIntosh points out that this tradition understands that creation was spoken into existence by the word of God, through the Word of God, and thus is patterned after or has the character or structure of the divine word. McIntosh then tries to show that this notion that reality has the character of a word (or has a noetic dimension) implies reality's intelligibility, and thus grounds the human possibility of knowing

72. Augustine, *On the Gospel of St. John* (3:15), as quoted in Ruddy, *Christological Approach to Virtue*, 292.

73. McIntosh, *Discernment and Truth*, 216.

74. See McIntosh, *Discernment and Truth*, 215–33.

such reality. For instance, Augustine maintains that the divine ideas or reasons—*logoi* in Greek—are the ground for the creation's intelligibility. For Maximus also, all the *logoi* find their true meaning and relationship in the overarching *Logos* who is none other than "Christ the Lord implanted within the community by the Spirit" (219).

This is not merely saying that because God is truth, any forms of truth must derive from God. Rather, McIntosh wants to highlight the point that there is a trinitarian character in God's knowing of the truth of all things, because creation came to be made as an overflowing of the trinitarian self-sharing of love and truth-speaking. In other words, within the Trinity, the event of knowledge is a "communal or indeed communion-like" event of joyful self-sharing (219–20). McIntosh states: "the truth of things originates in the divinely truthful self-knowing, in the perfect imaging and correspondence between the Father and the Son," and this divine truthfulness itself "springs from the eternal yearning (to know) of the Holy Spirit" (ibid.). McIntosh thus argues that it is in the *relationship* between the Father and the Son (through the Holy Spirit) that God knows all creatures-to-be—as eternal divine ideas contained in the Word. Since the trinitarian God is the source and origin of all things, any truth about the universe is necessarily the radiance of the trinitarian or relational knowing and loving of God: "truth springs precisely from the *relationship* of the Father and Son, that what is true is the perfect *likeness* and expression of the Father which the Word is and freely chooses to be. Or as the Letter to the Hebrews says regarding the Son, 'He is the reflection of God's glory and the exact imprint of God's very being' (Heb 1:3)" (222–23). So McIntosh emphasizes that because creation itself is the result of eternal events of trinitarian knowing and loving, the created reality has a word-like as well as a relational structure, and the process of human (themselves part of creation) knowing of truth also has a relational or trinitarian underpinning.

Christological Grounding of Knowing: Participating in the Paschal Mystery

McIntosh then explores what the intelligible cosmos means for human knowers. McIntosh suggests that human knowing of the truth of the world can only happen when humans are drawn into or participate in "that infinite knowing and loving which is God's life" (221). To journey into such mystical truth, one must first be aroused to desire such truth and, according to Bonaventure, such desire can only be animated by "the fire of the Holy Spirit"; or as McIntosh puts it: "The Holy Spirit must inflame and carry one into God, thus inducing within human knowing a participation in the divine knowing . . . ." (222). For Bonaventure, this journey means going through a dying process—being consumed and transformed in fire—the very image of burnt offerings in the Temple, even the perfect offering of (the Temple of) Christ's body. McIntosh thus comments: "For Bonaventure, Christ, who is the perfect offering—of the Father to the world and of the world to the Father—accomplishes in this liturgy of his dying and rising the consummation of the journey of truth. . . . He is the appearing in our present world of the truth of all things as they have passed from mendacity to reality, from death to life. In the bitter economy of lies, Christ, who is the truth of all things, appears as alienated and accursed by God; the resurrection reveals the truth of all things as vindicated and beloved of God" (ibid.).

Thus Bonaventure sees that not only is there the trinitarian grounding of truth, but also a christological grounding as well. For Bonaventure, coming to know the deep truth structure inherent in all things is crucially linked to the sharing or participating in truth's historical embodiment in the paschal mystery (220). Bonaventure likens the journey of knowing truth to a birthing process of conception, laboring, and giving birth—alluding to the second person of the Trinity respectively as the primordial Wisdom, the suffering Son, and the resurrected Christ. For Bonaventure, just as the truth of all things was conceived in the womb of Wisdom from all eternity, and just as the existence of all things in time is the expression of divine self-knowing in the Word, the *full* truth of all things comes to be realized or known in the Son's return to the Father (in the Spirit)—in Christ's journey through this world, by way of the cross and resurrection. As McIntosh puts it, "the events of Jesus' life, death, and resurrection are not simply the earthly, historical manifestation of the trinitarian life but a constitutive moment in the journey of creation into its fullest truthfulness" (223).

Divine Illumination: Knowing Truth through Loving Communion

McIntosh proceeds to an understanding of illumination as an event taking place in the (inner) noetic realm that is analogous to the mission of the Word and Spirit in (outer) history—the Passion and Pentecost. Here McIntosh suggests that because of sin's distortions, the creation's self-understanding became "fallacious and corrupted," which prevents it from realizing its consummate truth as conceived by God. The alienation of the creatures from (their truth in) the Father is overcome through the historical work of the Word and Spirit, which offers the opportunity for the creatures to participate in this redemption "through obedience to Christ in the power of the Spirit" (223–24). McIntosh then suggests that it might well be the case that the same Word and Spirit "who bring to birth all truth within the mind of God and who 'reconceived' and resurrect that truth within the brokenness of history are also at work mystically (or hiddenly) throughout the creation—and especially through creatures imbued with intellect—to foster this healing and reconciling discernment of the truth of things" (224).

McIntosh notes that such questions as "How do you know?" have arisen from the peculiarly modern preoccupation with the certainty or even the possibility of any human knowledge of God. The problem lies, McIntosh observes, in that since early modernity (ca. 1600), "knowing" has become a private, individual act of cognition, while the ancient Christians hold that knowing is an act of communion—with reality (the "known")—that can be distorted or harmed by sin.[75] Modern Christian theology, however, has tended to "sidestep the question of sin and instead to label revelation as the problem in and of itself."[76] McIntosh states, "Instead of realizing that our problem in hearing God aright has to do with sin, we have become convinced that the whole business of revelation hinges on whether the very idea of God speaking can make sense. Disobedience and infidelity to God make us increasingly insensitive to God's call to us in the prophets of Israel and the gospel of Christ, to say nothing of God's loving desire to address us in creation itself and in our relationships with one another."[77] However, for generations of Christians before modernity, knowing reality deeply has not so much to do with reading a book or observing through a microscope, but with faithful practice in the way of Christ: "By sharing in Jesus' ministry of reconciling love, Christians have found growing in themselves those habits of heart and intuitions of soul that draw them into God's own knowing of God, the Word's knowing of the Father. In other words, for most of Christian history, *understanding* reality has been integrally con-

75. McIntosh, *Mysteries of Faith*, 72–74.
76. Ibid., 72–73.
77. Ibid., 72.

nected with *loving* it."[78] McIntosh notes that because humanity has fallen into sin (especially its anxious self-making and fearful suspicion), the divine life—a communal and loving life—could not reveal itself to the world with outstretched arms without being hung on the cross. Thus to be able to receive divine revelation truthfully, our very life needs first to be transformed: "God can only really show us who God is by transforming us as fit partakers of God's life."[79]

After studying the extensive history of interpretations of illumination theory, McIntosh argues that from its inception the illumination theory of knowledge was never meant to be a purely philosophical theory, and particularly not a narrowly epistemological account of the human process of cognition. But rather, McIntosh attempts to show, from Augustine and Bonaventure, that illumination is a "way of thinking about the mystical interaction between the divine and the creaturely within the cosmic event of divine truth-expression."[80] Contemporary thinkers tend to conceive of epistemology in individualized terms and, notes McIntosh, such a peculiarly modern pattern of thought falls short of the grand vision of Augustine that is cosmological—in the majestic context of creation. McIntosh analyzes Augustine's reflection—in his *Literal Meaning of Genesis* (usually accounted as one of the three major works of the mature Augustine)—on the significance of light in the creation, especially for intellectual beings. Augustine sees that intellectual creatures—unlike non-intellectual ones (such as sea and dry land) that simply reflect the divine light in a passive way—are capable of receiving the divine light in an appreciative way and offering their response of praise. Augustine further envisions that the paradigm case of such illuminated appreciation and praise of the divine rationale in creation is the activity of angels in heaven, in which humanity will share only provisionally on earth, but will share fully in the life to come. McIntosh notes that in contrast to ordinary human knowing which corresponds to knowledge of the temporal "fact" of things, in Augustine's view, illumination is a human sharing in the angels' vision—always ordered toward praise—of the eternal "reason" for things (230–32). Knowing the truth of creation in this way naturally implies knowing God in an intimate way, for such knowing only happens in the moment when hu-

78. Ibid., 73.

79. Ibid., 79.

80. McIntosh, *Discernment and Truth*, 271n15.

man beings—companioned by the divine Wisdom—touch the Word's expression of the eternal reason of created things, in such a way that they can appreciate the wonderful divine rationale and intention of God's creativity, which in turn orders them toward profound wonder and praise.

Thus McIntosh suggests that illumination theory clarifies the point that there is a crucial link between human knowledge of truth and loving communion with the other—both the human other and the divine Other. Drawing from Bonaventure, McIntosh sees that the very purpose of God in creation, out of the unfolding (truth) event of abundant love and freedom in the Trinity, is to provide the space (analogous to the mutual "space" between the triune Persons) and thus the possibility for the creatures (especially the intellectual ones) to freely choose to love—to give themselves freely to one another and ultimately to the triune God. In other words, God gives the creatures their historical existence in finite form so that the truth of the creatures can come to its fullness or consummation when they choose to give themselves in love and freedom to one another. Here then each creature's apparent "autonomy" from each other and from God, McIntosh suggests, "is exactly the self-destructive counterfeit of the truth to which the creatures have been subjected . . ." (224), for the divine intention is for the creatures to move toward communion and, within their deep desire for knowing and loving one another, discover "their calling toward that infinite knowing and loving that is God's own life" (225).

According to McIntosh, for Augustine and Bonaventure—and to a great extent for Maximus as well—illumination can be understood in terms of Christ as the interior teacher and as the companion and friend for believers (229). Thus the event of knowing truth turns out to be an event of communion. In other words, "divine illumination theory . . . points to the spiritual encounter within which knowing takes place" (233). McIntosh states: "Christ, in whom the truth of all creatures dwells as spoken by the Father, teaches the mind to discern the reality of creatures by imbuing the mind with an intuition of the full truth of creatures *as intended by God* and by opening the mind to that yearning desire (the outpouring of the Holy Spirit) for the creatures to come to their fullness as events of divine communion" (ibid.). Further, knowledge thus gained (through illumination) is free from egoistic possession or manipulation, because the event of knowing bears the knowers up toward their consummate truth through an event of praise and communion. In short, McIntosh champions the trinitarian and christological groundings of truth, and as a result, the human process of truth-knowing as a relational event of loving communion. With this understanding of McIntosh's views of divine illumination theory, let us proceed to an evaluation of some controversial issues in Nee's views.

NEE AND MCINTOSH IN DIALOGUE

This section will attempt an evaluation of some controversial issues related to Nee's views on revelation and illumination. Leung Ka-lun notes that the spiritual theory adopted and developed by Nee shares much in common with heretical Gnosticism of the second and third centuries, and Leung suggests that Nee's tripartite anthropology and its resultant spiritual theology can be called a kind of "Chinese Gnosticism."[81] Since what is disputed is closely related to Nee's tripartite anthropology as well as his views of revelation or "hearing God," and since McIntosh does not deal with these topics explicitly, we will first attempt to assess Nee's tripartite anthropology in light of some recent biblical and theological studies, and then explore his idea of revelation in the contexts of both classic Reformed theology and contemporary pentecostal/charismatic thought. Finally, building on these discussions, we will bring Nee's thought into dialogue with McIntosh's work on the broadly Augustine tradition of divine illumination. We will then see whether Nee's view on revelation is consonant with the understanding of this Augustinian tradition.

Body, Soul, and Spirit: Scriptural Views

Nancey Murphy notes that questions about the nature of the human person have gained little speculative attention in the scriptures, nor have such questions been a central matter throughout the course of Christian history—in comparison to such central Christian concerns as Christology, soteriology, and eschatology.[82] Nonetheless, biblical writers usually worked with certain assumptions about the human person—"sometimes

---

81. K. L. Leung, "Huaren nuosidi zhuyi" [Chinese Gnosticism], 185–275, esp. 189, 197. Liao also notes the similarity and connection between Gnosticism and Nee's tripartite anthropology. See Liao, "Sanyuan renlun guan" [Tripartite anthropology], 102, and "Nee's Theology of Victory," 203.

82. Murphy, "Human Nature," 19, 23. See also Green, "Bodies—That Is, Human Lives," 149.

in order to counter competing portraits."[83] Most thinkers in the history of Christian thought, including the Reformers Luther and Calvin, affirmed or presupposed a dualistic—soul and body—conception of the person.[84] Murphy, however, points out that biblical scholars and theologians in the modern era began to question the scriptural basis for such body-soul dualism. In the early twentieth century, H. Wheeler Robinson argued that New Testament anthropology is largely continuous with that of the Old Testament, and that the Hebrew notion of the person is an integrative "animated body"—as opposed to the Greek idea of a dualistic "incarnated soul." Yet Robinson's rejection of radical dualism was still moderate, and his view is considered as a qualified dualism.

The mid-twentieth-century biblical theology movement—as well as neo-orthodox theologians Karl Barth and others—made a sharp distinction between the Hebraic and Hellenistic notions, and strongly favored the restoration of the earlier, Hebrew understanding. Rudolf Bultmann later shifted decisively from a qualified dualism to a thorough monism or physicalism.[85] Yet the debates about anthropological dualism and monism—inevitably tied to eschatological issues such as the intermediate state (after death and before resurrection) as well as to developments from contemporary science and philosophy—have continued throughout the century up to the present.[86] Joel B. Green points out the considerable difficulties in reconstructing the biblical views of the person's composition. Since New Testament writers were informed by a variety of traditions, our interpretation of the scriptures must be set within their own contexts. After exploring texts from Luke and Paul, Green concludes that the central concern of these New Testament authors is the notion of soteriological holism—emphasizing the person's embodied and communal existence, especially in relation to God within the community of God's people.[87] Murphy notes the tendency among scholars "to juxtapose incompatible accounts of

83. Green, "Bodies—That Is, Human Lives," 149.

84. Cf. Murphy, "Human Nature," 19; and Cooper, *Body, Soul, and Life Everlasting*, 1.

85. Murphy, "Human Nature," 20–29.

86. See Cooper, *Body, Soul, and Life Everlasting*. In this book, Cooper offers a survey of different modern critics of classical dualism, as well as a sustained argument—integrating biblical, theological, philosophical, and scientific studies—for a more traditional "holistic dualism" which upholds the integration of the human person on the one hand, and on the other allows a disembodied intermediate state after death.

87. Green, "Bodies—That Is, Human Lives," 169, 172–73.

biblical teaching," and concludes her survey of recent scholarship with these statements: "So it is clear that recent theological and biblical scholarship has not conclusively settled the issue. . . . the dichotomy 'Greek dualism versus Hebraic holism' is an oversimplification, and the typical method used to address this issue—studies of word usage—is now recognized to be inadequate."[88]

That being said, there seems to be a consensus among some scholars to view spirit, soul, and body as representing different functions or orientations of the holistic human person. Noting the influence of the tripartite anthropology propagated by Penn-Lewis and mediated sometimes by Nee, John Yates attempts to examine the scriptural evidence for understanding spirit as distinct from soul (or mind), and for positing the Spirit-spirit link as the nexus for receiving divine knowledge or transrational knowledge. Yates first points out that there are numerous difficulties in trying to establish a full-blown tripartite anthropology from scripture, since when viewed in context, the two popular proof texts of 1 Thessalonians 5:23 and Hebrews 4:12 (which are also the major biblical supports for Penn-Lewis and Nee) are not to be seen as making an anthropological statement *per se*. Further, there are examples of parallel use of spirit and soul such as Luke 1:46–47: "My soul [*psyche*] glorifies the Lord and my spirit [*pneuma*] rejoices in God my Saviour."[89] Other scholars also note that the simplistic study of word usage in the Bible does not do justice to the complex historical and literary contexts within which words were used in the scriptures.[90] Thus a full tripartite anthropology that regards the human person as consisting of three separate entities of body, soul, and spirit does not seem justifiable from scripture.

While *pneuma* (spirit) cannot be established as a separate constituent of human personality, can it be shown from the New Testament to be distinguishable from *psyche* (soul) at least functionally? Yates observes that even in terms of the human function, spirit and soul cannot be shown to be completely divisible aspects since both *psyche* and *pneuma* are used to describe similar emotions, but there are arguably crucial distinctions between *psyche* and *pneuma*. While *psyche* can be used as a source of evil (such as 1 Pet 2:11, 4:19; 2 Pet 2:14; Heb 13:17),

---

88. Murphy, "Human Nature," 21, 23.

89. Yates, "How Does God Speak," 110–11.

90. See Murphy, "Human Nature," 23; and Jewett, *Paul's Anthropological Terms*, 447–60.

pneuma is never used as the site of any negative ethical impulse. Besides, *pneuma* is not used for describing nonbelievers' relation to God, but it can be regarded as the special object of God's attention. Yates notes that in the non-Pauline literature, *pneuma* denotes a realm of "sensitivity and responsiveness to the divine"; and in the Pauline usage, scholarship broadly accepts that "the Holy Spirit is largely concerned with the human spirit."[91] For instance, in Ray S. Anderson's view, spirit is "an orientation towards God summoned forth by the divine Word and enabled by the divine Spirit."[92] For E. Schweizer, spirit is "the organ that receives the Spirit of God."[93] G. E. Ladd also insists that it is precisely "because man possesses *pneuma* that he is capable of being related to God."[94] Yates thus suggests that the human spirit is the locus for receiving divine knowledge from the Spirit, as Gordon Fee writes in his comments on 1 Corinthians 14:32: "he [Paul] tends to use the term ['spirit'] in a much more flexible way than most of us are comfortable with. The Spirit who speaks through the prophets is understood to be speaking through 'the spirit' of the prophet . . . 'my spirit prays' seems to mean something like 'my S/spirit prays . . .'"[95]

Anderson also suggests that while scripture does not support viewing body, soul, and spirit as separate *entities* or substances within a person, these terms are used to denote the whole person with different emphases or different orientations. He sees that scripture depicts a threefold orientation of the human life: emerging from the created world, interacting with other human creatures, and destined for eternal life with the Creator. He thus suggests that we should view body, soul, and spirit as different terms—while overlapping in meaning—describing different *functions* or *orientations* of human existence.[96] He notes that biological life (*bios*) is a necessary but insufficient condition to be a human being, who is destined to the abundant life (*zoe*) inseparable from Jesus Christ as the source of life. Noting that the image of God does

91. Yates, "How Does God Speak," 111.

92. Anderson, "On Being Human," 212, as quoted in Yates, "How Does God Speak," 111.

93. Schweizer, "Pneuma," as quoted in Yates, "How Does God Speak," 111–12.

94. Ladd, *Theology of the New Testament*, 463, as quoted in Yates, "How Does God Speak," 112.

95. Fee, *1 Corinthians*, 596, 670, as quoted in Yates, "How Does God Speak," 113.

96. Anderson, "On Being Human," 182; and Murphy, "Human Nature," 28.

not refer to the physical body, but to the "embodied soul," Anderson sees that scripture allows for a *duality* of the human person without a *dualism* or opposition between body and soul. Anderson writes: "What is distinctive about human beings is . . . that, as 'ensouled body' and 'embodied soul', the 'spirit' of that existence is opened towards God in a unique way as the source of life. The whole of human life, body and soul, is thus oriented towards a destiny beyond mortal or natural life. This endowment of life is experienced as the image and likeness of God. While the physical body itself is not held to be in the image of God, human beings as 'embodied souls' are in the image of God."[97] Thus while recent biblical scholarship does not support a hard version of Nee's tripartite anthropology, it does seem to allow for a soft version of it—maintaining a linguistic and functional distinction between spirit, soul, and body without insisting on an ontological identification or separation of each.[98]

Transrational Knowing: Reformed Theology and Pentecostal Thought

Leung's critique of Nee is from a conservative evangelical perspective which finds Penn-Lewis's—and by implication Nee's—views too mystical to stay within the safety bound of classic Reformed orthodoxy.[99] Similar questions have also been addressed by Yates in his analysis of the tension between the rationalism of conservative Reformed evangelicals and the enthusiasm of contemporary pentecostals/charismatics, both of which were part of Nee's theological heritage. However, Nee's idea of revelation can be seen as much closer to contemporary charismatic thought in its insistence on the possibility and even the necessity of "hearing God" in the present time. Yates's discussion appeals directly to scrip-

97. Anderson, "Christian Anthropology," 7.

98. Anderson also argues that since the term "soul"—as commonly used in Western culture—denotes the deeper concerns of human life (such as ethics or spirituality), "soul" can be employed to designate a distinctive aspect of the human person (without subscribing to dualism). See Anderson, "On Being Human," 175–94; and Murphy, "Human Nature," 28.

Kees Waaijman explores the multivalence and multidimensionality of the scriptural term *nephesh* (soul). Seeing that the soul unites the various dimensions that are constitutive of the humanness of human life, he argues that "soul" plays a preeminent role as a term denoting the human pole in the relationship with God, for it can "simultaneously surrender itself to the other and to God" and "it is that which is transformed in all its dimensions by God in love." See Waaijman, "Soul as Spiritual Core," 5–19, esp. 5–6.

99. See K. L. Leung, "Fenxing yundong dao shenmi zhuyi" [From revivalism to mysticism], esp. 2–56, 13.

tural data—which all parties in the debate claim to give their highest regard—and can shed light on many of the concerns that Leung raises. Yates notes Luther's rejection of the Roman Catholic appeal to the Holy Spirit's infallible guidance in the *magisterium* (the teaching authority of the Roman Catholic Church) on the one hand, and on the other, the enthusiastic claim of some Anabaptists for divine guidance apart from the scriptures. In their stead, Luther held that the Holy Spirit is bound both to the word of the scriptures and to the sacraments. Calvin also maintained a similar position: the Spirit and Word are inseparable in their mutual bond. And the Westminster Confession codified Calvin's distinction between the *revelation* that led to the writing of scripture and the *illumination* of the Spirit for reading and understanding the scriptures. While the classic Reformed tradition teaches that revelation ended with the authoring of the Bible, it nonetheless believes that the Spirit does guide believers into all truth—yet such Spirit guidance is bound within the limits set by scripture, and it is only for understanding biblical truth and applying it to current situations.[100]

Noting that contemporary pentecostal theology holds that a sort of divine revelation or transrational knowledge is available to believers (in such operations as tongues, prophecies, or "hearing God"), Yates points out that a similar kind of transrational knowing is also assumed in classical Reformed theology. Calvin speaks of the "internal testimony of the Holy Spirit" which testifies to believers that scripture is the word of God;[101] and he at times refers to an illumination of the heart that later Reformed theology designated as "illumination," sometimes regarded as "a reason beyond reasons, the reason of the heart."[102] In Calvin's words:

> Such, then, is the conviction that requires no reasons; such,
> a knowledge with which the best reason agrees—in which the
> mind reposes more securely than in any reasons; such, finally a
> *feeling* that can be born only of heavenly revelation. . . . the only
> true faith is that which the Holy Spirit illumines our hearts. . . .
> faith is much higher than human understanding . . . it will not be
> enough for the mind to be illumined by the Spirit of God unless

100. Yates, "How Does God Speak," 104–5, 107.

101. Cf. the second way that divine illumination theory (as formulated by Augustine and some medieval theologians) envisions how divine influence works in the human mind (i.e., providing the justification of knowledge). See Pasnau, "Divine Illumination" as well as the discussion in this chapter above.

102. Yates, "How Does God Speak," 108.

> the heart is also strengthened and supported. . . . the Word of
> God is not received by faith if it flits about in the top of the brain,
> but when it takes root in the depth of the heart. . . .[103]

While Reformed theology after Calvin focused strongly on the intellectual nature of faith, Yates notes that the knowledge of the heart did obtain prominence in one particular area, namely, that of assurance. Appealing to such biblical texts as 2 Corinthians 1:22, 5:5, Ephesians 1:13–14, and Romans 8:16, Reformed theology holds that the Holy Spirit testifies to the heart of believers that they are children of God. Yates thus suggests that this Reformed idea of the inner witness of the Spirit refers to a kind of transrational knowing that intersects with similar notions in contemporary charismatic/pentecostal thought.

Yates then observes that contemporary pentecostal views of transrational knowing are in line with a broader notion of revelation based on New Testament usage of the term. Yates notes that in 1 Corinthians 14:2 and 14:14—where Paul talks about speaking in tongues as uttering mysteries with the human spirit while the mind remains unfruitful—the implication is that there is a kind of communication or communion between God and the human spirit that bypasses the mind. In the same chapter, as Paul develops the notion of interpretation of tongues, the further implication is that the "mysteries" uttered in the spirit actually contain information—bearing knowledge that is transrational in origin. However, Yates argues that in the context of either Romans 8:16 or 1 Corinthians 14, it cannot be established that there is a necessary bond between such transrational knowing and scripture, a bond insisted on by the conservative Reformed and evangelical traditions. Rather, within the contexts of both Romans 8 and 1 Corinthians 14, this transrational knowledge is best understood as an immediate or direct operation of the Holy Spirit upon the human spirit. Yates therefore suggests that the contemporary charismatic view of transrational knowledge is compatible with the teaching of the scriptures.

Yates also attempts to show that the theological notion of revelation is too narrow according to biblical usages—there is no biblical basis for either the strict distinction between revelation and illumination maintained by some heirs of the Reformers or the corollary assumption that there can be "no new revelation" in the present era; there is "no

103. Calvin, *Institutes*, 80–81, 580–81, 583, as quoted in Yates, "How Does God Speak," 108 (emphasis Yates's).

neat biblical antithesis between objective revelation and uncontrolled mysticism" in the Bible.[104] Yates notes that there is a wide range of uses of *apocalypto/apocalypsis* (reveal/revelation) in the New Testament,[105] and that too much emphasis has been placed on the narrow sense of revelation (as pertaining only to the written scripture) in later Christian theologizing. Yates especially notes the use of the *apocalypto* word group in 1 Corinthians 12–14, in which there is not only a most intimate link between the Holy Spirit, the human spirit, and revelation, but also the equation of revelation with prophecy. Yates thus suggests that the much broader notion of revelation—that is used in the scriptures—can be applied to "hearing God" in other areas of Christian life.[106]

As to the relation between such "hearing God" and scripture, first Yates proposes thinking of "hearing God" as a lower level or subordinate revelation given by the Holy Spirit for mere "specific application of the core truths" recorded in the Bible.[107] Secondly, Yates holds that for matters necessary to salvation, the witness of the Spirit should be tied to the contexts of the scriptures—as maintained by traditional Reformed theology. Yates, however, suggests that for "nonessential matters" concerning the historical life of the church, there can be "private revelation"—equivalent to what Paul calls "prophecy"—as guidance for Christian life and service, although such private revelation can never dispute or contradict biblical standards for faith and practice. In this way, Yates sees that such an understanding of subordinate revelation need not threaten the centrality of scripture, and need not lead to unrestrained enthusiasm.[108]

How is one to discern whether such private or extra-biblical revelation is indeed from God? Such witness of the Holy Spirit is often described as a special sense of authority and peace in some spiritual writers. Yates points out, for instance, what Teresa of Avila says: "The first sign that a locution comes from God, is the sense of power

104. Yates, "How Does God Speak," 114. Yates cites D. A. Carson and G. C. Bingham as his supports (127n122).

105. Yates notes examples of such uses in Matthew 11:27, 16:17, Galatians 1:16, 1 Corinthians 2:10, Philippians 3:15, and Ephesians 1:17. See Yates, "How Does God Speak," 114.

106. Ibid., 114–15. Yates also notes a related example in Galatians 2:2 (127n128).

107. Ibid., 115.

108. Ibid., 115–17.

and authority the locution bears with it, and the sense of confidence and peace that follows it."[109] Yates also notes that other affects Teresa speaks of include tranquility, upwelling praise, and ease of recollection. Likewise, Jonathan Edwards also pays attention to "holy affections" that accompany the Spirit's influence on the human heart: "The gracious and most excellent assistance of the Spirit of God in praying and preaching is not by immediately suggesting words to the apprehension . . . but by warming the heart, and filling it with a great sense of things to be spoken, and with holy affections, that these may suggest words. . . ."[110] Noting the certitude expressed in Romans 8:16, philosopher William J. Abraham writes: "Subjects who experience the inner witness of the Holy Spirit are naturally inclined to treat their experience as veridical. Descriptions of their experience that construe it as an encounter with the Holy Spirit appear luminously correct to those who speak of this kind of religious experience. Thus it leads to a deep sense of certainty of the reality of God and his profoundly personal love for human agents."[111] Yates suggests that it can be supposed that the human spirit acts as a sort of sensor in receiving divine revelation analogous to the role of conscience in the moral realm. Just as the conscience bears a certain authority—yet not infallible—in moral situations, the spirit may well be playing a similar role in transrational knowing, thus imperfection in such spiritual guidance does not need to discount such guidance's significance. If Yates's analysis on these issues makes sense, then it is plausible that Nee's similar convictions of both the possibility and the significance of receiving direct divine guidance today are theologically well founded. As Nee's views of revelation as well as his tripartite anthropology are in peaceful company with some contemporary biblical and theological studies, let us proceed to a dialogue between Nee and McIntosh on their perspectives on revelation and illumination.

Hearing God and Spiritual Knowledge: Encountering the Living Word

Both Nee and McIntosh are concerned with the issue of spiritual knowledge, knowledge that is in some sense of divine origin, not conventionally

109. Teresa of Avila, *Interior Castle*, 116.

110. Edwards, *Great Awakening*, 437–38, as quoted in Yates, "How Does God Speak," 116.

111. Abraham, "Epistemological Significance," 441, referred to in Yates, "How Does God Speak," 116.

or customarily discernible. There are important similarities and differences between the two authors. Nee often speaks in terms of receiving divine illumination by an individual concerning certain scriptural passages, both for general understanding of the sanctification journey (such as victory over the power of sin and purifying the spirit from soulish mixtures), and for specific guidance in particular situations such as healing an illness or discerning direction for the future. McIntosh, however, while speaking also of illumination on the book of scripture, focuses more on divine illumination found in such areas as creation and other human creatures. Especially for McIntosh, while Jesus Christ is the very Word of God, the revelation of God to humankind is communicated through a union of scripture as the written Body of the Word and the church as the eucharistic (or mystical) Body of the Word.[112] While Nee regards revelation as a process of "hearing God" that must continuously happen today, McIntosh also regards revelation or illumination as an ongoing present-day event of encountering God. McIntosh writes:

> Revelation takes place as God speaks the divine life through different forms of embodiment, from creation and history to the incarnate form of the Word as Jesus, and from there to the resurrection life of Christ poured out through the church in Pentecost, and living still in eucharist and scripture. Revelation is the *whole* sweep. . . . each form it takes (in this case, the Bible) is crucial to the ongoing encounter of humanity with God. The biblical witness, in other words, tells of prior historical events, but does not stop there; it moves on to encounters of the community with God today and mediates that encounter.[113]

How then do we interpret scripture as God's Word? McIntosh rejects both the fundamentalist equation of the literal words of scripture with the Word of God, and the liberal revisionist treatment of the Bible as primitive cultural myths and symbols (as unreliable historical records) expressive of universal religious experiences. Instead, McIntosh finds a more tenable position in the middle way of the Episcopal priest Hans Frei, who regards the Bible as far more like a sacrament with visible forms (stories, prophecies, poetries, letters, etc.) for revelation of the invisible presence of God. For Frei, the miracle of the bodily resurrection of Jesus is a real historical event; but the fragmentary text is not

112. McIntosh, *Mysteries of Faith*, 84.

113. Ibid., 86–87.

like a photograph, rather it depicts a series of miraculous events that are mysterious and often beyond our linguistic and conceptual grasp. In McIntosh's view, the sometimes-ambiguous language of scripture is precisely the divinely chosen site for divine-human encounter:

> Rather, the biblical language is *itself* the place of encounter. As human language it could never tell us everything about these particular historical events because Jesus' death and resurrection have infinite and eternal significance. Nevertheless, the biblical language *is* adequate and absolutely necessary for our journeying into the mystery.
>   . . . the meaningfulness and truth of the scriptures, like the meaningfulness and truth of the church's life, does not rest finally in either the history behind the text or existential feelings beyond the text, but in God's will to speak to us by means of the text.[114]

While Nee insists on biblical inerrancy doctrinally, his practical uses of the Bible seem to have much in common with the middle path of Frei as expounded by McIntosh, since Nee also regards scripture mainly as the medium through which God speaks to humans. However, unlike McIntosh who places a high premium on interpreting the Bible within the communal life of the church, Nee's approach to biblical interpretation in practice seems to derive more from revelation or illumination that he personally received without paying much conscious attention to community discernment.

Both Nee and McIntosh agree that spiritual knowledge acquired through revelation or illumination is not antirational (at least to the renewed mind), though such divine knowledge is often beyond conventional rationality, or might be called transrational. Nee's distinction between divine revelation and intellectual knowledge bears much resemblance to Augustine's distinction between wisdom (*sapientia*) and knowledge (*scientia*). While the understanding of rational knowledge in Nee and Augustine seems to be identical, there are different emphases in Nee's notion of revelation *vis-à-vis* the Augustinian idea of divine illumination as expounded by McIntosh. Nee stresses revelation as an event of shining or illumination received as an immediate spiritual intuition in an instant, and then ascertained and understood by the mind in a longer process, although he does also hold that illumination itself could be a gradually deepening process. In McIntosh's view, while such

114. Ibid., 87–88.

divine knowledge is usually discerned by the human subject with the Holy Spirit's illumination, the accent is placed on the goal of a gradual transformation, that is, to attain a continual capacity "to intuit the presence of God in all things" after the manner of Christ, who desires "to act for the Father in all things, to interpret the will of the Father in all things, and to remain through all things in 'converse with Him.'"[115] Nee would certainly concur with McIntosh on this aim for believers to be transformed into Christ's likeness with such discerning consciousness and volitional orientation.

Nee maintains that such revelation often imparts new understanding as well as giving certainty or conviction of a doctrine that is received by the rational mind. The Augustinian tradition, according to some interpreters, places almost exclusive emphasis on this latter function of illumination, that of giving justification or certainty of knowledge. For instance, Robert E. Lauder suggests that Augustine's illumination theory is to be understood as neither a theory of a direct vision of God nor a theory of innate ideas (it is "not concerned with the formation of concepts"); rather, Lauder proposes to see Augustine's illumination theory as concerned with "the truth of judgements"; in other words, under the light of illumination, the human mind "can make true judgements and can see the truth of its own judgements."[116]

Other interpreters of Augustine, however, read that Augustinian illumination also includes the idea of concept formation or information acquisition. Pasnau, for instance, argues that illumination in Augustine's texts can be understood as including the formation of concepts as well as the judgment of truth.[117] At any rate, in McIntosh's view, illumination of the divine Word, analogous to sunlight, enables the mind to "see" clearly and with full color what the mind is considering: "just as the sun shining in the world lights up the colors and forms of things for our eye, so the Word (in whom all creatures are eternally known and created) shining in the mind lights up the intelligible beauty and truth of whatever the mind is considering."[118] It would be natural that such brilliant light not only enable the eyes to see more clearly (and thus have more confidence with) what is seen, but also let the eyes perceive what was not seen be-

115. McIntosh, *Discernment and Truth*, 183.
116. Lauder, "Augustine," 183.
117. Pasnau, "Divine Illumination."
118. McIntosh, *Discernment and Truth*, 227.

fore when the light was dim. Besides, while Augustine's understanding of general divine illumination could be interpreted as encompassing the realms of both natural and divine knowledge, he does make a distinction between the created light of human reason and the uncreated light of divine illumination. In this regard, then, Nee's notion of revelation as illumination coming from the divine source seems to fall in line with the Augustinian notion of uncreated light.

Revelation and Illumination: Gnosticism or Christian Mysticism?

Leung has suggested that Nee's spiritual theory contains heavy Gnostic elements, shown especially in its radical dualism and its emphasis on supernatural illumination or gnosis.[119] Leung has rightly pointed at two distinct characteristics of the otherwise quite amorphous philosophical and religious movement in the second to fourth century CE known as Gnosticism: emphasis on the antithesis between the spiritual (which is good) and the material (which is evil), and stress on the necessity of secret knowledge for the spirit to escape from the inner prison and to travel to the heavenly realms.[120] Salvation thus has to do with removal of ignorance rather than with forgiveness of sin. As we have seen, the terms Nee uses such as "release of the spirit" as well as his view on the need of revelation for the sanctification journey do bear some resemblance with Gnostic terminology and teaching. Yet more careful readings of Nee will show that these similarities are more apparent than real, as Nee's spiritual theology is far too body-affirming and Christo-centric to be labeled as Gnostic.[121]

First, Nee's view is far from the Gnostic perspective that the human body is "either unreal or evil."[122] Rather, his attitude toward the

119. K. L. Leung, "Huaren nuosidi zhuyi" [Chinese Gnosticism], 189, 197, and "Sanyuan renlun" [Trichotomistic anthropology], 196.

120. Grant, "Gnostic Spirituality," 44–60.

121. One should also note that scholars have identified (based on the discovery around 1945 of the original Gnostic texts near Nag Hammadi in Egypt) that historically, both the Gnostic writers and New Testament authors shared some common cultural settings and ideological heritage; thus there are parallel elements between Gnostic writings and those of Paul and John, as well as the tradition of Jesus's sayings. Such parallels, however, do not necessarily imply that one proceeded from the other, but only mean that they are branches of the same historical and cultural trunk. See Perkins, *Gnosticism and the New Testament*, 1–5.

122. Achtemeier et al., *New Testament*, 412–13.

body is quite positive due to his deep appreciation for the Incarnation: "The body is needed and important; otherwise, God would not have given man a body. If we carefully read through the Bible, we can see the importance that God places on the body of man. Nearly everything that is recorded in the Bible has to do with the body. The incarnation is the most conspicuous and convincing point. The Son of God took a body of flesh and blood. Though He has passed through death, He still has this body throughout eternity."[123] Moreover, in his comments on 1 Corinthians 6:13, Nee explicitly criticizes those who—thinking that salvation only has to do with "saving souls"—neglect or despise the body and its role in the spiritual life. Nee states: "'The Lord [is also] for the body.' This is a marvelous word. Ordinarily we think that the Lord came to save the soul. But this verse tells us that 'the Lord [is also] for the body.' Many believers despise the body too much. They believe that the Lord only cares to save souls and that the body does not have any use. They consider the body worthless in the realm of spiritual life and that there is no provision of grace for it in God's salvation. But this verse tells us that 'the Lord [is also] for the body.' God says that the Lord is also for the body that man despises."[124] It thus seems clear that Nee's view cannot be construed simply as a radical antithesis between the spiritual and the material. To be sure, Nee does preach often for the need of dying to self through the practices of obedience and humility, yet these teachings are in concurrence with the gospel messages of self-denial and the way of the cross as well as the Christian ascetical tradition.

Secondly, Nee's stress on the essential importance of grace offered in Christ for salvation—sanctification as well as justification—distances him from the Gnostic emphasis on securing secret knowledge for one's liberation. Nee holds that not only is justification by faith made available through God's forgiving grace offered by Jesus on the cross, but the whole sanctification process is a continual journey of grace made available by Christ's finished work of the cross. For Nee both the revelation and the faith that are needed for believers to enter the narrow gate and to continue throughout the narrow way of the cross are from the grace of God. In other words, Nee maintains that sanctification is as much a gift of grace as justification, and the key to receiving such grace is to become aware that one is without any resource in one's self to make any

123. Nee, *The Spiritual Man*, 3:659.
124. Ibid., 3:669.

true spiritual progress—an awareness that makes one willing to come to the point of dying to one's self or natural life, namely, ceasing from all forms of self-striving:

> And now the good news is that sanctification is made possible for you on exactly the same basis as that initial salvation. You are offered deliverance from sin as no less a gift of God's grace than was the forgiveness of your sins. . . .
>
> For years, maybe, you have tried fruitlessly to exercise control over yourself, and perhaps this is still your experience; but when once you see the truth you will recognize that you are indeed powerless to do anything, but that in setting you aside altogether God has done it all. Such a discovery brings human striving and self-effort to an end.[125]

Nee's stress on following in the way of Christ's humility—in his death and resurrection—as the path to transformation leading to receiving divine revelation, as well as his overall Christo-centric emphasis, sets him clearly apart from the variegated Gnostic striving for a return to the heavenly realm through possessing secret *gnosis* (often assisted by elaborate maps and charts for the journey).[126] Nee states: "How can we know more of Christ in this way? Only by way of an increasing awareness of need. Some are afraid to discover deficiency in themselves, and so they never grow. Growth *in grace* is the only sense in which we can grow, and grace, we have said is God doing something for us. We all have the same Christ dwelling within, but revelation of some new need will lead us spontaneously to trust Him to live out His life in us in that particular."[127] Moreover, scholars have pointed out that one of the distinct features of Nee's theology lies in its Christo-centrism,[128] and that the bread-breaking communion occupies the first place in Nee's mind among different church meetings.[129] We will explore in more detail about Nee's view on the observance of bread-breaking communion in chapter 5; for now it suffices to note that Nee's high regard for the Eucharist Communion shows again the Christo-centrism in his spirituality, as May comments: "the breaking of bread celebrated one's ongoing com-

125. Nee, *Normal Christian Life*, 36.
126. Grant, "Gnostic Spirituality," 44–60.
127. Nee, *Normal Christian Life*, 123.
128. Pamudji, "Little Flock Trilogy," 182.
129. G. Y. May, "Breaking of Bread," 334–36.

munion with Christ and his body."[130] Further, Nee's emphasis on weekly partaking of the elements of bread and wine exhibits his deep appreciation of the Incarnation and the embodiment of the spiritual realm. As May notes: "Eating and drinking could be transformed into a subversive act, abolishing the sharp divide between the physical and the spiritual realms that exists in so many conservative Christian churches."[131] Such Christo-centric and body-affirming emphases again demonstrate that Nee's theological orientation is far from the Gnostics' penchant toward dualism as well as toward the purely spiritual ascent to the One.[132]

Furthermore, Nee's accent on grace and humility is wholly comparable with such distinguished Christian thinkers as Augustine. Louth points out that Augustine's distinction between *scientia* and *sapientia*, as well as his idea that *sapientia* is the aim of the soul, are derived from his Platonic background. But Augustine clearly cuts himself off from his Neoplatonic roots in his emphasis on grace in the Incarnation. Human beings cannot, by their own efforts, move their concern from *scientia* to *sapientia*, from the temporal to the eternal. They can only free themselves from the effects of the Fall by faith in the Incarnation. While various forms of Platonism and Neoplatonism also stress human dependence on the divine, Augustine moves beyond Neoplatonism in his understanding that grace is inevitably linked to God's self-emptying and coming down to us, to God's humility that manifests in the Incarnation. God's humility calls for human response also in humility. For Augustine, while the mind must be purified in order to obtain the eternal—because its impurity has resulted from its attachment to the temporal—this purification must be done by means of the temporal. Since it is in the Incarnation that the eternal is given to humans within the temporal, the way to purification is by faith in the Incarnation and by humble submission to temporal things.[133] According to Louth, Augustine holds a view such as this:

> In Christ, the Incarnate Lord, are hidden 'all the treasures of wisdom and knowledge', as St. Paul says (Col 2:3). So in God

130. Ibid., 332.

131. Ibid., 348.

132. I owe my thanks to Professor Philip Wickeri for suggesting that the weekly communion is significant for spiritual formation in Nee's view, and that the Christo-centrism in this practice makes a Gnostic interpretation of Nee even more implausible.

133. Louth, *Christian Mystical Tradition*, 144–46.

Incarnate there are the treasures both of *scientia* (which we can reach) and *sapientia* (which we want to reach). . . .

The truths of faith, the truths concerning the Incarnate Word, are the means whereby we pass from the temporal to the eternal. . . . We must submit to the way of faith, we must accept what the Incarnate Word has done for us, if we are to attain to contemplation. We must submit to being purified through temporal things. And that requires humility: only the humble mind can submit to the Incarnate One, who himself teaches us the way of humility.[134]

Augustine sees that the response that God requires of humans is purity of heart or single-minded devotion to God. Yet humans can only obtain purity of heart through humility, and this humility can only be awakened in them by the humility and love of God manifested in the Incarnation. In Augustine's view, without a humble and loving response to God's humility and love in the Incarnation, humans will either be provoked to despair by their consciousness of sin, or be led to pride by their own inspiration and striving for God. Thus the goal of human life is no longer conceived in a Platonic fashion as the natural culmination of the restless heart longing for God. Rather, in a characteristically Christian way, Augustine, the doctor of grace, regards that the end of the quest is to be perfected in the image of God as something God gives, or to obtain true wisdom as something disclosed—to receive it as grace.[135] Louth comments thus: "So we come to the perfection of the image of God—the image of the Trinity—in the soul, when the soul attains wisdom, or rather receives wisdom, and remembers, understands, and loves God. Augustine is insistent that the soul can only be reformed in the image of God by God."[136] This emphasis on wisdom as divine grace freely bestowed is reinforced by Jesus's teachings in the Gospels that only by becoming like little children, one can receive divine revelation (see Matt 11:25) as well as entering the kingdom of heaven, as Richard B. Gaffin notes: "The exclusive necessity of revelation is reinforced by the 'infants,' 'little children' (νηπτοῖζ) as the recipients of revelation, in counterpoint to the 'wise and intelligent.' This reference is explicated by what Jesus teaches elsewhere: the necessity of repenting and becoming like a little

134. Ibid., 155.
135. Ibid., 144–46.
136. Ibid., 157.

child for entering the kingdom of heaven and of becoming humble like a child to be great in the kingdom (Matt 18:3–4), the necessity of receiving the kingdom like a little child in order to enter it (Mark 10:15)."[137]

While a precise definition of mysticism is difficult, D. D. Martin points out that mysticism is not primarily interested in such phenomena as special voices or visions, and it is "not the same as magic, clairvoyance, parapsychology, or occultism."[138] Martin continues: "Nearly all Christian mystics relegate these phenomena to the periphery and avoid the occult arts entirely. Briefly and generally stated, mystical theology or Christian mysticism seeks to describe an experiential, direct, non-abstract, unmediated, loving knowing of God, a knowing or seeing so direct as to be called union with God."[139] This focus on direct knowing and union with God, however, is better understood as the goal of mysticism, for in Bernard McGinn's view, "mysticism is always a process or a way of life": "Although the essential note—or, better, goal—of mysticism may be conceived of as a particular kind of encounter between God and the human, between Infinite Spirit and the finite human spirit, everything that leads up to and prepares for this encounter, as well as all that flows from or is supposed to flow from it for the life of the individual in the belief community, is also mystical, even if in a secondary sense."[140] Thus McGinn proposes "the presence of God" as a more fitting term to describe Christian mysticism, or more precisely, to think of the mystical element in Christianity as that which "concerns the preparation for, the consciousness of, and the reaction to the immediate or direct presence of God."[141] In addition, Martin notes that while many Christian mystics adapted the Neoplatonic doctrine of emanation (procession) from and return to union with the One, some of them are also emphatically "Christocentric, ecclesial, and liturgical"; thus Christian mysticism cannot be simply characterized by such "meta-historical categories" as Neoplatonism: "While a concern to relate the Creator to creation both immanently and transcendentally has from the earliest centuries led Christian mystics to make use of Neoplatonic philosophy, equally prominent are those (especially in the Franciscan school) whose theology is

137. Gaffin, "Epistemological Reflections," 105.
138. Martin, "Mysticism," 806.
139. Ibid.
140. McGinn, *Foundations of Mysticism*, xvi.
141. McGinn, *Growth of Mysticism*, xi.

Christocentric, ecclesial, and liturgical. One of the most cosmologically sophisticated medieval mystics, Nicolas of Cusa (1401–64), drew deeply from Neoplatonic and Eckhartian emanationism but was also profoundly Christocentric. The issue cannot be resolved solely with broad brushstrokes of meta-historical categories such as Neoplatonism."[142]

It would be helpful to note a distinction von Balthasar draws between two kinds of Christian mysticism; one more inclined toward Neoplatonism and the other more genuinely christological and trinitarian. According to McIntosh, on the one hand, von Balthasar is uneasy with a kind of Christian mysticism "which has not quite freed itself from the common Neoplatonic inheritance of the ancient Mediterranean world," and "in which the soul is urged to transcend itself in order to rediscover its unity with the One in an eternal silence of union without distinction. . . ."[143] On the other hand, von Balthasar points out a more authentic kind of Christian mysticism "which has truly emerged from the paschal mystery (and leads back to it)" that is "more inherently trinitarian."[144] As McIntosh comments: "For the mystical journey which takes place in union with Jesus in his prayer to the Father in their Spirit is finally a mysticism of communion and dialogue. Such a trinitarian mysticism tends inherently towards the expressivity of concrete form—whether in the obedience of a particular state of life or in the mystagogical structures of a spiritual text."[145] As we shall see in chapter 5, Nee's teaching of spiritual formation emphasizes obedience to Christ and union with God's will, as well as stressing the need to carry one's cross daily in order to walk after the Spirit. It could well be said that for Nee, as for Bonaventure, the spiritual journey is "a *descent* into the passion of Jesus" as opposed to "an anonymously metaphysical ascent" of the Neoplatonic or Gnostic strive.[146] In sum, Nee's emphatic Christocentric concern and overall trinitarian orientation, as well as his profound appreciation for the body and the (descending) way of humility and obedience, set him clearly apart from the basic orientations and preoccupations of both Neoplatonism and Gnosticism.

142. Martin, "Mysticism," 808.
143. McIntosh, *Mystical Theology*, 101, 116n24.
144. Ibid., 101.
145. Ibid.
146. Ibid., 77.

~

In this chapter, we have looked at the understandings of both Nee and McIntosh on various issues related to revelation or divine illumination. The issues explored in this chapter correspond roughly to the *what* questions underlying revelation or illumination: What does revelation or illumination look like? What are its functions in the spiritual life? We have also investigated some controversies about Nee's views. Regarding Nee's teaching of tripartite anthropology, we have suggested that while there is no consensus on this issue yet among biblical scholars and theologians, and although there is not enough biblical support for viewing spirit, soul, and body as three different *entities* in the human person, there is sufficient reason to see these as representing three different *aspects* or *orientations* in human functioning. And we have shown that Nee's views of revelation exhibit substantial similarity with the broadly Augustinian tradition of divine illumination as articulated by McIntosh. Through thus interpreting Nee's view in light of McIntosh's perspective, we have contended that the suspicion of Gnostic orientation in Nee's views is in fact not grounded, especially in light of Nee's strong Christocentric emphasis. This chapter, then, is the first of three major building blocks toward substantiating the thesis of this book, namely, that Nee's major theological convictions have strong parallels with related aspects of the Christian spiritual traditions, and that some major weaknesses in Nee's thoughts perceived by his critics can be overcome or substantially ameliorated. Let us now turn to the second major building block of this book, namely, on Nee's views on the relationship between illumination and intellectual studies, between spirituality and knowledge.

4

Knowledge and Spirituality
The Mind's Role in the Spiritual Journey

WHAT IS THE ROLE of the mind in the spiritual life? How might the seeking of intellectual knowledge help or hinder one's progress in the faith journey? What are the values and limitations of theology or doctrines for the ultimate concern of encountering the living God of love? Why is divine illumination or revelation significant, especially as compared to knowledge gained through intellectual inquiries? These and related questions in the writings of both Nee and McIntosh will be explored respectively in this chapter's first two sections, which will mainly be an exposition of their views without proceeding to an evaluation. In the third section then, we will attempt to bring these two authors into a constructive dialogue, to note their similarities and differences, and to explore in particular the question as to whether Nee's views are anti-intellectual as some of his critics perceived.

NEE ON KNOWLEDGE AND SPIRITUALITY

In this section, we will look at Nee's views on issues revolving around the relation between knowledge and spirituality, between intellectual activity of the mind and spiritual pursuit of the heart. We will first analyze his somewhat negative diagnosis of the role of the mind in the journey of faith and his recommendations for ways to overcome such negativity. These will include such themes as the dangers of independent pursuit of knowledge, the necessity for a broken mind, the battlefield of the mind, and the importance of the mind's renewal. We will then explore his more positive views on the function of the mind in the spiritual journey, including the mind's role in receiving revelation, and the use of the mind for assisting the spirit in spiritual practice and spiritual discernment.

Dangers of Independent Pursuit of Knowledge

Nee notes that God originally intended for Adam to eat from the tree of life, since in the book of Genesis this tree was mentioned before the tree of knowledge of good and evil, and God commanded that the fruits of *all* trees—except the tree of knowledge of good and evil—could be eaten. Nee believes that God's intention was for Adam to partake of the tree of divine life, so as to live in continual human-divine communion as well as in complete dependence on God. Yet Adam and Eve partook of the tree of knowledge of good and evil instead. Consequently their spirits were dead, and their souls rose up rampantly and pursued an unbridled development independent of God. Nee thus suggests that the tree of life and the tree of knowledge signify two kinds of life: spiritual versus soulish, or dependent versus independent (of God). The problem with the fruit from the tree of knowledge is that it leads humanity into illusionary confidence in their own judgment of good and evil, to independent self-sufficiency apart from God (in both knowledge and power), and to prideful alienation from each other, as well as to a false self-centered and individualistic perception of their own personal identity. Nee writes:

> The tree of life signifies dependence. . . . The tree of the knowledge of good and evil signifies independence. . . . For man to try to know good and evil is also a sign of independence. He is not satisfied with what God has given him. The difference between being spiritual and being soulish is very clear here. To be spiritual is to fully trust in God and to be satisfied with what God has given. To be soulish is to turn away from God and to freely seek after what God has not given, in particular, to seek after knowledge. Independence is a characteristic of the soul. . . . This rebellion and independence is the principle of transgression for all sinners as well as for the believers.[1]

Since the Fall of the first couple has to do with eating from the tree of knowledge of good and evil, Nee believes that the curious pursuit of knowledge, even spiritual knowledge and wisdom, is usually a

---

1. Nee, *The Spiritual Man*, 1:35–36.

kind of fleshly activity that is detrimental to the spiritual life; he thus warns of several dangers or pitfalls in seeking knowledge for its own sake. First, one such pitfall is that it distracts the seekers from attending wholeheartedly to God and it diminishes their trust in God's Spirit: "The activity of the soul can many times be detected in the pursuit for wisdom and knowledge, including spiritual knowledge. To give no time to wait on God, to have no trust in the leading of the Holy Spirit, and to try to increase one's knowledge with the help of one's mind and books, these are the activities of the flesh. The result of this is damage to the spiritual life."[2] Secondly, another danger Nee sees in seeking intellectual knowledge with the mind alone is that it often leads to personal pride and thus gives the devil grounds to work:

> When the mind is working, believers should be careful not to let it work alone. This means that it should not work apart from the ruling of the spirit. . . . when it becomes independent, it expresses the fallen flesh. For example, many Bible studies are simply pursuits of men's own minds according to their own thoughts and by their own strength. . . . This kind of independent action of the mind is very dangerous because this kind of knowledge will just provide more information to one's mind for his thinking and more of a basis for his boasting . . . Believers have to awaken to the fact that any knowledge, secured by the mind alone, provides a way for the devil to work. This kind of craving has to be restrained.[3]

Thirdly, Nee cautions that mere intellectual pursuit of knowledge can lead to grave errors: "Indeed, unless intellectual power comes under the leading of the Holy Spirit, it is unreliable and is very dangerous. It will take right as wrong and wrong as right. If one is not careful, he will not only suffer temporary loss but will suffer permanent damage. The dark thoughts of man usually lead him into the place of eternal death."[4] In addition, Nee notes that the fallen mind has a tendency to be critical and judgmental, a tendency that prevents it from receiving spiritual edification from others:

> Unless a head-strong person is confronted with another strong mind, he will not receive any help from anyone. . . . He has a

2. Ibid., 1:33.

3. Ibid., 3:568.

4. Ibid., 1:39–40.

shell in his mentality, and he can only receive help in the mental realm; he cannot receive any spiritual edification. But if the Lord steps into his situation . . . , the shell of his mentality will be broken. He will realize the futility of his mentality. He will become like a child, and it will be very easy for him to listen to others. He will no longer dare despise others. When he listens to another brother, he will no longer try to catch flaws in his pronunciation, mistakes in his teaching, or ambiguities in meaning. He will instead touch the speaker's spirit with his own spirit.[5]

In short, Nee believes that human thinking alone—without the spirit's rule and guidance—is dangerous and should be avoided with vigilance:

Our thoughts are confused, wild, self-motivated, and undisciplined. We think that we are clever, that we know everything, and that we can think of things that others cannot think of. Because of this, the Lord allows us to make mistakes, and stumble again and again so that we would be wary of our own thoughts. If we find great grace in the Lord, we will shy away from our thoughts as much as we shy away from fire. As soon as the hand touches fire, it pulls back. In the same way as soon as we touch our thoughts, we turn back and tell ourselves, "This is not what I should think. I fear my own thoughts."[6]

With this understanding of Nee's views on the dangers of the mind's pursuits independent of the spirit, let us turn to a need Nee perceives in order for the mind to be governed by the spirit, that is, the need for the mind to be "broken."

Need for a Broken Mind

Nee believes that because of the death of the human spirit after the Fall, humanity's communion and communication with God is severed to the extent that they are no longer able to hear from God or to have true knowledge of God. In other words, the eyes of their heart are blinded and they cannot perceive the light of divine revelation; now all their attempts to seek God by the powers of the soul are futile: "When man sinned, this sin corrupted the keen intuitive knowledge of God that existed in man's spirit so that he became dead to the things of the spiritual

5. Nee, *Breaking of the Outer Man*, 108.
6. Ibid., 74.

realm. Thereafter, man may have religion, morality, education, ability, power, and mental and physical health, yet he is dead to God."[7] Thus for Nee, intellectual power alone will not attain divine revelation: "Although these ones can be very intelligent and can come up with wonderful ideas and theories, they cannot say anything about the things of the Holy Spirit of God. They cannot receive the revelation from the Holy Spirit."[8]

The remedy to the noetic blindness from the Fall, notes Nee, is to renounce the wisdom of the world, and to believe in the foolishness of the tree of the cross:

> God used the foolishness of the cross to destroy the wisdom of the wise. Intellectual power is the source of the fall. Therefore, if a man desires to be saved, he has to believe in the foolishness of the cross in order that he would not trust in intellectual power. The tree of knowledge led to man's fall, but God used the foolish tree (1 Pet 2:24) to save man. Therefore, "if anyone thinks that he is wise among you in this age, let him become foolish that he may become wise. For the wisdom of this world is foolishness with God" (1 Cor 3:18–19; 1:18–25).[9]

Nee distinguishes between two different approaches to the Christian life. The first is the way of human thinking including doctrines and scriptural expositions—this is the outward way, the way of increase. The second is the way of illumination of the Holy Spirit—this is the inward way, the way of decrease or breaking (of the outward person). Nee believes that true Christianity consists in the second way:

> What is edification? It is not the increase of thoughts, ideas, or doctrines. Edification is when our spirit touches God's Spirit. . . .
> There are two entirely different approaches to edification. One way is outward, involving thoughts, doctrines, and expositions of the Scriptures. Some can claim that they have received help in this way. The other way is entirely different, involving the touching of spirit with spirit. When spirits touch, spiritual help is found. We only touch true Christianity as we touch the second way. This is true edification.[10]

---

7. Nee, *The Spiritual Man*, 1:36–37.

8. Ibid., 1:39.

9. Ibid., 1:33.

10. Nee, *Breaking of the Outer Man*, 109–10.

Looking at the life of Jacob in the book of Genesis, Nee comments that Jacob reached his spiritual maturity only after his outer person had been broken through "numerous misfortunes" or "repeated dealings" from God (14–15). Noting that "It is the Spirit who gives life" (John 6:63) (17), Nee maintains that true spirituality has to involve the spirit that resides in the inner person, and that the outer person has to be broken or cracked open for the inner spirit to be accessible so as to receive edification or to impart edification to other spirits. For instance, in order to receive spiritual nourishment from the Bible, the hard shell of one's mind (part of the outer person) needs to be broken: "A man often approaches the Bible with his rebellious, confused, and seemingly clever mind. What he gets out of the Bible is the product of his mind; he does not touch the spirit of the Word. If we want to meet the Lord through the Bible, our rebellious and uncooperative mind must be broken" (57–58). By the same token, Nee insists that to be a real minister of God's word, the most important thing is for one's outer person to be broken—only so can the minister have true understanding of the word of God, and can impart or deliver to others the life of the Spirit: "We must remember that the outer man constitutes the greatest hindrance to the ministry of the word. Many people think that cleverness is somewhat useful. This is wrong. . . . The inner man will come up with the right thoughts and proper words to flow out only as the outer man is broken and smashed. The outer shell must be broken by God. The more this shell is broken, the more the life in the spirit will be released" (61–62). For Nee, without the breaking of the outer person, mere doctrines or theology in the mind are useless: "Doctrines and theology will not work. Mere Bible knowledge will not profit us. The only thing that is useful is for God to come out of us. . . . Unless the outer man is broken, everything we have is in the mind and in the realm of knowledge and is useless" (15).

Further, Nee insists that no amount of theology would be able to break the outer person; this breaking can only be accomplished by the Spirit's discipline through one's circumstances: "No teaching, doctrine, or memorization will destroy the outer man. Only God's chastisement and the Spirit's discipline will destroy it" (77). Similarly, for distinguishing and separating the soul from the spirit, Nee holds that mere doctrine or analysis will not do the job: "We cannot make this matter clear with doctrines. If we try to discern doctrinally what is of the self, what is of the Lord, what is of the flesh, what is of the Holy Spirit, what is of the Lord's grace, what is of the outer man, and what is of the inner man, we can spell out a long list and can even memorize the list, but we will still be in darkness. . . . Deliverance does not come this way; it comes from God's light. . . . We foolishly think that we possess what we know in our mind" (87–88). Not only is the prideful mind in need of being broken after the Fall, in Nee's view, but the mind also has been the site of warfare that both demonic forces and divine powers have been aiming to conquer since the very beginning. We will now turn to Nee's understanding of the battlefield of the mind.

Battlefield of the Mind

Nee defines the mind as the "thinking organ": "Through the mind, we know, think, imagine, recollect, and understand. The intellectual power, rationality, wisdom, and intelligence of man all belong to the mind. Broadly speaking, our mind is everything related to our brain. *Mind* is the psychological term, while *brain* is the physiological term."[11] Looking at 2 Corinthians 10:3–5, Nee sees that the mind is a battlefield where evil spirits wage war in order to capture a believer's will and spirit. The reason why the mind is so close to the forces of darkness, Nee believes, is that from the beginning the devil has always been enticing human beings by suggesting to them various tempting thoughts. Nee maintains that while believers receive a new life or a new heart after their conversion, they nonetheless still have an old mind or an old head. Nee explains that this is why throughout history many heretics had "holy" character, because the head did not catch up with the heart. Thus Nee cautions believers not to place complete confidence in the words of any supposed saintly person or spiritual authority, but to trust only in the words clearly written in the scriptures.

Nee underscores that it is important to watch and engage the mind's movements actively so as not to lose ground to demonic attacks. Noting that God gives humans a free will, Nee believes that human beings have the authority to rule over all of their own faculties, and so "the mind should come under the rule of the will" (3:504). Nee says that since God does not do the job of managing the mind for humans, believers should be wary when they are not in control of the state of

11. Nee, *The Spiritual Man*, 3:497.

their own mind, for the other possibility (except for illness) is that their mind is being controlled by the forces of darkness (3:504–5). Nee notes that a mind under demonic influence would exhibit such constant traits as confusion, restlessness, fanaticism, hesitation, poor focus, deficient memory, or inability to be watchful, as well as inexplicable fearfulness, disarray, or fretfulness (3:538). Yet evil spirits can come and attack only if a believer—often unintentionally or unconsciously—gives ground for their foothold. Such ground includes entertaining improper thoughts or accepting demonic lies, and being in an empty or passive state of mind, as well as having a generally unrenewed mind (3:545).

First, entertaining improper thoughts or accepting lies from the enemy would cause the loss of ground, albeit often gradually or imperceptibly: "All filthy, haughty, unkind, unrighteous, and similar thoughts give ground to evil spirits. Believers who yield in their minds and do not refuse these kinds of thought will find these kinds of thought coming back more easily the next time. It also becomes harder to ward them off because evil spirits have already occupied a place in their minds" (3:509). Nee thus continues: "Evil spirits often inject a thought into the believers. If they receive it, the thought becomes a ground for the evil spirits to work on" (ibid.).

Secondly, Nee highlights the danger of our mind being in a state of emptiness or idleness (not engaging in any mental activity), and especially in a state of passivity (waiting to be moved by an external force) (3:512). Nee holds that believers are to co-labor or corroborate with God in an active way: "In trying to follow the leading of the Holy Spirit, many believers consider that henceforth they do not need to weigh, consider, or decide whether any seemingly God-given thoughts are according to the light of the Bible. . . . Many believers do not understand that God does not want man to be passive, but to co-labor with Him in an active way. . . . God does not want men to become machines in order to receive His revelation. Only evil spirits want men to behave this way. Hence all passivity affords convenience for evil spirits" (3:513). Nee especially emphasizes that believers should be diligent in exercising their mind—to bring "every thought unto the obedient of Christ" (2 Cor 10:5), for using the mind properly is "profitable and necessary" for the spiritual life: "Many believers think that their thoughts are hindrances to their spiritual lives. Little do they know that the real hindrance is when their head stops working or when it works in disarray. They do not realize that the proper functioning of the head is profitable and necessary because only by functioning in this way will one be able to co-labor with God" (3:514).

How then can believers manage their mind for the spiritual life? First, Nee exhorts the importance of keeping an open mind that is not determined by one's presuppositions and preconceived notions or biases. Secondly, Nee teaches that believers should pray to God for a purified mind that is no longer affected by their old nature or old conception. Thirdly, Nee insists that believers should fill their mind with the word of God by reading and memorizing the scriptures. Fourthly, while idleness of the mind is to be avoided, Nee also notes that believers should restrain from too much activity of their mind in order to give it proper rest. Fifthly, the mind should not be given to restlessness, but should be kept at peace and should dwell on good and worthy things. Commenting on Philippians 4:6 and 4:8, Nee notes that believers are not to allow any anxious thoughts to remain in them; rather, they are to take account of things that are true, dignified, righteous, pure, lovely, well spoken of, virtuous, and praise-worthy. In addition, the state of the mind should not depend on or be swayed by feelings—either natural emotions or supernatural voices and visions. Rather, the mind should be governed by faith and follow the intuition of the spirit. Finally, believers should keep the mind in humility, and not let it be given to "self-justification, self-boasting, and self-satisfaction" lest they deceive themselves (3:567–71). In short, Nee maintains that the ways to deliverance from demonic influence in the battlefield of the mind include rejecting the enemy's lies (through seeking divine truths and speaking scriptural words to the evil spirits), overthrowing passivity (by actively using the mind as well as exercising the will), and renewing of the mind. It is to Nee's discussion on the importance of the mind's renewal that we now turn.

Renewal of the Mind (Nous)

In *The Spiritual Man* (1928), Nee teaches that the initial step of receiving or sensing divine revelation in the spirit's intuition needs a further step of comprehending the meaning of such revelation through an operation called "spiritual understanding." Nee regards that there are two kinds of "understanding": a spiritual one versus a soulish or natural one, and that spiritual understanding is the result of receiving light or enlightenment from the spirit. Nee writes: "Revelation is what we receive from God;

understanding is comprehending the revelation we have received from God. . . . Our fellowship with God relies on our spirit receiving God's revelation, on the intuition of the spirit sensing this revelation, and on the spiritual understanding to interpret the meaning of this revelation. Our own understanding can never resolve anything. When our spirit enlightens our understanding, the latter knows the purpose of God's movement" (2:327). In his later book *Renewal of Your Mind* (1933), Nee explicitly locates understanding as part of the function of the soul. While he maintains that the mind—*nous* in Greek—includes both understanding and thought, Nee seems to regard the renewal of *nous* as primarily the renewal of understanding. This is probably because Nee regards the mind as "the thinking organ" (3:497), thus the renewal of the mind (or understanding) would necessarily entail the renewal of its thinking function including its thoughts. In discussing the renewal of *nous*, Nee often uses the terms *nous*, mind, and understanding interchangeably.

Nee notes that the Bible describes the *nous* (mind) of nonbelievers as fleshly, corrupt, defiled, and futile, as well as blind and in darkness. He regards that when nonbelievers are saved, they are given both a new spirit and a new heart, and their eyes of faith are opened to see the light of salvation, which is the greatest revelation in their whole life. Yet their *nous* needs to be constantly renewed, otherwise they cannot receive further divine revelations. Nee sees that an unrenewed *nous* will have problems such as lack of trust in God, inability to understand the Bible or to discern the will of God, suspicion of and prejudice toward (usually looking down at) others, proneness to introspection or self-judgment (as opposed to waiting for the righteous judgment of divine light), confusion in thoughts, and inability to communicate to others the words of God. By contrast, a renewed *nous* will be able to receive divine light for understanding the Bible, to discern the will of God, to judge things and people rightly, to understand and receive others' words correctly, to manage thinking activities properly, and to deliver spiritual messages effectively and efficiently. Thus it seems that for Nee a renewed mind (*nous*) would be able to receive light and perform functions of discernment that he otherwise often attributes only to the spirit.

An explanation can perhaps be found in Nee's reading of the biblical heart as the point of connection (and the conduit of passage) between the spirit and the soul. He maintains that the heart includes both the spirit's conscience and the soul's mind (or understanding), thus there are interconnections between the spirit (including intuition, fellowship, and conscience), the heart (including both conscience and mind), *nous* (as mainly mind or understanding), and thoughts. Nee holds that the problems of an unrenewed *nous* are only symptoms: the root of illness lies in the heart. Thus the heart needs to be healed first, which will then lead to the healing of the *nous* (or mind). Nee regards the basic issues of the heart to be its hardness (for both nonbelievers and believers), willfulness, or non uprightness. He sees that the non-upright heart is biased, perceiving oneself to be wise, self-righteous, self-asserting, lazy, or containing sin, while the upright heart as having such characteristics as humility, teachability, openness, and fairness. Besides exhorting for a change in the basic posture of the heart, Nee especially emphasizes that believers need to ask God to search out their heart for any hidden sins, and to single-heartedly seek (and trust) God for a renewed *nous*.[12]

Nee sees *nous* (mainly as understanding) to be the key link between intuition and thought, and he reads in scripture the critical importance of the renewal of *nous* for spiritual discernment (especially Rom 12:2). Following Penn-Lewis, he maintains that if the *nous* is closed or unrenewed, the spirit will also be closed or without a path to come out.[13] Nee thus holds that spiritual understanding has nothing to do with one's natural intellectual capacity or the amount of knowledge one possesses; rather, it has to do only with the extent to which one's *nous* (or understanding) is renewed.[14]

Nee notes that in Romans 12:1–2, the renewal of *nous* has to do with a wholehearted dedication of one's entire being to God, a total dedication that is nonetheless continual and gradually increasing according to what the believer knows at any given point of their spiritual journey.[15] Thus, Nee stresses the crucial importance of one's actions for

---

12. See Nee, *Wuxing de gengxin* [Renewal of the mind], 7–63, esp. 8–9, 15–17, 23, 43, 58. Nee's treatment of the term heart in *Renewal of the mind* is not wholly consistent with some of his statements in *The Spiritual Man*, in which he sometimes regards the heart to mean merely understanding, mind, or intellect. See Nee, *Shuling ren* [The spiritual man], 240. Since *Renewal of the mind* was published later in 1933, Nee's view in it can be regarded as a later development, possibly influenced by his 1929 translation of Penn-Lewis's article on *nous*. For these datings, see http://www.lsmchinese.org/big5/07online_reading/nee/read.asp?no=1-11-17.

13. Nee, *Wuxing de gengxin* [Renewal of the mind], 57.

14. Ibid., 33.

15. Ibid., 58–60.

the renewal of *nous*. He cites Ephesians 4:22–24 to exhort a continual vigilance in one's daily living—for putting off the old person and putting on the new person. He notes that putting off the old person here is different from the co-crucifixion of the old person with Christ spoken of in Romans 6:6. Here, Nee maintains that putting off the old person is a denial or rejection (with conscious efforts of the will) of anything—in one's thoughts, words, deeds—that belongs to the old person, namely, that are of one's self as well as of the devil. And putting on the new person means acting in accordance with righteousness and holiness.[16] Nee maintains that for a believer whose mind has been renewed, the mind cooperates with the spirit, and its rationality is in one accord with the spirit: "A spiritual believer should walk according to the spirit; but he should not negate the mind with its understanding of the intentions of the spirit. In genuine guidance, the spirit and the mind are in one accord. There is no such thing as the reasoning in the mind going against the leading in the spirit. . . . Of course, we are talking about believers whose minds have been renewed."[17]

In short, perceiving different dangers in the often unrecognized battlefield of the mind, Nee teaches different strategies for Christian soldiers to "take every thought captive to obey Christ" (2 Cor 10:5) as well as renewing their mind so that they can become "more than conquerors" (Rom 8:37). We will now look at Nee's views of how the mind, especially the renewed mind, can play a more positive role in the spiritual life, including in the process of receiving revelation and in cases when the spirit is so weak that it needs assistance from the mind.

The Mind's Role in Receiving Revelation

Nee affirms that the soul contains many "gifts from God," most importantly the mind and the will.[18] The problem comes only when these gifts are used apart from the spirit's direction, and when the soul becomes the very source of one's life.[19] Nee maintains that God's redemptive work of breaking the outer person does not mean annihilation of the soul's functions of will, thought, or emotion; rather, it aims at bringing all these

---

16. Ibid., 52, 54–56, and *The Spiritual Man*, 3:545–48.

17. Nee, *The Spiritual Man*, 3:562.

18. Ibid., 1:29–30.

19. Nee, *Normal Christian Life*, 152–53.

powers under the direction and service of the Spirit. These powers are in fact an indispensable channel or media for the Spirit to work, and Nee holds that the believer's goal is not to become merely *spiritual*, but to become a spiritual *person*. Nee states: "Today God's Spirit must be released through man. Man's love must be available before others can see God's love. Man's thoughts must be available before others can see God's thoughts. Man's decision must be found before others can touch God's will. But the trouble with man is that his outer man is too busy with his own things. . . . This is the reason God has to break the outer man. . . . In this way the inner man will find a mind, an emotion, and a will that are available for use."[20] Nee thus holds together the indispensable instrumentality of the outer person for doing God's work as well as the absolute necessity for the outer person to be broken for it to have any use for the ministry of God: "God does not destroy our outer man. But neither will He allow it to remain intact and unbroken. He wants to pass through our outer man. He wants our spirit to love, think, and make decisions through the outer man. God's work can only be accomplished through a broken outer man."[21]

Nee maintains that the thinking faculty has its role to play in the spiritual life, albeit only a secondary one; it is the role of a submissive servant—rather than a controlling master—of the spirit. Nee sees that human rationality mainly has two proper functions: interpreting (to one's own outer person) and communicating (to others) what one already knows in the spirit. In other words, for Nee the thinking mind in the soul is not the faculty for gaining spiritual knowledge, but only for processing and delivering divine revelations that are already received via the spirit. Here Nee distinguishes between the source of knowledge and the handling of such knowledge, and notes that Paul's proclamations of the gospel in his epistles are just such examples of the divine source of revelations being communicated with the assistance of human understanding and language.[22]

While Nee is emphatic about the supreme importance of the spirit (or its intuition) in receiving revelation or spiritual knowledge, as well as the contrast of such divine revelations versus rational knowledge acquired by intellectual activity, he is also adamant in insisting on the

20. Nee, *Breaking of the Outer Man*, 36.

21. Ibid.

22. Nee, *Shuling ren* [The spiritual man], 238, 244–45.

paramount significance of the renewed mind in receiving revelations. He maintains that while the mind is not the primary faculty for obtaining spiritual knowledge, it plays a secondary yet absolutely essential role in the whole process of receiving divine revelation. Commenting on Ephesians 1:17–18 ("That the God of our Lord Jesus Christ, the Father of glory, may give to you a spirit of wisdom and revelation in the *full knowledge* of Him, the eyes of your heart having been enlightened, that you may *know* . . ."), Nee suggests that the "eyes of your heart" here refers to "the faculty of understanding, which is our mind."[23] Nee sees that what is known in the spirit of the inner person needs to be conveyed to the mind of the outer person, so that the body can take action accordingly. He reads that the two knowings mentioned in the above passage have two different references—one in the spirit and the other in the mind: "The first knowing is the knowing in the intuition. The second knowing is the knowing or realization of the mind. The spirit of revelation is the deepest part of our being. . . . Scripture tells us that our spirit needs to enlighten our mind, so that our mind can understand the notion of our spirit and our outer man can also have the knowledge. Our outer man apprehends things through the mind. . . . The mind in turns tells the whole body and causes it to walk according to the spirit" (ibid.). Thus Nee sees that there is an intimate relationship between the mind and the spirit: "nothing has a closer relationship with the spirit than the mind. . . . Because both the spirit and the mind are the faculties of 'knowledge,' their relationship is closer than anything else. In our life of walking according to the spirit, the mind is the best assistant of the spirit, we must know how these two assist each other" (3:560). Nee notes that only with the cooperation of the mind and the spirit, can one fully know and understand the will of God: "We receive the will of God in our intuition first, then our mind enables us to know that it is God's will. The Holy Spirit impresses our spirit and gives us a spiritual sense. Then we apply our mind to study and understand this sense. In order to comprehend fully the will of God, there must be a co-working of the spirit and the mind. The spirit causes our inner man to have the knowledge, while the mind causes our outer man to understand" (3:561).

The mind's role here is to receive light from the spirit for understanding; such understanding in the mind (as well as the knowing in the spirit) happens in an instant, although describing it in words would

23. Nee, *The Spiritual Man*, 3:560–61.

usually take a long time: "This cooperation of the spirit with the mind causes the believers to fully know the will of God, and it happens in an instant. It may take us a long time to describe it in words. . . . the spirit knows it in the twinkling of an eye and causes the mind to understand" (ibid.). Nee maintains that the mind needs first to be renewed and becomes spiritual—being governed by the spirit—and the renewed mind "requires the light of the spirit for its guidance" lest it fall into darkness; this mind can then pay close attention to the activities of the Spirit (3:562–63). Nee also notes that since revelation is very short, like the illumination of sudden lightning, it needs to be stabilized by the utilization of one's thought; yet such thought pattern needs to be trained or dealt with often.[24]

Further, Nee emphasizes that believers need to use their mind to help the spirit—by examining whether the supposed revelation they receive is truly from God, or whether it is in accordance with the scriptures. In other words, the mind performs the functions of checks-and-balances and confirmation, since humans are prone to making mistakes and are vulnerable to counterfeit deceptions: "The intuition is the organ that knows God's will. But we still need the mind to examine and see if our feeling proceeds from the intuition or if it is a counterfeit of our own emotions. We have to know if the inner feeling is God's will and according to the Bible. We know with our intuition, but we confirm with our mind. How easily we are prone to make mistakes! If we do not have the assistance of the mind, it is hard for us to decide what is of God."[25] So even in the case of already receiving a revelation in one's spirit, one still needs to use the mind to "examine and consider" the received revelation to "further brighten the revelation," and sometimes the mind could find out that the supposed revelation is not really from God:

> A believer . . . has to apply his thoughts to everything. He should be a spiritual person with a full consciousness. . . . Do not think that after he has a revelation in his spirit he can act accordingly. He must apply his mind to examine and consider what he is about to do and find out if there is still any self-intention, anything not according to God, and anything that proceeds from the flesh. . . . This kind of consideration will help the spirit to further brighten the revelation in the intuition. If it is not God's

24. Lam, "Huaren shenxue" [Chinese theology], 69–70.
25. Nee, *The Spiritual Man*, 3:514–15.

revelation, it will be exposed. . . . God does not want us to follow blindly. He wants us to apprehend His will clearly. Anything
which is not thoroughly apprehended is not reliable. (3:567–68)

Nee's teaching here to use the mind to examine if there is anything
from the flesh seems to be contrary to his warning elsewhere, about not
to engage in self-examination, but only to wait for the Spirit's light to
search out one's inner intention. This seeming contradiction can perhaps
be explained by Nee's pastoral concerns when speaking to believers with
different orientations, maturities, or experiences. The warning not to
engage in self-introspection is probably issued to a perceived audience
who is less mature in their spiritual journey or whose mind is not quite
renewed yet; thus the advice is not to use the mind to figure out whether
a certain inner movement is from the spirit or from the soul. By contrast,
the exhortation to use the mind to ascertain a supposed revelation is
probably targeted toward an intended audience who is more mature or
who has progressed a longer way in the renewal of their mind; thus the
mind in this case can be relied on more and should be employed more
in discerning spiritual matters.

While Nee teaches that the right path of seeking guidance and discernment requires the right use of the mind, the use of the mind here
is not to engage in arguments or deliberations against what seems contrary to reason, but simply to engage in a more neutral or open kind
of mental activity—that of considering and pondering. Nee holds that
by going through such a process of conscious investigation, the original
intuitive feeling will prove or disprove itself—either by growing even
more certain in the intuition or by arousing unrest and protest from
the conscience. Nee writes: "Therefore, a rational investigation for the
purpose of *understanding* whether or not something is from God in not
an impediment, but an opportunity for the intuition to prove itself. If a
matter is truly from the intuition, it will not be afraid of any investigation by the reason in the mind. On the contrary, many of the leadings
that fear investigation probably originate from the self!" (3:515). So
Nee maintains that while the mind should not take the lead in matters
of guidance, it should definitely follow up in examining any supposed
"leadings" or intuitive movements. Stressing that God does not want
blind or ignorant obedience, Nee teaches that a believer's passive following—without using the mind and exercising the will—often leads
to demon possession. Thus Nee strongly discourages blindly seeking

extra-ordinary experiences—such as voices, visions, and wonders—especially through the process of emptying the mind or waiting passively. But he does hold that such supernatural experiences can be of divine origin—if they occur at a time when the mind is able to control itself and is fully conscious (even in an "enlivened" state), and if such experiences are in concurrence with scripture as well as with God's nature or character (3:515–21).

The Mind Assisting the Spirit

Not only does the mind play an important role in the process of receiving revelation, Nee observes, but also the spirit can be weak or asleep sometimes, and during such times, the mind needs to act first to assist the spirit into its proper movement. Nee notes that the mind can remember, guard, and apply spiritual knowledge previously received by the spirit, and by recalling such knowledge of truths, the mind can assist the spirit in a range of activities such as prayer, spiritual warfare, preaching, and discerning God's will. Nee says: "The truths were originally acquired in the spirit and preserved in our mind. Now because of our prayer according to the mind, they reenter our spirit" (2:395–96). Here Nee sees that the mind's role is to activate the dormant spirit, and then let the awakened spirit take the lead for the main course; thus the mind is merely assisting, rather than leading, the spirit. Noting the exhortation to pray with the mind (or understanding) as well as with the spirit in 1 Corinthians 14:15, Nee believes that praying with the mind will stir up the spirit, even though initially the prayer may seem dry and empty. Nee writes:

> When the spirit is sleeping, we should use our mind to work in place of the spirit, and before very long, the spirit will also join in to work. The mind and the spirit are closely related; they are a help to each other. . . . sometimes the spirit does not move. Therefore, it is necessary for the believer to activate the spirit by exercising his mind. . . . After the spirit moves, the believers are able to move according to the spirit. Activating the spirit by the mind is called the principle of the mind assisting the spirit. There is a principle in the spiritual life: in the *beginning* we should use the sense of the spirit to perceive the knowledge given to us by God; later we should guard and apply this knowledge with our mind. (2:394)

Similarly, in the process of discerning the will of God, there are often times when the spirit is lethargic. At such times the mind could help the spirit by considering, pondering, and praying about the uncertainties, in order that the spirit may rise up to the occasion and take charge in the final discernment. Nee uses the analogy of a water pump that requires a cup of water to be poured into it first before it will start running and drawing water from a well. Likewise, the spirit sometimes needs just such a jump from the mind for it to get started for the real work. Nee suggests that the cooperation of the mind and spirit is especially critical in the case of spiritual warfare: "When our spirit wrestles with the evil spirit, the strength of our entire being is one with the spirit for the battle. The most important part is our mind. The entire strength of the spirit and the mind must be united together for the attack. If the spirit becomes suppressed and loses its strength to resist, the mind should continually fight for the spirit. When the mind fights by praying, resisting, and opposing, the spirit will receive a supply to rise up once again for the battle" (2:400–401).

Moreover, Nee observes that the mind is crucial in the spiritual life also in its everyday action of either minding the Spirit or minding the flesh (Rom 8:5–6), which will eventually cause one to become either a spiritual or a fleshly person:

> Whatever the mind is minding, that is what we will walk after. If the mind is minding the flesh, we will walk according to the flesh; if the mind is minding the Spirit, we will walk according to the spirit. Therefore, we do not need to ask if we are walking according to the spirit; we only need to ask if we are minding the Spirit . . . In our daily life, what is our mind thinking about, paying attention to, and setting itself on? Are we minding the Spirit or the flesh? Minding the things of the Spirit will cause us to become spiritual men; minding the things of the flesh will cause us to become fleshly men. (3:564)

Minding the things of the Spirit is important, notes Watchman Nee, because the Spirit's movement—usually gentle and quiet—would only be noticed by a "watchman" whose mind is not distracted by "what is earthly" or "what is from below" (3:564–65).

Furthermore, while insistent on the importance of receiving direct revelation from God as well as not letting the mind work independently, Nee nonetheless notes that "most of the time" divine truth comes to believers through other children of God. Such truth taught by others is understood by the mind first, and only later reaches the spirit through divine enlightenment. Here Nee stresses that the attitude or orientation of the mind—whether it is opened and not occupied with its own presuppositions—is key to receiving such divine truth:

> This kind of truth is first accepted by our mind, and then it reaches our spirit. We use the mind to contact the speaking and writing of others. If we did not have a mind, it would be impossible for the truth to reach our life. Therefore, an opened mind is very crucial to our spiritual life. If our mind is fully occupied with opinions, whether they are about the truth or about the person who preaches the truth, there will be no way for the truth to enter into our mind or life. . . .
>
> . . . Many times a believer receives a truth which seems meaningless. But after a while, the light of the spirit comes in, and the believer seems to understand everything. . . . Yet without the enlightening of the spirit, it will remain useless. (3:565–66)

In sum, while Nee sometimes appears to be downplaying the role of the intellectual mind in the spiritual life because of its possible interference with the realm of the spirit, he does unequivocally speak of the mutual interaction and interdependence of the mind and the spirit in the spiritual journey—especially with the case of the renewed mind. Not only is the mind indispensable, but also it plays an important role in the spiritual life. Particularly with regards to receiving divine revelations, in Nee's view, the mind's function is to examine and help ascertain whether a supposed revelation is indeed of divine origin—by considering and comparing it with what one already knows about what the scriptures say and what the nature of God is. In the case of having received a genuine revelation, the mind's task then is to carry on the process of understanding its meaning as well as communicating such understanding to others. Further, when the spirit is in a state of dormancy or weakness, it needs the mind's assistance to activate it so that it can rise up to its proper function and vocation. Thus neither the spirit nor the mind can work alone: both need the other in the process of spiritual discernment and spiritual warfare. Moreover, the mind, especially an "open" mind, is crucial for acquiring spiritual knowledge from other people—usually the major way of acquiring spiritual knowledge—which will become true understanding of one's own when it is illuminated by divine light. With this understanding of Nee's views on knowledge and spirituality, let us now turn to McIntosh's exploration of some similar issues that concern Nee.

MCINTOSH ON KNOWLEDGE AND SPIRITUALITY

In this section, we will explore McIntosh's views on the relationship between knowledge and spirituality, between theology and the spiritual life. We will investigate his analysis of several related problems: the weakness of the mind susceptible to impulses and biases, the malfunction of human reason distorted by contentious and prideful self-conceit, and the deeper root of this noetic distortion in anxiety and fear of lack. We will then look into McIntosh's proposed remedies to these pathologies, namely, confidence and peace from seeing the infinite love and abundance of God revealed in the cross, and loving self-abandonment to encountering the mystery of divine love so as to be known by (and thus truly know) the God of loving and knowing.

Weakness of the Mind: Susceptibility to Impulses and Biases

McIntosh observes that different classical spiritual authors have given attention to the unrecognized influence that various factors have brought to bear upon the human mind. These authors' common concern seems to be that the mind is oftentimes unsuspecting of the various impulses at work in it, assuming that "it is making an assessment of things in a quite transparent manner."[26] For instance, Origen (ca. 185–254) sees that as the mind is easily moved unaware by impulses, it is also often oblivious to its own biased interpretations and judgements. For Origen, our mind is so weak that with our usual conceptions, we are very likely to constrict or misconceive the mysterious and almost unfathomable depths of truth inherent in both providence and scripture: "Just as providence is not abolished because of our ignorance . . . so neither is the divine character of scripture, which extends through all of it, abolished because our weakness cannot discern in every sentence the hidden splendour of its teachings."[27]

26. McIntosh, *Discernment and Truth*, 83. This line of thinking seems to concur with scriptural verses such as Jeremiah 17:9 ("The heart is deceitful above all things and beyond cure. Who can understand it?") and Psalm 139:23–24 ("Search me, O God, and know my heart. . . .").

27. Origen, *On First Principles*, 4.1.7, 267, as quoted in McIntosh, *Discernment and Truth*, 83.

Yet the mind is not totally helpless in this matter. McIntosh notes that Origen "assumes an underlying freedom and coherence in human thinking,"[28] and John Cassian (ca. 360–436) believes that while the origin of various impulses and thoughts does not depend on us, "their refusal or acceptance does depend on us."[29] Thus McIntosh suggests that the first step in forming a discerning mind is "becoming aware that one's thoughts are not entirely one's own," and especially, becoming aware of the mind's tendencies toward "all-too-tidy consistency" as well as its many other urgencies and its own narrowness.[30]

What can generate or foster the kind of self-awareness needed for authentic discernment of truth? McIntosh turns his attention to the discussion by Cassian's older contemporary Evagrius Ponticus (ca. 346–399) on several successive stages of spiritual progress marked by "growing gifts of perception and insight."[31] These stages for Evagrius begin with (1) faith and fear of God, progress through (2) *apatheia* (balanced and untroubled by desires and obsessions) and (3) *agape* ("availability to the divine will for all things"), move on to (4) "natural" contemplation for "attaining to the inner meaning (*logoi*) of created things" and, finally attain to (5) true theology as sharing directly in God's speaking or God's knowing (*theo-logia*) of God.[32]

Looking backward from the final goal of the above spiritual progress, McIntosh points out that for Evagrius, before one can share directly in the divine self-knowing, or before one can obtain the divine gift of perfect discernment, one must first attain "natural" contemplation understood as knowledge of the inner truth of the created world.[33] Yet in order to attain to this crucial stage of being able to discern clearly the truth of the universe, one must be free from all self-centered desires, obsessions, or passions. For Evagrius the mind is clouded and rendered undiscerning by the passions, which are "stirred up by demons" in the battleground of the soul. Evagrius thus recommends the ascetic life of practicing the virtues as aids to gaining freedom from the passions,

28. McIntosh, *Discernment and Truth*, 83.

29. Cassian, *Conferences*, 1.16, 56, as quoted in McIntosh, *Discernment and Truth*, 84.

30. McIntosh, *Discernment and Truth*, 83.

31. Ibid., 85.

32. Ibid.

33. Ibid.

leading then to liberation from a blinded or distorted perception of reality, so as to attain finally the purity of heart that can "see" God.[34] This inextricable link between virtue and knowledge (of divine truth) was a common belief for ancient Christians; as Evagrius says, "the virtues have knowledge as their fruit."[35] McIntosh thus underscores "the personal transformation of the would-be knower" as the prerequisite for discerning divine truth.[36]

Soulish vs. Spiritual: Prideful Self-Conceit vs. the Crucified Christ

McIntosh articulates some significant insights on discernment through an investigation into the notion "the mind of Christ," as named by the apostle Paul (1 Cor 2) and as given fresh expression in two great desert fathers, Evagrius Ponticus and Diadochus of Photike (mid-400s). McIntosh's interest lies in exploring how human perception and understanding are recreated or reformed by the death and resurrection of Christ, or how the paschal mystery becomes "the fundamental context of discernment."[37] Exploring recent scholarship on 1 Corinthians, McIntosh observes that the social context of the letter is a key to understanding some of Paul's rhetorical statements. Seen in this light, McIntosh suggests that the mind of Christ is characterized by peace and loving unity in the community, thus peace and unity is the precondition for any truthful discernment.

Regarding Paul's context as he writes 1 Corinthians, there have been different opinions among New Testament scholars. McIntosh notes that for a good part of the twentieth century, the dominant view was that Paul is targeting toward various misguided religious tendencies— either Jewish, Hellenizing, or Gnostic, or even all three at once. In these interpretations, then, Paul was seen as asserting the authority of divine revelation (or faith) against human rationality of any kind. Contrary to this dominant view, McIntosh points out, some recent scholars have observed that it is very difficult to ascertain the actual existence of one or more of these religious currents in Corinth. Paul's concern here, then, unlike his letter to the Galatians which focuses on some erroneous

34. Ibid., 87.

35. Evagrius, *Praktikos and Chapters*, §90, 38–39, as quoted in McIntosh, *Discernment and Truth*, 86.

36. McIntosh, *Discernment and Truth*, 86, 8.

37. Ibid., 127.

theological views, is more with the painful antagonism and disunity of the local church. Paul's concern with unity and love can be seen throughout the whole letter beginning with his appeal for unity in 1 Corinthians 1:10 and climaxing with the great hymn of love in 1 Corinthians 13.[38]

Interpreted from this social context, McIntosh points out that Paul's rejection of human wisdom is seen not as a rejection of human reason *per se*, but as an indictment of the malfunction of human reason due to its rebellion against God the Creator (as seen also in Romans 1:18 and following). This rebellion against God has "created a false world" and subsequently false criteria of wisdom for "securing and validating the very falsity itself."[39] One characteristic of people living in this false world is that rather than putting trust and hope in the abundant love of God, they derive security and satisfaction from the applause of each other. Drawing from Diadochus as well as from contemporary scholar Stanley K. Stowers, McIntosh notes that such an idolatrous disposition will give rise to a whole range of fantasy or "epistemological vices" such as "conceit, bragging, boasting, envious comparisons, arrogant attachment to one's own positions, prudish disdain for the new ideas of others."[40] Such prideful attitudes among them naturally lead to contests with each other and to divisions in their midst. That is why Paul battles against their "social-climbing" value system by noting that God exalts the weak, the foolish, the lowly, and the like.[41] Paul works to undo their boasting by boasting in Christ crucified as well as by pointing out that whatever gifts they now possess have been given to them by the sheer grace of God (1 Cor 4:6–7).[42] Thus in this diagnosis of the Corinthians, their problem begins with a prideful alienation from God that results in envious alienation among themselves—which then leads to the "noetic self-importance and rivalry."[43]

McIntosh highlights that a preliminary step to discerning truth is to become aware that one's own critical instincts may very well be wrong

---

38. Ibid., 130–31.

39. Scroggs, "New Being," 177, as quoted in McIntosh, *Discernment and Truth*, 131.

40. McIntosh, *Discernment and Truth*, 131.

41. Ibid., 132.

42. Many biblical scholars have recognized that "boasting" is a central concept for understanding Paul's critique in 1 Corinthians. McIntosh especially draws on Gooch, *Partial Knowledge*, 26 (McIntosh, *Discernment and Truth*, 132).

43. McIntosh, *Discernment and Truth*, 132.

or misdirected, and that the conventional criteria of judgment are too tidy and self-gratifying. And such complacent and blinded "diagnostic schemes" need to have something far more than mere refinement; rather, they ought to be wholly subverted.[44] McIntosh notes that St. Paul confronts the Corinthians "who are busy judging, evaluating, discerning, and comparing themselves according to a variety of apparently satisfying critical schemes," which include their baptismal lineage, class status, cultural sophistication, and others (1 Cor 1:12, 26).[45]

The soul-spirit (*psychikos-pneumatikos*) distinction that Paul employs in 1 Corinthians 2:14 has been debated by scholars. Some believe that there is probably a measure of the spiritual elitism that some of the Corinthians have received from Gnostic influence, and Paul here simply adopts their own words (now using them for different connotations) for rhetorical purposes in order to subvert their very distinction. The contrast, rather than being the soul versus the spirit, is the conventional human categories of conception as opposed to divine grace or the Holy Spirit's gifts of discernment. McIntosh points out that in Alexandra Brown's view, Paul's soulish (*psychikos*) and spiritual (*pneumatikos*) distinction is a distinction between *gnosis* and *pneuma*, between the world's wisdom and the Spirit's revelation, namely the crucified Christ.[46]

McIntosh further suggests that Paul here is not attacking the human criteria in use in Corinth but simply proposing another criterion or noetic norm—the message of the cross—which McIntosh believes "requires just as much deployment of human rationality, intelligence, and skill to apply it."[47] McIntosh sees that the light shining through the paschal mystery is God's generous love in rescuing fallen humanity. So the contrast here is between loving actions and envious factions, between divine generosity and conventional tests of spiritual improvement—or, we might say, between a descending (humble) bestowal of divine love and an ascending (prideful) pursuit of human wisdom. Drawing from Diadochus again, McIntosh points out that the pitfall here is that rather than focusing on what God is doing, one is unconsciously driven by others' perception of one's own spiritual status, and this kind of compulsive

---

44. Ibid., 128.

45. Ibid., 129.

46. Cf. Brown, *Cross and Human Transformation*, 138, as quoted in McIntosh, *Discernment and Truth*, 135.

47. McIntosh, *Discernment and Truth*, 129.

concern for worldly regard leads a person toward fantasy and blindness that satisfy the ego but fabricate an illusory perception of reality.
Following Paul Gooch, McIntosh suggests, again, that Paul is blaming
neither the "fallenness of reason per se," nor the "sheer incapacity of the
unaided human mind" as philosophy against faith.[48] Rather, the problem
lies in the "pathology . . . toward noetic error" or the "'logic' of distorted
reason."[49] In Gooch's words, it is "human conceit that shuts itself up
against truth," so the remedy is not going to be an extreme form of irrational fideism, but "it asks for right reasoning and for the cognitive
modesty appropriate to all human intellectual activity."[50]

Noetic Pathology: Distortion through Fear of Lack

How does this unconscious "pathology" toward error happen? Or how
does the self-righteous "'logic' of distorted reason" become one's basic
noetic function? The problem, McIntosh notes, lies in envy, comparison, and competition, for in 2 Corinthians 10:12 Paul reprimands those
who commend themselves and "size-up" one another. Referring to 1
Corinthians 3:3 (where Paul asks "as long as there is jealousy and quar-
reling among you, are you not of the flesh and behaving according to
human inclinations?"), McIntosh points out: "Envious rivalry in cultural
and spiritual advancement, in Paul's view, only renders the parties to
the scheme blind and without understanding, stuck in that conflictual
and rapacious mentality that he calls thinking according to the flesh."[51]
Here McIntosh sees that Paul's indictment of their *acting* according to
the flesh includes or presupposes *thinking* according to the flesh.

McIntosh then draws from the desert fathers to develop the point
that such envious comparisons are the necessary result of an anxious
pursuit of pleasures—which unavoidably results in fears for not getting what others have, and throughout this whole process "the mind is
increasingly clouded and rendered insensible to the truth."[52] Evagrius
identifies that the problems lie in what he calls the eight kinds of deadly
thoughts or powerful imaginations: food, sex, things, anger, sadness,

48. Ibid.

49. Ibid., 132–33.

50. Gooch, *Partial Knowledge*, 42, as quoted in McIntosh, *Discernment and Truth*,
132.

51. McIntosh, *Discernment and Truth*, 133.

52. Ibid.

listlessness, vainglory, and pride. Here the obsession with more self-oriented pleasures, which derive from food, sex, and things, leads gradually to more relation-oriented compulsions such as anger (and the rest in the list), which usually manifest whenever we see that "the success of others dims our splendor."[53] Evagrius believes that anger especially renders the mind insensible to true knowledge, as he reports that an abba was saying: "For I know that anger constantly fights for pleasures and clouds the mind with passion that drives away contemplative knowledge."[54]

McIntosh points out that for Evagrius what is behind the eight deadly thoughts is "a persistent fear of lack and scarcity."[55] McIntosh notes that from Evagrius one could see that the noetic effect of sin—characterized by a heart blinded to divine generosity due to its alienation from God—is felt directly in the realm of the will, breeding feelings of insecurity, distrust, and fear. In other words, reality is interpreted as a realm of scarcity because the alienated self no longer knows how to receive freely from God, and so this hungry self seeks anxiously to extricate itself from its fear of lack—ultimately the fear of death—through extracting goods from others. McIntosh notes that such a fearful mentality gives rise to the need to rise above the world and "to boast of superior social status"; a more subtle form of such competition is a "wonderful elevating of the mind to bliss" or an "escapist mentality of pseudo-spiritual accomplishment" that the Corinthians are prone to have (ibid.).

In the selfish pursuit of pleasure, McIntosh notices that "everyone and everything else comes to be apprehended now, if at all, only in terms of the most atavistic needs and fears"; in such possessive pursuit, there is unavoidably "a fundamental anxiety about scarcity, a fear of somehow not getting what one is convinced one must have" (134). McIntosh points out that Evagrius's interest is not simply to expose the compulsive pursuit of the self, but to liberate it to see or appreciate "the infinitely greater joy of real life" (ibid.). Here McIntosh highlights the point that reality is filled with an enormous abundance, but the truth of such divine abundance and generosity is "hidden from minds in the grip of this mentality of deprivation" (ibid.). Thus in a sense we can say that there is a hermeneutic cycle here: the inability to perceive the divine abundance

53. Ibid.

54. Quoted by Evagrius, *Praktikos and Chapters*, §99, 38–39, as quoted in McIntosh, *Discernment and Truth*, 133.

55. McIntosh, *Discernment and Truth*, 135.

in reality causes an anxious and fearful grasping of illusionary pleasures, which in turn further drives the mind away from truth and constricts it from perceiving the reality of the abundant divine mercy and generosity.

Revelation of the Cross: Infinite Love and Unbounded Abundance

Besides identifying the pathologies of the human mind and their causes, McIntosh also proposes these illnesses' remedies derived especially from an apophatic tradition of Christian spirituality. Drawing from a tradition represented again by St. Paul, Evagrius Ponticus, and Diadochus of Photiki, as well as by the early Byzantine Maximus the Confessor (ca. 580–662), McIntosh underlines that the paschal mystery can be seen as a shining forth of the boundless divine mercy in giving life, the limitless abundance of God's love and provision for humankind. McIntosh highlights "the old-fashioned and quaintly unmodern point that moral and intellectual virtues are integrally related" (145), such that only a mind attuned to the overwhelming divine abundance can perceive reality truly. Put negatively, those accustomed to viewing reality "in terms of a fundamental lack" will live in self-seeking anxiety and fear and will inevitably have a distorted vision of reality (127). In other words, the truth of reality is inaccessible to such "vicious minds" that are habitually filled with anxieties, fears, and inordinate desires. McIntosh links this debilitating condition with what St. Paul identifies as living and thinking "according to the flesh" (1 Cor 3:3) (127, 133). McIntosh thus suggests that the *ascetical* process of purifying one's "evil thoughts" (Evagrius's phrase) through participating in the paschal mystery can lead to a *mystical* opening to the "mind of Christ" that discerns the fullness of reality in the boundless and gratuitous love of the Trinity (145). Again, McIntosh points out that this tradition sees a crucial link between transformation of the knowers' disposition and their capacity for discerning or seeing reality truly: "Here we notice immediately the indissoluble link that this tradition sees between knowledge and spirituality, between vision and the moral life" (127).

At the cross, McIntosh points out, God embraces humiliation and death which the pseudo-spiritual seek to escape "by assuming a higher status and comparing themselves with others," for it is through the cross that the power of death is overcome, as McIntosh quotes scripture: "Since, therefore, the children share flesh and blood, he himself likewise shared the same things, so that through death he might destroy the one who has the power of death, that is, the devil, and free those who all their lives were held in slavery by the fear of death" (Heb 2:14) (136). McIntosh thus observes that the cross of Christ grounds the mind in the reality of God's power over death and the overflowing divine abundance of mercy and love, and frees the mind from the distortions of fear and envy—in this way the cross is reshaping and reforming a truly discerning mind.

McIntosh suggests that the reason why Jesus is free from fears and distorted thinking is because of his personal identity as the Son—his intimate relationship with the one he calls Abba who is the infinite source of life, love, and abundance. McIntosh notices that Jesus calls people out to form a new community of sons and daughters through adoption: "for you did not receive a spirit of slavery to fall back into fear, but you have received a spirit of adoption" (Rom 8:15). By thus sharing in Jesus's loving relationship with the Father, one's mind will be renewed to trust in "the immensity of divine love" and to be able to discern the divine will that is "good and acceptable and perfect" (Rom 12:2) (ibid.).

Spirituality and Theology: Two Elements for Encountering the Living God

Noting the unfortunate divorce of theology from spirituality since the late Middle Ages, McIntosh wrestles with questions about the integrity of spirituality and theology, especially about "the challenge that spirituality issues to theology."[56] Proposing to think of spirituality as "the new and transformative pattern of life and thought engendered in people by their encounter with God" (9), McIntosh suggests that the common ground of spirituality and theology lies in "the believing community's encounter with God": "Spirituality is the *impression* that encounter has in the continual transformation of the members of the church; theology is the *expression* of that encounter in the attempt to understand and tell something true of the mystery whom the believing community encounters" (11). McIntosh points out that theological doctrines are "both shaped by and orient" Christians' encounters with God (41). Against modernity's impulse to separate theory from practice, McIntosh points out that a valuable insight in the feminist and liberationist perspectives has been the focus on praxis, that is, the affirmation that not only is

---

56. McIntosh, *Mystical Theology*, 14.

theory for the sake of praxis, but theory is also in some way coming out of praxis. This is in fact a recovery of "a fundamental assumption of earlier eras; namely, that living, practical involvement in reality is not a recipe for subjective beclouding of our understanding but is rather the prerequisite for true insight in conceptualization" (24). Drawing on the work of Pierre Hadot, McIntosh notes that in the ancient world, the philosophical schools "developed very concrete patterns of life" with particular exercises and practices that were required by those lovers of wisdom, because they believed that philosophical teachings were merely "second-order derivations" (ibid.). As Hadot comments: "Theory is never considered an end in itself; it is clearly and decidedly put in the service of practice."[57]

In McIntosh's view, therefore, the "second-order" enterprise of theology is not only arisen from, and shaped by, the believing community's more primary "data" of living encounter with the self-disclosing or self-revealing God, but such theology is also oriented toward the more ultimate goal of the community's life of journeying into union with God.[58] Noting Rowan Williams's view of doctrines as "a set of instructions for performance"[59] in the life drama of the divine-human encounter, McIntosh suggests that we think of doctrines as "a preliminary guide" for assisting believers in their life-long spiritual journey.[60] In this view, theology is placed within the larger context of the believing community's journey toward union with the divine life, which is the focal concern for mystical theology of the ancient Western theologians as well as Eastern Orthodox thinkers. Regarding Dionysius's mystical theology as a model for faith in search of understanding, McIntosh comments thus: "For theology is really an aspect of the mystical journey by means of which God is leading creation back into unity with the divine life. Theology is the attempt to notice how this is happening, to articulate the stages of the community's journey, to point ahead to the One who alone could mystically arouse the uplifting ecstasy that always leads beyond."[61] Drawing

---

57. Hadot, *Philosophy as a Way of Life*, 60, as quoted in McIntosh, *Mystical Theology*, 24.

58. McIntosh, *Mystical Theology*, 40.

59. Williams, "Teaching the Truth," 36, as quoted in McIntosh, *Mystical Theology*, 40.

60. McIntosh, *Mystical Theology*, 25, 40.

61. Ibid., 56.

from Vladimir Lossky, McIntosh notes that mystical theology measures all theological discourse by determining "how well does it safeguard the possibility for all Christians of becoming 'partakers of the divine nature' (2 Pet 1:4)."[62] The concern of mystical theology, in Lossky's words, "is always the possibility, the manner, or the means of our union with God."[63] Yet this approach of mystical theology does not concern itself primarily with such things as theories of prayer, but rather with the "mystical center" about which "all the history of Christian dogma unfolds itself,"[64] namely, "the central doctrinal truths" as McIntosh calls them: "What is paramount are the central doctrinal truths of Christianity: that there has been a true incarnation in true humanity of the true God, and that the church can only live as the true body of this incarnate Word by living ever more truthfully into Christ's dying and rising—thus to participate in that self-giving love which is truly the life of the triune God."[65] Following Lossky, McIntosh particularly favors this approach of mystical theology for theological thinking: "doctrinal reflection that is constantly alive to its spiritual sources and goals."[66]

Drawing from Andrew Louth, McIntosh proposes to see spirituality and theology as two elements that are held together in the activity of "the most intimate and transforming encounter with God" that ancient theologians referred to as contemplation, a term that has often been replaced by the term "mysticism" in today's academic discourse. McIntosh suggests that spirituality and theology can be viewed as mutually related "as the preparation for and articulation of the event of contemplation," or as the two basic impulses in the activity of contemplation: "the affective or loving impulse and the intellectual or knowing impulse."[67]

To Know and To Be Known: Loving Surrender to God's Loving and Knowing

Thus both spirituality and theology are all about encountering the living God who is ultimately a mystery to the human mind which can only "see

---

62. Ibid., 40.

63. Lossky, *Mystical Theology*, 10, as quoted in McIntosh, *Mystical Theology*, 40.

64. Ibid.

65. McIntosh, *Mystical Theology*, 40.

66. Ibid.

67. Ibid., 11–12.

through the glass dimly" (1 Cor 13:12) on this side of heaven. Especially with the advent of modern sciences and the split between subject and object, there has been a tendency to view God as merely another object (albeit the biggest one) to be investigated, grasped, or "known." For McIntosh, theology is about hearing and understanding (with the Spirit's power) God's own speaking, understanding, and knowing of God, which can be viewed in several successive moments:

> The first moment of theology is this divine speaking as it overtakes our lives. . . . The second moment of theology is when the loving power or Spirit of this Speaking inhabits us and transforms our hearts and minds so that we begin to hear and understand what God is saying. . . . The third moment of theology is when, by the Spirit's power, we have been so drawn into the Word's human life and death and resurrection that we are able to hear the loving call of the Father as Jesus does and to cry out "*Abba*" in loving response, as he does. And from there, you could say, theology becomes "*theo-logia*" in its truest and deepest sense, God-talk: not in the sense of our talk about God, but rather God's talk, God's conversation and loving communion with God.[68]

McIntosh therefore suggests that we need to become aware that "God is not an object which we could simply describe in the usual ways; as if God were like all the other items in the universe only bigger and invisible. Rather, to know and speak truly of God requires being drawn to share in God's own self-knowledge. . . ."[69] Thus if the goal of theology is "to speak truthfully of a God who is *not* simply the highest item of existence"—but rather the divine Subject to be encountered by the believing community—then ultimately theology can achieve its goal only "by helping the community to that moment in its encounter with God" when all our faculties are transcended and we are reduced to utter silence (126).

McIntosh thus highlights the apophatic or negative feature in human theological reflection. God is a mystery to us not only because of the finite limitation of our mental capacity, but also because our mind has fallen so much away that it is no longer able to comprehend the free self-giving of God's unbounded love: "in our world the trinitarian life of freely giving yourself away in love to the other is an act of blinding—even

---

68. McIntosh, *Mysteries of Faith*, 19.
69. McIntosh, *Mystical Theology*, 28.

incomprehensible—foolishness" (194). Again, McIntosh comments: "What renders this divine love *'mustikos'* or hidden, mystical and beyond comprehension, is not merely its infinity but the fact that *this infinity discloses itself in the activity of self-giving love*, in God's decision not to be God apart from the lost creation. . . . Indeed, the contrary and arresting sign of the Cross is the fitting revelation of this hiddenness, for it marks the very real, concrete, historical point at which this love passes into a darkness beyond human understanding" (43–44). This darkness in human understanding *vis-à-vis* the mystery of God, McIntosh notes, requires the continual and "painful undoing of all our attempts at fixity and foreclosure" (127); it is a warning against our proclivity to rely on any "particular beliefs, aspirations, feelings, or idols of any kind whatsoever in the encounter with the living God" (23). Thus theological questioning, in Rowan Williams's words, "is not our interrogation of the data, but its interrogation of us. It is the intractable *strangeness* of the ground of belief that must constantly be allowed to challenge the fixed assumptions of religiosity. . . . And the greatness of the great Christian saints lies in their readiness to be questioned, judged, stripped naked and left speechless by that which lies at the centre of their faith."[70] The other side of this "apophatic momentum," however, is "the intensifying of desire to such a point that one is left hungering only for the living God."[71] This can explain why, in contrast to "the cold and clever individual reasoner of today," the early Christians are ardently involved in witnessing to the truths—in John Henry Newman's words—"which they could not indeed understand, but by which they might gain life, and for which they could dare to die."[72] McIntosh thus suggests: "Spirituality calls theology to an honesty about the difficulty of understanding what is unfathomable (that 'suspended wonder' spoken of by Richard of St. Victor), an openness to what is never a puzzle to be solved but always a mystery to be lived."[73]

McIntosh notes that for the ancient world, the process of "knowing" (*noesis*) is "far more intuitive," because "it is not so much 'I' who am knowing but that 'the known' has drawn me into an encounter with

---

70. Williams, *Wound of Knowledge*, 1, as quoted in McIntosh, *Mystical Theology*, 17.

71. McIntosh, *Mystical Theology*, 123–24.

72. Newman, "Humiliation of the Eternal Son," 581, as quoted in McIntosh, *Mystical Theology*, 196.

73. McIntosh, *Mystical Theology*, 15.

itself" (70). In contemplation, the mystic is not the one who knows and loves, but the one who is *"known* and *loved* by God" (71). Noting that this notion of God as "the ultimate Knower" is evident in 1 Corinthians 13:12—"Now I know in part, then I shall know fully even as I have been fully known"—McIntosh points out that it is clear for St. Paul that "the most complete form of knowledge would not finally be our own act at all, but an event in which I yield myself to God" (70). McIntosh underlines that this unity of knowing and loving is not derived from an analysis of the human subject in which "knowing and loving are distinct . . . often in conflict with each other"; rather, it is from a looking into the divine Subject, for "knowing and loving are aspects of the one trinitarian act of existence" (71).

Rejecting modern epistemology's disjunction between subject and object as well as the modern "majority view" that there is an "unthematic, non-categorial" primal core to all mystical experience, McIntosh argues (drawing from von Balthasar) for a "more christological and trinitarian perspective" (112–13). This perspective, while holding that the "ever-greater" reality of God reduces *us* to silence, nonetheless sees that the superabundance of divine expressibility of love is *"eminently* 'thematic' and linguistic" as can be seen in the trinitarian "language of love" addressed to us through the historical missions of the Son and the Spirit (113). McIntosh thus suggests that "all human consciousness is irreducibly inter-personal, that is, I am aware of myself and of anything at all because 'I' have been addressed by another"; so "I will only know insofar as I am ready to love the other" (113–14). This kind of knowing is driven "not towards the ever more abstractly conceptual but towards the *concrete good* of the other," for it is a learning "to know as God knows Godself" in the patterns of "the trinitarian relations of infinitely giving love" (ibid.). In such relational dynamics of knowing and loving, oftentimes the infinite divine reality (or mystery) calls for "a renunciation of knowing according to our human ability to know," so that "by means of an abandonment to love, 'by growing in the practice of love and not by a theory of the desire to know,'" one can come to the only truthful "knowledge" of God possible (99). McIntosh notes that this faith journey of knowing God sometimes seems like "an increase in ignorance," as he quotes Herbert McCabe: "it is not information that we need. . . . What we need is to be taken up by God himself, to share in his knowledge of himself, a sharing that to *us* must look like darkness. So that our faith seems not like an increase of knowledge but, if anything, an increase in ignorance. . . . Not that we should speak more about him, but that *he* should speak to us."[74] McIntosh especially notes that the notion of "loving unknowing" or "the darkness of faith" is found chiefly in the Christian apophatic tradition: "In this form of negative theology, the supernal beauty and ineffable reality of God is understood to be so infinite, so dazzling to the human self, that the mystic is brought at last to the most crucial insight: loving *unknowing* is the only truthful knowing that one can have of God."[75] Yet McIntosh stresses that this is not proposing simply a kind of fideism, but rather suggesting that self-abandonment or "kenosis"—in the ultimate apophasis of Jesus's "full and loving surrender to the incomprehensible mystery of God"—is the mystical participation that can lead one to the true knowing and sharing in God's own revelation of God.[76]

In sum, we have looked at McIntosh's diagnosis and suggested treatment of our noetic pathologies. The remedies McIntosh proposes build substantially on an apophatic tradition of Christian spirituality, which begins with the ultimate apophatic moment of the cross of Jesus, continued through St. Paul and the desert fathers, and down to Maximus the Confessor, Pseudo-Dionysius, and others. A distinct characteristic of this apophatic tradition has been the emphasis on God as the ultimate mystery that is beyond usual human comprehension, conceptualization, and communication; yet it is a mystery that can be truly known and loved if we abandon ourselves to be drawn into the trinitarian life pattern of loving and knowing as it is disclosed in the life, death, and resurrection of the incarnate Son.

NEE AND MCINTOSH IN DIALOGUE

We have explored the views of both Nee and McIntosh on issues surrounding the relation between spirituality and knowledge. Nee's view is seen by some as "utterly anti-intellectual."[77] Others question the role or position Nee accords to the mind in the spiritual life.[78] In this

74. McCabe, *God Matters*, 20, as quoted in McIntosh, *Mystical Theology*, 16.

75. McIntosh, *Mystical Theology*, 191.

76. Ibid., 197, 99.

77. K. L. Leung, "Huaren nuosidi zhuyi" [Chinese Gnosticism], 248–64, esp. 255.

78. Lam, *Shuling shenxue* [Spiritual theology], 284–85.

section we will engage Nee and McIntosh in a mutual conversation—analyzing their important similarities and differences, and suggesting insights that are emerging from such a dialogue. I will suggest that there is a basic congruence between the thoughts of these two writers, and particularly that Nee's view of the role of intellectual activity in the spiritual life can find substantial parallels in the Christian apophatic tradition. I therefore contend that Nee's view is not anti-intellectual as some of his critics perceive.

Knowing and Loving: Relative Roles in the Spiritual Journey

Both Nee and McIntosh maintain a certain suspicion or vigilance toward a mere intellectual pursuit of knowledge. Nee's teaching about the dangers of the battlefield of the mind coincides with Cassian's dislike of excessive philosophical thinking because of its threefold pitfalls: distracting the mind from the spiritual pursuit, duping the mind toward "error in religion," and leading the mind to pride in knowledge.[79] Similarly, McIntosh notices certain warnings given by some desert and patristic writers. For instance, Evagrius understands the soul to be a battleground in which demons wage wars—by stirring up different passions or evil thoughts—to obstruct or distort the mind's discerning capacity.[80] McIntosh also sees that in Augustine's view, after the Fall the mind has the tendency to a private or self-centered perception of reality and, out of its illusionary need for security and control, the mind tends to settle for sheer analytical knowledge. In other words, the mind tends to "know things concupiscently and slightingly, and to slide into partiality and bias" with the concomitant anxious and fearful grip for certainties and possessions as well as self-preoccupying "resentment of others."[81]

Both Nee and McIntosh also notice the mind's proclivity to intellectualization and reductionism. Nee says: "We foolishly think that we possess what we know in our mind."[82] McIntosh points out that the mind is prone to different versions of reduction: the "shriveling of what the mind is willing to count as reality" due to its "frequent failures" of both moral and intellectual perception on the one hand, and on the

---

79. Chadwick, Introduction, 5, 24.

80. McIntosh, *Discernment and Truth*, 85–87, 93–103.

81. Ibid., 236.

82. Nee, *Breaking of the Outer Man*, 88.

other, the eagerness "to possess what reality it can perceive," which leads to its ceaseless reducing of reality to mere manageable propositions.[83] McIntosh comments:

> Augustine's suggestion is that while the grip of human reason is essential to productive life in the world, it needs frequent airing out and refreshing journeys up into the high country of wisdom. This exposure to the freely given and immeasurable outpouring of divine light relaxes the mind's self-defeating grip on its own small certainties. Otherwise the mind begins to draw back from the common joy of life in God and grows "busy reasoning in a lively fashion about temporal and bodily things in its task of activity, and along comes that carnal or animal sense with a tempting suggestion for self-enjoyment, that is for enjoying something as one's very own private good and not as a public and common good which is what the unchangeable good is."[84]

Nonetheless, there are subtle differences between the views of Nee and McIntosh, especially in their understandings of the role of the intellect in the spiritual life. Their different orientations can come to a better light with the help of the insightful analysis of the differing views of some Western Christian mystics in a medieval period by Bernard McGinn, a noted mysticism scholar who was also one of the supervisors for McIntosh's PhD dissertation. McGinn observes that there were three tendencies in which mystical theologians of this period understood the relation of the goal of mystical union (however it is conceived) to "the lower stages of human knowing."[85] McGinn summarizes the differences of these three tendencies as follows:

> One tendency, well expressed in classic Cistercian and Victorine mystical theory but found in many later authors, especially John of the Cross, emphasized the continuous dynamic activity by which Divine Love subsumes all spiritual activities toward a union with God where love and knowledge form one transcendent reality. Another tendency, represented by Thomas Gallus and the *Cloud of Unknowing*, was inclined to look with suspicion on the lower aspects of human intellectual activity and thus sought to establish a clear line of demarcation and separation between these aspects and the ultimate loving union lest human

83. McIntosh, *Discernment and Truth*, 190.
84. Ibid., 190–91, quoting from Augustine, *Trinity*, 12.3.17, 332.
85. McGinn, "Love, Knowledge, and *Unio Mystica*," 85.

discursive and conceptual thinking egotistically try to invade a realm where it could only do more harm than good. Finally, Meister Eckhart's insistence on the radical transcendence of union led him to emphasize that all loving and knowing (at least as we experience them) are negated in the *unitas indistinctionis*.[86]

McGinn is worth noting here for his contrast between the first and second tendencies, namely, in the first, love "subsumes" knowledge without giving it too much negative appraisal, whereas in the second, intellectual activity is watched vigilantly with suspicion and precaution. It seems apparent that McIntosh's position is closer to the first tendency, while Nee gravitates more toward the second.

The difference in emphasis between McIntosh and Nee can perhaps find some explanation in the two writers' different backgrounds. As a professor of theology educated at Yale, Oxford, and the University of Chicago, and having taught for many years in outstanding universities in both the United States and Britain, McIntosh has been shaped inevitably by the Western academic culture of the later twentieth and early twenty-first centuries. Nee, on the other hand, never underwent any formal theological training and (as we have seen in chapter 2) was influenced by various theological and spiritual strands that tended to place a more exclusive emphasis on the experiential encounter with the divine reality. Another factor that could have contributed to Nee's general disaffection toward speculative theology as well as his inclination toward the practical aspects of the spiritual life may lie in the pragmatism of the general Chinese culture in which Nee was imbedded. Lee Ken Ang has pointed out that one of the "underlying principles of Nee's theological system" is "Chinese ethico-pragmatism."[87] Peterus Pamudji has also noted such Chinese inclination toward the practical in Nee's teachings.[88] For the Chinese, intellectual endeavor—while being exalted in Confucianism—is generally a means to an end (for securing desirable social positions), unlike the Western mindset that would justify pursuing knowledge for its own sake. As Wu Kuang-ming, in his study of Chinese mysticism, also notes the contrast of the Chinese pragmatic approach to living *vis-à-vis* the Western speculative approach to understanding life.[89]

86. Ibid.
87. K. Lee, "Watchman Nee," 178, 182–92, 45–46.
88. Pamudji, "Little Flock Trilogy," 180–81.
89. K. Wu, "Chinese Mysticism," 233–34, 257.

Other scholars have pointed out that Chinese philosophy is usually "a philosophy of living"[90] or "a lived philosophy."[91] These deep layers of the Chinese consciousness have perhaps subtly influenced Nee's conviction regarding the place of intellectual studies—especially doctrines and theologies—in the journey of the spiritual pursuit.

The Mind and the Spirit: Anti-Intellectualism or Pastoral Sensitivity?

This brings up the issue of the so-called anti-intellectual tendency in Nee. One needs to note that the difference between the first and second tendencies of McGinn's schema is actually more apparent than real. Not only do both assume that love is in some way superior to knowledge, but the extreme forms of these two tendencies are best seen as two poles of a continuum (on the same plane nonetheless). The positions of McIntosh and Nee can be regarded as located somewhere between the two poles, with different degrees of orientation. In other words, their difference is just a difference in emphasis: the first emphasizes the continuity in the progression from knowledge to love, while the second stresses the discontinuity of the two. Thus these two tendencies are only different orientations in the Christian mystical tradition, as McGinn judges that "perhaps each of the three tendencies will always be present in Christian mysticism."[92] While McGinn does note that the first ("subsuming") tradition should be kept in mind (on the conceptual level) for "theologians and historians of mysticism" "as a corrective to those who have viewed mysticism as an anti-intellectual, purely emotional, and obscurantist phenomenon," it seems apparent that the overall balance of the Christian mystical tradition tips over to the side of love.[93] As McGinn notes, since Gregory the Great, "the majority of Western mystics have insisted that 'amor ipse notitia est.'"[94] Steven Chase also notes that Victorine spirituality (representing the first tendency in McGinn's schema) "has finally more [to] do with simplicity, humility, and compassion, than with criti-

90. Y. Lin, *Wisdom of China and India*, 569, as quoted in Hardy, "Interpretations of the *Tao-te-ching*," 171.

91. Hardy, "Interpretations of the *Tao-te-ching*," 170, referring to Fung, *Short History of Chinese Philosophy*, 10.

92. McGinn, "Love, Knowledge, and *Unio Mystica*," 85.

93. Ibid.

94. Ibid. The Latin sentence means "love is itself [a form] of understanding." See Chase, *Contemplation and Compassion*, 85.

cal analysis."[95] Thus not only does Nee's view fall within one of the major streams of the Christian mystical current (McGinn's second tendency), but it is arguable that this tradition's particular attitude toward the relative importance of intellectual activity in the spiritual life is also more or less shared by other Christian mystical streams (McGinn's first and third tendencies). It therefore does not do justice to dismiss Nee's conviction as simply "anti-intellectual."

It is also worth quoting at length here Nee's own comments against what might be called a species of anti-intellectualism of his day:

> Most teachings today emphasize a believer's spiritual life (the heart)—how one should love, be patient, humble, etc. These are surely *very* important, and nothing can substitute for these things. However, . . . It is equally important for a believer's mind to be renewed and enlarged and increase in strength so that it becomes strong. Otherwise, we will have an imbalanced life. Many people think that a spiritual believer should be one without any perception. It seems that the more foolish one is, the better. . . . Of course, we do not want worldly intelligence and knowledge. But the goal of God's salvation is not that we would continue to use the same mind that was defiled by sin. . . . God wants our mind to be restored to the perfect condition that existed at the time of His creation so that we will not only glorify God in our living, but also with our mind. Countless numbers of God's children have become narrow, obstinate, hard, and even defiled through the negligence of their minds. . . . Believers forget that after they are saved, they should still pursue the full renewing of their mind.[96]

Besides, Nee does teach on the importance of the mind for the spiritual life, as we have seen in his discussions of the mind's role in receiving and evaluating revelation and divine knowledge as well as in assisting and cooperating with the spirit during the journey of faith. These or similar comments of Nee, however, are noted by Leung as mere variants in Nee's views because they are few in number and are in contradiction to Nee's emphasis in his overall system of thought. While Leung's suggestion that Nee's inconsistency was probably due to different sources of his theological influence is debatable; Leung's dismissal of this whole strand in Nee's thought—because it is not in agreement with "his main idea"[97]—is

95. Chase, *Contemplation and Compassion*, 85.

96. Nee, *The Spiritual Man*, 3:502–3.

97. K. L. Leung, "Huaren nuosidi zhuyi" [Chinese Gnosticism], 259–64, and

not well-grounded. For it does not seem that systematic consistency was Nee's chief preoccupation. Nee's main concern, however, was more practical or pastoral, determined by different needs of the audiences that he perceived at the moment. Thus Nee's different teachings regarding the role of the mind's activity can best be understood with the view that he had in mind different believers that were under different developmental stages spiritually. On the one hand, Nee recognizes a great need to temper the independent activity of the believer's mind across the board, and even more so for those in the beginning stage of their faith journey. On the other hand, he nevertheless sees that for those who are at a later stage of spiritual maturity, their mind can now play a more actively assisting role for their spiritual development. This is particularly true for those whose mind has been renewed to the extent that it is brought under the rule of the spirit.

Nee's pastoral sensitivity in giving different, even contradictory, advice to people in different situations can find significant parallels in the history of Christian spirituality, with its classic characterization of the spiritual journey into the three main developmental stages of purgation, illumination, and union. For instance, Ignatius of Loyola, in his *Spiritual Exercises* (a manual for a four week retreat), shows such differentiated advice to retreatants in the First Week of the Exercises (corresponding to the purgative stage) and those in the Second Week (corresponding to the illuminative stage).[98] According to Michael Buckley, Ignatius sees that persons in the First Week usually operate on the pleasure-pain axis and are easily tempted by obvious evil. On the contrary, persons in the Second Week—usually having passed through the purification process of the First Week—do not function within the pleasure-pain axis anymore; they are no longer easily moved by the obvious evil, but are tempted more under the appearance of good.[99] For this reason Ignatius gives different sets of rules of discernment to different people, depending on the particular states they are in. It should be noted that Ignatius "warns seriously against giving the rules of the Second Week for those in the First Week. The criteria in each are almost the opposite. . . ."[100]

"Sanyuan renlun" [Trichotomistic anthropology], 208, 217.

98. Ganss, Introduction, 51–52.

99. Buckley, "Structure of the Rules," 224–25; and Spohn, "Pragmatism and the Glory of God," 34.

100. Buckley, "Structure of the Rules," 232.

Similarly, scholars have suggested that some seeming inconsistencies in Augustine's writings can be understood in light of the different motivations during the African bishop's career: his polemical stances (taken in his doctrinal treatises) when defending the true faith as opposed to his pastoral concerns (expressed in his sermons) when addressing the faithful.[101]

In short, we could say that the seeming contradictions in Nee's works regarding the mind's functions in the faith journey are probably good pastoral advice for believers with different levels of maturity. And the apparent negative assessments, in Nee, of the mind's role in the spiritual life can find substantial parallels in the Christian spiritual traditions, including the apophatic tradition on which McIntosh expounds. So while Nee's teachings may sound anti-intellectual to the ears of those accustomed to a certain standard of rationality or intellectualization, to categorize Nee's view as simply anti-intellectual does not do justice at all to the wisdom and subtlety in Nee's teachings and preachings.

∼

In this chapter, we have looked at the understandings of both Nee and McIntosh on the connection between knowledge and spirituality, especially regarding the role of the mind's activities in the spiritual life. The issues explored in this chapter can be understood as roughly related to the *why* question underlying divine illumination, namely: Why is illumination a significant concern for the spiritual life, especially when compared with the more conventional way of knowing through intellectual studies? After expounding on several relevant themes in Nee and McIntosh, we have demonstrated that there are substantial similarities between the two authors' views. While there are different tendencies between the two writers' understandings of the relative roles of knowing and loving in the journey of faith, their difference is more a matter of different emphases or orientations. In other words, the difference between Nee and McIntosh can be understood as difference in unity, since both represent part of a larger Christian mystical tradition whose common ultimate concern is to encounter the reality of divine Love that surpasses understanding. Through thus interpreting Nee's view in light of McIntosh's perspective, we have contended that the apparent negative

101. Drobner, "Studying Augustine," 19–20.

appraisal—in some of Nee's writings—for the role of the mind in the spiritual life can be shown as not anti-intellectual as some of his critics perceive. This chapter, then, forms the second of the three major building blocks toward substantiating the thesis of this book, namely, toward showing that Nee's major theological convictions have strong parallels with related aspects of the Christian spiritual traditions articulated by McIntosh, and also that some major weaknesses in Nee's thoughts perceived by his critics can be overcome or substantially ameliorated. It is to the third and last substantive chapter that we now turn.

5

Discernment and Formation

The Transformation of Spiritual Perception

BOTH NEE AND McINTOSH recognize the significance of revelation and illumination for the spiritual life. Both of them also highlight the crucial point that receiving revelation (or illumination) is not so much a matter of intellectual study, but rather, it is contingent upon a spiritual sensibility that is largely determined by one's spiritual maturity. How then can one foster the capacity of receiving revelation or illumination? How can one facilitate the growth toward spiritual maturity? Or how can a would-be discerner be formed or transformed in order to better discern the divine will in everything? These and related questions will be the focus of this chapter's exploration. In the first two sections of this chapter, the views of Nee and McIntosh will be expounded respectively on their own terms. Then in the third section, the two authors will engage in a critical dialogue as a way to evaluate Nee's view, examining especially the perceived tension in Nee's works between the human will and the divine will.

NEE ON REVELATION AND SPIRITUAL FORMATION

Nee affirms that all believers receive the Holy Spirit right from the beginning of their rebirth, although many still do not feel like they have the Spirit within even years after their conversion. Nee explains that this is because they are still babies in the spirit and so their intuition has yet to grow up to sense various spiritual realities. Just as natural babies can only drink milk that their mothers produce from digesting solid food, spiritual babies usually cannot receive divine revelations directly, but can only rely on mature believers to feed them spiritual foods. In other words, in Nee's view, the ability to receive revelations directly is closely related to growth in spiritual maturity and in its byproduct, spiritual intuition. Looking at 1 Corinthians 1:5—3:2, Nee believes that while the Corinthians possessed eloquence, knowledge, and various spiritual gifts, these are merely outward things or forms lacking spiritual essence or substance, for the Corinthians were still regarded by Paul as immature babies. By contrast, growth in intuition or spiritual knowing is the inward thing that really matters. Since for Nee intuition is part of the spirit, so growth in the spirit or the spiritual life must include, and often be indicated by, growth in the intuition. Nee says: "Please remember that God wants us to grow not in our knowledge, eloquence, or gifts. He only wants the growth of our spirit, our spiritual life, and the intuition of our spirit."[1] In Nee's view, the growth of intuition also makes possible true spiritual discernment, including discerning the will of God and discerning the true condition of people.[2]

So for Nee growing in spiritual intuition and discernment is intimately connected to becoming a spiritual person. What then could facilitate such spiritual growth or spiritual formation? In this section, we will look at Nee's perspective on various ways for facilitating one's growth in the spirit, including such themes as breaking the outer person, cooperating with divine grace in the circumstances of life, participating in the life of the corporate church (the bride of the Son), and dying to self-will in order to attain union with Christ and with Christ's body—the church.

Breaking of the Outer Person: The Way of the Cross

Nee's teaching on spiritual formation is quite comprehensive including various spiritual disciplines and practices such as scripture reading, prayer, communion with God, praise and singing, fellowship, breaking bread, witnessing, and others.[3] Yet Nee lays paramount importance on "breaking the outer person" as the way of the cross for the disciples of

---

1. Nee, *The Spiritual Man*, 2:321.
2. Nee, *Shuling ren* [The spiritual man], 226–54, esp. 232–35, 246–49.
3. See esp. Nee, *Xintu zaojiu* [Building Christian virtues].

Christ. Drawing from the Pauline notions of outer person and inner person (Rom 7:22, 2 Cor 4:16, and Eph 3:16), Nee holds that the outer person includes both the body and the soul, whereas the inner person is the seat of both the human spirit and the divine Spirit.[4] As we have seen in chapter 3, Nee's overall schema of sanctification includes two major sequences: first dealing with the "body" part of the flesh or deliverance from the power of sin; and secondly dealing with the "soul" part of the flesh or liberation from the bondage of the self (called also by Nee the natural life or natural person). It is this second phase of the soul-life (the self or natural life) that Nee usually focuses on when he treats the topic of breaking the outer person—with much attention to distinguishing the function of the soul from that of the spirit.

Nee sees that there are two kinds of work to be done to foster one's spiritual life: building up and tearing down. Building up has to do with strengthening the inner person, and tearing down has to do with breaking the outer person. Drawing apparently from Wesley's notion of the "means of grace," Nee teaches that the usual means of grace or spiritual practices—such as prayer, reading scriptures, listening to sermons, meditation, praise, or fellowship with other believers—function only to nourish the inner person. In contrast, tearing down or breaking the outer person can be accomplished only through outward means, or through what Nee calls "the discipline of the Holy Spirit," by which he means all the circumstances in one's life—inevitably orchestrated by the all sovereign Spirit of God.

Nee sees that at conversion, two things happen simultaneously to believers: their inner spirit is quickened, and they receive the divine Spirit. For Nee the human spirit and the divine Spirit within the human person are distinct but not usually separable,[5] so "the release of the spirit is not merely a release of man's spirit but a release of the Holy Spirit through man's spirit, because the two spirits are one."[6] As Nee is concerned with the formation of servants (or ministers) of God, he insists on the crucial importance of breaking the outer person in order for the inner person to be released, or to let the inner spirit have free access to and from outside: both ministering to others and receiving nourishment from outside resources:

4. Nee, *Ling de chulai* [Release of the Spirit], 10–11, 41.

5. Ibid., 26. See also Nee, *Breaking of the Outer Man*, 18.

6. Nee, *Breaking of the Outer Man*, 19.

> The breaking of the outer man leads to the free release of the
> spirit. The free release of the spirit is not only necessary to our
> work; it is profitable to our personal walk as well. If the spirit is
> released, we can constantly abide in God's presence. If the spirit is
> released, we spontaneously touch the spirit of inspiration that lies
> behind the Bible. We spontaneously receive revelation through
> the exercise of our spirit. If the spirit is released, we spontane-
> ously will have power in our testimony when we deliver God's
> word with our spirit. . . . When a person comes and speaks to us,
> we will be able to "measure him" with our spirit. We will know
> the kind of person he is, . . . the kind of needs he has. Our spirit
> will be able to touch his spirit.[7]

Thus for Nee one's ability to receive revelations (from God's word—read
or heard), to discern others' true spiritual conditions and needs, and
to release power to "touch" others is directly related to whether or how
much one's outer person has been broken.

What does Nee mean by breaking the outer person? We could trace
it back to his understanding of the fourfold aspects of Christ's work of
the cross. First, in Nee's view, Christ's blood satisfies God's righteous
judgment on—and brings about forgiveness for—*sins* (plural) or sinful
behavior, accomplishing objective, positional justification. Secondly, the
cross of Christ offers God's salvation for humanity's *sin* (singular) or sinful nature, leading to subjective, experiential victory over the power of
sin. Thirdly, like a grain of wheat that dies into the ground and brings
forth many new lives, Christ's death and resurrection releases his divine
life to believers, and gives birth to a new creation, that is, the corporate
Body of Christ. Fourthly, the cross of Christ makes it possible for his disciples to bear their cross daily—after the pattern of their Master—dying
to their own self or natural life, so as to manifest, and impart to others,
the divine life they have within.[8]

Nee suggests that the above third and fourth aspects of the cross are
two sides of the same coin: to release Christ's life into the believers' spirit
(a positive side) and to subdue the natural soul-life (a negative side) that
lurks around, vying ever for independence and control. Nee holds that
only to the extent that the believers have died to their soul-life—which
will then not be blocking the spirit-life—can they thus manifest the life
of Christ within. Besides, such dying to the natural person is a process

7. Ibid., 21–22.
8. Nee, *Normal Christian Life*, 139.

of undoing the result of eating from the tree of knowledge of good and evil: "On the one hand God is seeking to bring us to the place where we live by the life of His Son. On the other hand He is doing a direct work in our hearts to undo that other natural resource that is the result of the fruit of knowledge. Every day we are learning these two lessons: a rising up of the life of this One, and a checking and a handing over to death of that other soul-life. . . . So Paul says: 'We which live are always delivered unto death for Jesus' sake, that the life also of Jesus may be manifested in our mortal flesh' (2 Cor 4:11)."[9] The issue here is the over-development of the natural soul-life, its self-reliance or independence, which chokes the divine life newly acquired within: "Many of us Christians to-day are men with over-developed souls. We have grown too big in ourselves. When we are in that condition, it is possible for the life of the Son of God in us to be confined and crowded almost out of action."[10]

Nee notes that the life of a grain of wheat is contained within its shell and that unless the shell breaks (or dies), the kernel (the life) within would not come out to bear many fruits. In a similar vein, the life of Christ within a believer would not come out to produce life in others unless the believer's outer person is broken.[11] For Nee the main issue then is not about acquiring more of Christ's life, which believers have already had within themselves; the issue, rather, lies in how this life can be freely flowing out of their inner being: "The problem with us today is not how we can have life, but how we can allow this life to flow out of us."[12] Thus Nee maintains that a major work of the cross is to break the outer person: "The meaning of the cross is the breaking of the outer man. The cross puts the outer man to death and breaks open the shell."[13] This work of the cross is to bring the natural person into submission to, or alignment with, the Holy Spirit: "our co-operation in the daily inworking of His death whereby way is made in us for the manifestation of that new life, through the bringing of the 'natural man' progressively into his right place of subjection to the Holy Spirit."[14]

9. Ibid., 153.

10. Ibid., 154.

11. Nee, *Breaking of the Outer Man*, 8–9.

12. Ibid., 9.

13. Ibid., 12.

14. Nee, *Normal Christian Life*, 150.

Nee teaches that to be qualified for ministry, the fundamental issue is not about learning more doctrines; rather, it is about whether one's very self has been broken down and become submissive to God's dealing hand: "Unfortunately, many people think that what they lack is doctrines. . . . But this is absolutely the wrong way. . . . God has to break us down completely. The trouble with us is that while God stops us time after time, we blame this and that for the blockage. We are like the prophet who did not see God's hand; instead, we blame our 'donkey' for halting."[15] In Nee's view, breaking the outer person is not only needed for one to better receive revelations from scripture, sermons, and spiritual books, but is also necessary for a minister to acquire the capacity to discern the needs and problems of other people. Such discerning ability has nothing to do with the sharpness of one's mind: "Neither slowness in feeling nor sharpness of mind have anything to do with discerning men. We cannot discern men with our mind or our feelings. No matter how sharp our mind is, we cannot bring the hidden things in man to light, nor can we touch the depth of man's condition" (42). Nee maintains that unlike medical doctors who can treat certain illnesses without having to suffer the same illness themselves, physicians of the soul are to undergo an essential training, namely, going through a process of suffering from—and being broken by—various adverse conditions or situations. Such formation is necessary for the would-be ministers to become "medical instruments" themselves for diagnosing others' sickness. Nee thus preaches: "We are the thermometers; we are the medical instruments. Therefore, we have to go through strict trainings and dealings. What is untouched in us will remain untouched in others" (44). Only through each particular experience of being broken, can one acquire the spiritual sense or discernment in that particular area:

> Spiritual senses are acquired one by one, time after time. . . .
> Suppose a person condemns pride in his mind. He may even be
> able to preach on the subject of pride. But in his spirit he does not
> feel the evil of pride. . . . When God's Spirit operates on him, he
> will see what pride is. . . . As soon as a proud spirit comes out of
> a brother, he will feel that something is wrong. In fact, he will feel
> sickened. . . . From that point onward he will be able to serve this
> brother because he knows his illness; he has passed through the

---

15. Nee, *Breaking of the Outer Man*, 39.

> same illness and has received healing from it. . . . This is how we
> acquire our spiritual knowledge. (50–51)

Therefore, to the extent that the ministers are broken in certain areas, they can then become "wounded healers"[16] for others in the same areas: "Only those who suffer much loss will have much to give others. If we try to save ourselves in a certain matter, we will lose our spiritual usefulness in that matter."[17]

Moreover, Nee sees that breaking of the outer person is usually accomplished by "the discipline of the Holy Spirit," which means that all happenings around one's circumstance are deliberately arranged by the divine Spirit for one's discipline and ultimate good: "Everything that comes our way is meaningful and under God's sovereign arrangement. Nothing accidental happens to a Christian. . . . May the Lord open our eyes to see that God is arranging everything around us; He has a purpose in us. Through everything He is crushing us" (39). Nee underscores that such discipline of the Holy Spirit is a unique "means of grace"—a way for receiving divine grace—which cannot be replaced by other means of grace such as prayer, scripture reading, fellowship, or fasting (76). Further, Nee believes that such discipline of the Spirit is the greatest means of grace, because it is measured out precisely to each believer for his or her specific needs that only the Spirit of God can see—it is a grace that cannot be achieved or surpassed by any humanly contrived efforts of spiritual pursuit: "Our consecration cannot satisfy God's heart because our knowledge is limited and our light is limited. But the discipline of the Holy Spirit is altogether different; it evaluates our need in God's own light. It is not what we see, but what God sees" (68). Nee also contrasts the radical availability of this means of grace with other means of grace: "The discipline of the Holy Spirit is a lesson that will never slacken in us. Sometimes we lack the ministry of the word or, other means of grace. . . . But the discipline of the Holy Spirit is not limited by any circumstances. In fact, it becomes more manifest through limitations in the circumstance. . . . The Holy Spirit is arranging things every day and providing us with plenty of opportunities to learn our lessons" (76). Nee thus preaches that everything we encounter in our daily life is orchestrated by the Holy Spirit for our highest profit: "All

---

16. This term is borrowed from Henri Nouwen, *The Wounded Healer*.

17. Nee, *Breaking of the Outer Man*, 49.

the things that come upon us every day in the family, in our school, in our work, or even on the street are arranged by the Holy Spirit for our highest good and profit. If we have not received profit from them and if we remain ignorant and closed to this greatest means of grace, we will suffer the greatest loss. The discipline of the Holy Spirit is too crucial; it is a Christian's main means of receiving grace throughout his life" (72).

In short, Nee sees an interlocking link between the Spirit's discipline through one's circumstances and the breaking of the outer person, as well as between such brokenness and the capacity to minister to others: "In whatever matter we receive the Spirit's discipline, we are broken in that same matter. . . . as we have been disciplined by the Holy Spirit and broken in a certain aspect, we are able to touch a brother in that same aspect" (49). Let us now explore further Nee's teaching on submitting to the Spirit's discipline as a way of cooperating with God for better receiving divine grace.

Submitting to the Spirit's Discipline: Cooperating with Divine Grace

Nee elaborates on several points on how believers can cooperate with God for better receiving the grace of the Spirit's discipline. A first prerequisite is that believers must make a complete dedication of themselves into the all-wise hand of God, so that the gentle Spirit can freely administer to them what is deemed best from the divine perspective. Nee teaches: "If we have never consecrated ourselves to the Lord in a thorough way in the past, we have to do it now. We have to say, 'Lord, . . . I commit myself unreservedly and unconditionally to Your hand. Lord, I gladly put myself in Your hand. I am willing to let You find a way to release Yourself through me'" (12). Another point Nee notes is that at some time in their lives, many ministers would come to the realization that their very self is the major obstacle in their ministry: "Sooner or later a servant of God discovers that he himself is the greatest frustration to his work" (7). Many would receive a light, however dim, to see that their life is going nowhere if they are living for their self or with their own strength: "At a certain point, a man will feel that he can no longer live by himself or for himself. Under the feeble light that he apprehends, he will come to God and say, 'I consecrate myself to You. Whether the outcome is death or life, I will consecrate myself to You'. . . . 'Lord, accomplish in me what is most profitable in Your sight!'" (70–71). Nee teaches that it is important to ask for such light to see God's hand in one's circumstances—especially amidst difficulties and oppositions—and to acknowledge that whatever God arranges is the best for oneself: "Our responsibility is to ask for a little light from God so that we will know and acknowledge His hand. We want to be humbled under the mighty hand of God to confess that whatever He does is right" (112). Indeed, such light could make sense of all of our past experiences. In other words, seeing that breaking our outer person is the very purpose of God can become the hermeneutical key to unlock the meaning and significance of all happenings in our personal history: "When the Lord opens our eyes, we will see that everything that has happened to us throughout our lives is meaningful. The Lord never does anything in vain. After we realize that the Lord's goal is to break our outer man, we will realize that everything that has happened to us is significant" (11).

Nee points out that a major hindrance for the discipline of the Holy Spirit to be effective in one's life is a self-love that tries desperately to save oneself as well as a kind of attachment to earthly things. Nee states: "Some people are particularly bound by certain things. . . . We may love a certain thing without even realizing it ourselves. Yet God knows, and He will deal with us in a very detailed way. When all these things are taken away, we will be completely free. . . . The Holy Spirit . . . goes after their cherished items relentlessly. . . . Sometimes God deals with us through men. He puts men around us whom we hate, envy, or despise and deals with us through them. He also puts lovable men around us to deal with us" (73). Thus Nee sees that in order not to impede the Spirit's disciplining work, believers need to learn to be submissive to God's dealing hand in all the circumstances of their life, especially in difficulties and sufferings as well as when facing discouragement and opposition from annoying or "troublesome" people around them. Nee notes that complaint and resentment under such circumstances are counter-productive: "Many people cannot submit themselves. They murmur with their mouth and resent in their heart. This is indeed foolish. We have to remember that everything is measured to us by the Holy Spirit and is the best that it can be" (70). Thus while God is sovereign in arranging our circumstances, it takes our cooperation—a yielding, thankful, even joyful heart—to receive the hidden grace or "camouflaged blessing" that lies behind all circumstantial incidents or "accidents" which are measured out specifically and precisely to each one of us.[18] "If we yield to the arrangement of the

18. Nee, *Yao changchang xile* [Be joyful always].

Holy Spirit, we will reap the benefit. The very act of yielding will bring us benefit. But if we do not yield, instead arguing with God and walking according to our own will, we will end up taking the crooked path no matter what way we take. The basic issue is whether or not we can give ourselves to God unconditionally, unreservedly, and unequivocally for Him to deal with us freely."[19]

Nee says that when we can yield to God, the discipline of the Holy Spirit will prove to be a very effective means of grace to us, "more so than the ministry of the word" (76). Nee thus preaches:

> Our attitude before the Lord should be as the psalmist said, "I did not open my mouth; for You have done this" (Ps 39:9). We have to remember that it is not our brother, sister, friends and relatives, or any other person who is dealing with us. . . . Because of our ignorance we have put the blame on others or even on fate. . . . We have to remember that everything has been measured to us by our God. The amount, the length, and the intensity of what befalls us are all measured by Him. He orders everything around us, the only purpose of which is to break our conspicuous, obtuse, and hard spots. (100)

Moreover, Nee emphasizes that this principle of breaking the outer person (in order to release the inner spirit) is a law or a way of God that cannot be changed by human prayer. Thus the proper attitude is to cooperate with God, by submitting to the way of God: "Submission to God's law is better than many prayers. A minute of revelation of God's way is better than an incessant, ignorant pleading for God's blessings and His help in our works. . . . We have to ask for light. We have to learn to humble ourselves under His hand and obey this law. With obedience there is blessing" (40).

Besides the importance of breaking the outer person through submitting to the Spirit's discipline in one's circumstances, Nee further maintains that even when one's outer person is broken and the spirit can be released, such a release of the spirit may still be impure—or mixed with soulish elements. Thus there needs to be a further step of separating the soul from the spirit, which cannot be accomplished by self-introspection; rather it can only come from the revelation of the Spirit. Nee appeals to Hebrews 4:12–13 for the need to separate the soul from the spirit, and for the necessity of the Spirit's revelation—through the word

19. Nee, *Breaking of the Outer Man*, 73.

of God that is both living and operative—for such a separation. In other words, only through the revelation of God's word can the human heart have the capacity to discern what is of the soul and what is of the spirit.[20]

While the release of the spirit and the separation of the soul from the spirit are critically important for the spiritual life of a person, Nee teaches that the corporate church, rather than the individual, is the focus of both the creative and redemptive purpose of God. This grand vision of God's corporate purpose—as seen in the biblical languages that the corporate church is the Body of Christ as well as becoming the Bride of the Son—in turn has intimate implications for the spiritual formation of the individual person, especially in one's response to aligning the personal will with the divine will. In the remaining expositions on Nee, we will look at Nee's particular understandings of God's eternal purpose for the church, the bread-breaking communion in the Body of Christ, and union with Christ and with Christ's Body through union of the will.

God's Eternal Purpose: The Church as the Son's Bride of Love

Based on his study of Romans chapters 3 and 8, Nee believes that God's eternal purpose in creation and redemption is "glory, glory, glory"— which includes both "the glory of God (Rom 3:23)" and "the glory of the children of God (8:21)."[21] In other words, Nee sees that God's purpose is to have many children—after the pattern of the firstborn Son—who will enter into the everlasting glory of God. Thus for Nee God's eternal purpose in creating and redeeming humanity goes far beyond restoring the original paradise of Eden, or the mere salvation of individual sinners. Rather, God aims at gaining a corporate race that, through its cooperation and union with God, will secure the glory of God by finally defeating the devil's rebellion:

> God was moving towards the fulfillment of His purpose in creating man, a purpose which went beyond man himself, for it had in view the securing to God of all His rights in the universe through man's instrumentality. But how could man be instrumental in this? Only by a co-operation that sprang from living union with God. God was seeking to have not merely a race of men of one blood upon the earth, but a race which had, in addition, His life resident within its members. Such a race will eventually compass

20. Nee, *Ling de chulai* [Release of the Spirit], 115–36.
21. Nee, *Normal Christian Life*, 73.

Satan's downfall and bring to fulfillment all that God has set His
heart upon. It is this that was in view with the creation of man.[22]

This new creation of the corporate race consists of spiritual persons who
are in communion with God who is Spirit; persons who are therefore
capable of winning the ultimate spiritual warfare against the enemy:
"God wanted to have a race of men whose members were gifted with
a spirit whereby communion would be possible with Himself, who is
Spirit. That race, possessing God's own life, was to co-operate in securing His purposed end by defeating every possible uprising of the enemy
and undoing his evil works."[23]

For Nee this new race is none other than the church. Linking Genesis
2:21–23 (God created Eve out of Adam's rib) and Ephesians 5:25–27
(husbands should love their wives as Christ loved the church) together
and interpreting the scriptures typologically, Nee regards Adam and Eve
as the (allegorical) types respectively for Christ and the church. Since
Eve was created out of Adam's sleep for love and this happened before
their fall, Nee sees that the purpose for the death of Christ, the Second
Adam, goes beyond mere redemption of sin. In other words, parallel to
Adam's sleep and Eve's creation, Christ's death (and resurrection) issued
in a new creation—the church—also for the purpose of love. For Nee the
central message of the gospel is found in Ephesians 5:25: Christ loved
the church and gave himself up for it. In Nee's view, then, Eve expressed
"most perfectly God's original and eternal intention to have a Bride for
His Son."[24] The ultimate purpose of God, then, is to prepare a glorious
Bride of love (holy and without blemish) for the glorious Son—in the
new heaven and new earth of the new age of glory.[25]

Bread-Breaking: Corporate Communion and Personal Sanctification

Upon studying the apostolic age as recorded in the New Testament, Nee
sees that there are five kinds of meetings that are necessary for building
up a strong church as well as nurturing the growth of individual believers. These five kinds of meetings are: gospel meeting, bread-breaking

22. Ibid., 151.

23. Ibid., 140.

24. Nee, "Glorious Church," 88, as quoted in G. Y. May, "Breaking of Bread," 256.
May also comments that Nee's development of his ecclesiology around the image of Eve
is an "evidence of the ongoing matriarchal presence of his mentors" (p. 257).

25. Nee, *Normal Christian Life*, 140–44.

(*bobing*) meeting, prayer meeting, fellowship meeting, and meeting of preaching.[26] According to Grace May, the bread-breaking communion occupies "the first and most important" place in Nee's mind among the different meetings.[27] Intersecting at the bread-breaking event are two axes: the vertical and the horizontal—worship and fellowship[28]—which for Nee correspond respectively to the distinctive notions of the Lord's *Supper* and the Lord's *Table*.[29]

Vertically, Nee teaches that the Lord's Supper has two significances: remembrance and proclamation (1 Cor 11:24–26).[30] Here the bread refers to Christ's physical body. Nee says that because we are humans who would forget things, the Lord wants us to keep partaking the bread and wine in remembrance of him. We therefore are to observe the supper for commemorating Christ's grace of salvation, just as the Israelites observed the Passover feast to remember their deliverance from Egypt.[31] If we do not always remember the Lord's redemption, Nee cautions: "Our loss will indeed be very great."[32] Nee is convinced that the remembrance of Christ in bread-taking is a great means to receiving the Lord's grace, for just as Christ humbled himself in the Incarnation to save us, today he still humbles himself out of love to request our remembrance and to beseech our hearts so as to give us spiritual blessings:

> The Lord has condescended Himself and has beckoned us to remember Him. He first condescended Himself to be our Savior. He also condescended Himself to win our hearts and gain our remembrance. He does not want us to forget Him. He desires that week after week we continuously live before Him and remember Him. He asks this so that we may gain spiritual blessings from Him. . . . This is why the Lord wants us to remember Him. We are blessed when we remember Him. This

---

26. Nee, *Xintu zaojiu* [Building Christian virtues], 1:211. Earlier Nee held that five essential types of meetings were bread-breaking meeting, Bible-study meeting, gospel meeting, prayer meeting, and brothers' or sisters' meeting. See G. Y. May, "Breaking of Bread," 334.

27. G. Y. May, "Breaking of Bread," 334–36.

28. Ibid., 318–19.

29. Nee, "Bobing" [Bread-breaking], 315, 319.

30. Ibid., 308–15.

31. Ibid., 306–8.

32. Nee, "Bread-Breaking."

is one way to receive His blessing. We receive the Lord's grace through remembering Him.[33]

Thus the exclusive note for the eucharistic communion should be praise, blessing, and thanksgiving.[34] Nee's view and language, notes May, would have been appreciated by Calvin. As May comments: "For the Reformed theologian saw all of life as a grateful response to God, who condescended to create and redeem humanity. The eucharist, in Calvin's opinion, best captured the dynamic of God's initiative in love towards humanity and humanity's response to God in gratitude."[35]

The other vertical significance for the supper is to declare or display the Lord's death, as Nee notes that the separation of Jesus's flesh and blood on the cross is itself an indication of death, and that bread and wine are products coming from the death of grains and grapes. Nee states: "Jesus of Nazareth, the Son of God, has died. This is a tremendous fact displayed before us."[36] These and other words in the preceding context, especially in the original Chinese, are reminiscent of the note Nee wrote probably on his last day (or night) on earth (see chapter 1 of this book). The connection here is striking because Nee also noted that the Lord's Supper was instituted in the Passover evening—in Jesus's last evening and last meal on earth—which, Nee would certainly have realized, was at the threshold of the passing-over to the new life of resurrection.[37]

Nee thus preaches on the paradox or mystery of the cross and resurrection: "The cross always leads to His coming; it always leads to glory. . . . He wants us to declare His death continually and proclaim His death till He comes."[38] May notes that Nee does not subscribe to the doctrine of transubstantiation but instead articulates a Zwinglian theology, which holds that the elements symbolize Christ's broken body and shed blood that recall "the once and for all sacrifice of the savior of the world."[39] Yet in reality, according to May, Nee's view is closer to Calvin's "intermediary position."[40] While Calvin, and Zwingli as well,

---

33. Ibid.

34. Nee, "Bobing" [Bread-breaking], 309, 321.

35. G. Y. May, "Breaking of Bread," 319, referring to Gerrish, *Grace and Gratitude*.

36. Nee, "Bread-Breaking."

37. See Nee, "Bobing" [Bread-breaking], 306.

38. Nee, "Bread-Breaking."

39. G. Y. May, "Breaking of Bread," 333.

40. Ibid.

emphasize the special action of the Spirit on the community gathered
to remember Christ, Calvin's perspective accords the elements of bread
and wine a stronger instrumentality.[41] According to B. A. Gerrish, "one
of the most distinctive features" of Calvin's sacramental theology lies in
his appropriation of the Council of Chalcedon's understanding about
Christ's two natures—"distinction without separation"—for describing
the nature of "the sacramental union of sign and thing signified."[42] It was
by this christological formula that Calvin "defined his position against
the Zwinglians on the one side, and the Roman Catholics and Lutherans
on the other."[43] Nee's position does seem closer to Calvin's because of
Nee's stress on the grace available in the bread-breaking communion.

The Assembly's weekly observance of bread-breaking set them
apart from other independent or indigenous movements of the era.
Nee's high view of the eucharistic service had probably been shaped at
least partly by his own experiences of Christ's unique presence during
the communion. As Kinnear thus recounts the first bread-breaking
communion in which Nee participated after he had withdrawn for two
years from the local Methodist church: "One Sunday evening in 1922 a
small group of just four persons, Wang Tsai and his wife and Watchman
and his mother, remembered the Lord together in the breaking of bread.
They found such joy and release in thus worshipping Him without priest
or minister that they began to do this frequently. . . ."[44]

Horizontally, Nee also points out two significances of the Lord's
Table: fellowship and unity (1 Cor 10:16–17). In contradistinction to 1
Corinthians 11:24–26 where the bread refers to Christ's physical body,
Nee notes that in 1 Corinthians 10 the bread refers to Christ's (mystical) Body—the church; the emphasis here is on partaking the one bread
and one cup *together*.[45] Nee underscores that partaking from the *one*
cup signifies intimate communion shared among the children of God.
The one bread, on the other hand, signifies the unity not only among
all the sons and daughters of God, but also among all the churches of
God. Nee understands the one bread as a symbol of the whole church,
encompassing all believers throughout the world and across the ages:

41. Gerrish, *Grace and Gratitude*, 7.

42. Ibid., 53n9.

43. Ibid.

44. Kinnear, *Against the Tide*, 56; cf. G. Y. May, "Breaking of Bread," 339.

45. Nee, "Bobing" [Bread-breaking], 315–19, esp. 317.

"I break off a piece of the bread and eat it in remembrance of the Lord. Every Christian throughout the world in all ages has taken a little portion of this loaf and eaten it. If we take all the pieces that have been eaten and put it together, then this is the whole church."[46] While Nee discourages Assembly members from attending the eucharistic services of other churches,[47] he nonetheless emphasizes an openness to allow other brothers and sisters (particularly those from the denominations) to partake at the communion table of the Assembly.[48] Nee's inclusiveness goes even farther, as he states thus: "even those brothers and sisters who are not breaking bread with us are also included in this bread."[49] May notes that for Nee the one Christ is being scattered—dwelling in the many members while at the same time holding an undivided unity. Nee's language, May observes, bears "a striking resemblance" to that of the Didaché of the early church fathers.[50] Such resemblance probably indicates a patristic influence on Nee, since Nee indeed has knowledge of the ancient writing of the Didaché as well as that of Ignatius, Justin Martyr, Clement of Alexandria, Tertullian, Origen, and others.[51]

Such corporate communion, Nee regards, has crucial significance for individual sanctification and formation for ministry. For Nee, sanctification is a lifetime journey of following Christ through the daily bearing of one's own cross—through which one's (outward) self is being gradually broken. Only after the old self is broken or dealt with, can one be blessed by God and become a blessing to others. Referring to the bread that the Galilean boy gave to Jesus for feeding the five thousand, Nee teaches that what is important here is to consecrate or dedicate oneself wholly to God, as exhorted by Romans 6:13 and 12:1.[52] In other words, the requirement is to present oneself as an offering on the altar, or "handing oneself over" to the Lord.[53]

---

46. Nee, *Glorious Church*, 29, as quoted in G. Y. May, "Breaking of Bread," 295.

47. G. Y. May, "Breaking of Bread," 164.

48. Nee, "Bobing" [Bread-breaking], 319.

49. Nee, *Messages for Building Up*, 269, as quoted in G. Y. May, "Breaking of Bread," 323. *Messages for Building Up* is an English translation of a slightly different version of Nee's *Xintu zaojiu* [Building Christian virtues].

50. G. Y. May, "Breaking of Bread," 322.

51. Nee, "Appendix—Ancient Writings."

52. Nee, *Normal Christian Life*, 67–72, and *Wuxing de gengxin* [Renewal of your mind], 58–63.

53. Nee, *Ministries*, 56, as quoted in G. Y. May, "Breaking of Bread," 326.

There is a close connection between the process of being broken and the maintenance of loving fellowship and unity among brothers and sisters. In order to join with other believers in Christ's Body, one must allow oneself "to be limited by the other members."[54] As May notes: "Nee was emphatic that Christians should not insist on their own way. Upon entering the church, Christians gave up the prerogative to choose their brothers and sisters or to associate with only the people they liked. As a member of the body, one needed to learn how to submit and blend in with others."[55] Especially, appealing to 1 John 4:20, Nee highlights that the real test of love lies in how one deals with difficult brothers and sisters in the everyday life.[56] This would involve the often painful and humbling process of obedience and mutual submission.[57] Just as bread is made from grains that are ground into powder and wine is brewed from grapes that are pressed into juice, Nee underlines the necessity of going through the process of death in order to enter into the new life abundant.[58] Thus, similar to baptism (which is also held in high regard by Nee), the bread-breaking communion "celebrated the victorious death of Christ and invited the believer to enter into Christ's death and resurrection."[59] In addition, Nee sees that only love derived from the divine Source can make possible love in the human community, and unity among Christian members requires nothing less than holding together onto Christ their common head.[60] Furthermore, May notes that for Nee, "Without the filling of the Holy Spirit, Christians could not unite with Christ in his death and resurrection."[61] While Nee never fully identifies himself with the Pentecostal movement, the Assembly does not reject charismatic experiences.[62] Nee himself had a quite dramatic experience

54. Nee, "Protection, Limitation, and Ministry," 805, as quoted in G. Y. May, "Breaking of Bread," 314.

55. G. Y. May, "Breaking of Bread," 314, referring to Nee, "Protection, Limitation, and Ministry," 805.

56. G. Y. May, "Breaking of Bread," 299.

57. It is reported that some churches of the Assembly heritage also observe a foot-washing or humility practice preceding the bread-breaking communion.

58. Nee, "Bobing" [Bread-breaking], 312; cf. G. Y. May, "Breaking of Bread," 320.

59. G. Y. May, "Breaking of Bread," 336.

60. Ibid., 316.

61. Ibid., 325.

62. K. L. Leung, "Fenxing yundong dao shenmi zhuyi" [From revivalism to mysticism], 56.

of being filled by the Spirit,[63] and insisted that believers need to "live in the Holy Spirit" for both personal sanctification and effective ministry.[64]

Dying to Self-Will: Union with Christ and with Christ's Body

Because of the Fall, Nee notes, God's eternal purpose (to prepare a bride for the Son) is thwarted, and so Christ's work of redemption becomes a necessary measure for the "catastrophic break in the straight line of the purpose of God."[65] Nee points out the crucial role that the will plays in both the Fall and salvation, since sin came from Adam's disobedience, while salvation came from the obedience of Christ, the Second Adam—both are a matter of the will. Nee also holds that there are two kinds of union between believers and God: union of life and union of will. The first kind of union (that of life) happens at the starting point of the faith journey, at the time of conversion, when believers receive the life of God. At this beginning point, through faith believers are already in union with Christ in his death and resurrection—because scripture exhorts them to abide (which means they are already there) in Christ and to live their lives by the Holy Spirit.[66]

The second kind of union (that of the human and the divine wills), however, is the end goal of the sanctification journey. Here Nee holds that "the greatest work of salvation"[67] consists neither in the emotion (such as peace or happiness) nor in the mind (such as spiritual knowledge); rather it is in the will. Thus Nee sees that union (by submission) of one's will with the divine will is far more important than such extraordinary spiritual gifts as dreams, visions, prophecies, or laborious ministerial works and services:

> Among all our sins, there is one common principle—rebellion. Adam brought us to perdition through this sin, while Christ brought us to salvation through obedience. . . . The whole purpose of God's salvation is to have us forsake our will and be in union with His will. Today believers often make a big mistake in this matter. They think that spiritual life is happiness in the

63. See chapter 1 of this book, n110, n111.

64. Nee, "Anointing of the Body," 817, as quoted in G. Y. May, "Breaking of Bread," 325. See also G. Y. May, "Breaking of Bread," 327.

65. Nee, *Normal Christian Life*, 143.

66. Nee, *The Spiritual Man*, 3:583, and *Normal Christian Life*, 57.

67. Nee, *The Spiritual Man*, 3:582.

feeling and knowledge in the mind. . . . He desires to see a believer wholeheartedly seeking after what He wants and willingly
obeying all that He says. Unless he [the believer] unconditionally
submits to God . . . , his so-called spiritual life is superficial. . . .
All visions, strange dreams, voices, prophecies, zeal, works, activities, and labors are outward.[68]

Seeing that "it may be more or less accurate to say that the 'self'
is the 'self-will,'"[69] Nee holds that breaking the outer person ultimately
comes down to breaking one's stubborn willfulness: "the result of every
dealing is to make us weaker than before. He deals with us repeatedly
until our self is wounded and we are weakened. Some are touched in a
particular way in their emotion. Others are touched in a particular way
in their mind. Whatever area a man is touched in, the end result is the
breaking of the will."[70] Noting that "Pliableness is a mark of a broken
man,"[71] Nee underlines that when the work of breaking is complete in
someone's life, this person will exhibit a kind of pliableness or meekness
that resembles the dove-like Spirit: "In symbolizing the Spirit's nature,
the dove is used. The Spirit's nature is a dove's nature—pliable, peaceful,
and meek. It is not hard. As the Spirit of God works His nature into us
step by step, we acquire a dove's nature."[72] Such meekness or submission
to the divine will also means a change of one's basic posture from that of
self-centeredness to God-centeredness, particularly from self-initiating
activities to responsive actions in accordance with the movements of
God's Spirit: "If our will is in union with God . . . We are dead toward
ourselves, but alive toward God. . . . It means that we move according to
the moving of God. . . . In other words, this kind of union is a change
of who is the center, a change of who is the initiating one. In the past all
of our works were centered upon the self, and all of our activities were
initiated by the self. Now everything is unto God."[73]

Furthermore, Nee notes that the problem of the Fall lies in humanity's illusionary attempt for self-sufficiency apart from God, which
also led to alienation and jealous competition among people. Thus Nee

68. Ibid., 3:583–84 (brackets mine).

69. Ibid., 3:582.

70. Nee, *Breaking of the Outer Man*, 104.

71. Ibid.

72. Ibid., 106.

73. Nee, *The Spiritual Man*, 3:584.

stresses that dying of the self-will also includes dying to independent individualism, especially via practicing fellowship and union with other members of the Body of Christ: "There is no union, no fellowship in sin, but only self-interest and distrust of others. As I go on with the Lord I soon discover, not only that the problem of sin and of my natural strength has to be dealt with, but that there is also a further problem created by my 'individual' life, the life that is sufficient in itself and does not recognize its need for and union in the Body. . . . I want holiness and victory and fruitfulness for myself personally and apart, albeit from the purest motives."[74] Noting that the new life of Christ within believers would incline them to such fellowship and union, Nee emphasizes again that God's redemptive purpose is to gain a new race, a corporate church, to display the glory of God: "The vessel through which the Lord Jesus can reveal Himself in this generation is not the individual but the Body. . . . It requires a complete Body to attain to the stature of Christ and to display His glory."[75]

In short, Nee sees that the capacity for true spiritual discernment is closely linked to personal formation or maturity in the spiritual journey. For Nee the goal of the lifelong journey of sanctification can be conceived in terms of union of the individual will with the divine will. In order for this to happen, the individualistic and independent natural life of the self needs to be broken, usually by difficult or unpleasant life circumstances (often by people around) as deliberately arranged by the disciplining hand of the all-wise and all-loving Spirit. The key to better receiving such disciplining grace from God lies in a submissive and thankful heart. In addition, Nee teaches that other means to receiving divine grace for spiritual growth include such practices as early morning devotions, praise, and fasting, as well as scripture reading, prayer, fellowship, service, and observance of the eucharistic communion. With this understanding of Nee's view on the connection between spiritual formation and spiritual discernment, let us now turn to McIntosh's exploration of some similar issues that concern Nee.

74. Nee, *Normal Christian Life*, 147.
75. Ibid., 146.

MCINTOSH ON DISCERNMENT AND TRANSFORMATION

In this section, we will first look at McIntosh's view of why personal transformation is a great prerequisite for authentic discernment. We will then explore his understanding of how spiritual transformation can happen for the would-be discerners of divine knowledge, including such themes as participating in the paschal mystery as ascetical noetic transformation, sharing in the mind of Christ in the mystical unity of knowing and loving, joining the life of the church in the communal search for truth, responding to the call for assisting all things in fulfilling their divine destiny, and awakening to the love of the Holy Spirit in the journey of personal transformation.

Transformation in Love: The Great Prerequisite for Discernment of Truth

McIntosh is concerned with questions about discernment and knowledge of truth. What then is truth? McIntosh accepts, as his initial premise, the basic Christian notion that God is truth. From this starting point, McIntosh reasons that there must be a deep connection between how truth is known and how God is known, or "between how people come to know truth and how people come to be related to God"—between perception and relationship.[76] This connection is referred to in Romans 1:20–21, in which the apostle Paul sees that creation is permeated with the light of God's truth that humankind ought to be able to perceive and understand, yet because humanity refused to give honor and thanks to God—their relationship with God was not right—their minds were darkened and their thinking became futile. Thus a problem in the human-divine relationship results in a problem in the human noetic realm—the inability to discern and know the truth of God (ibid.).

Drawing from the apostle Paul, McIntosh notes that the divine remedy to this noetic illness was to shine into the world a new transforming light—from the same divine radiance shining forth at creation—that radiates from the face of Christ risen from the dead. Reconciling humanity's relationship with their Creator, this healing light of the resurrected Christ is now being reflected—by the Holy Spirit—into believers' hearts, presenting the knowledge of the glory of God; as 2 Corinthians 4:6 states: "For it is the God who said, 'Let light shine out of darkness,'

76. McIntosh, *Discernment and Truth*, 4.

who has shone in our hearts to give us the light of the knowledge of the glory of God in the face of Jesus Christ" (ibid.). Moreover, McIntosh sees that it is nothing less than Jesus's own relationship with the Father that the Spirit is restoring in the believers (Romans 8, especially verses 14–17), and such restoration is not merely an individual matter, for the Spirit is to establish a new community of love that is now positioned for "a renewed perception of all truth" (ibid.). Furthermore, McIntosh points out real knowledge is less like what humans possess, and more like what God knows (1 Cor 8:1–3)—it is through loving friendship with God that believers come to be sharers in "God's own knowing and loving of reality" (4–6).

McIntosh observes perceptively that throughout history Christian spiritual writers have discussed five different aspects or phases of discernment as follows:

1. Discernment as faith: spiritual discernment as grounded in a loving and trusting relationship with God.

2. Discernment as distinguishing between good and evil impulses that move people.

3. Discernment as discretion, practical wisdom, moderation, and generally good sense about what to do in given practical situations.

4. Discernment as sensitivity to and desire to pursue God's will in all things.

5. Discernment as illumination, contemplative wisdom, a noetic relationship with God that irradiates and facilitates knowledge of every kind of truth. (5)

McIntosh points out that these different aspects are usually dealt with by writers on discernment in a discrete manner such that the link between them is often obscure. While only the fifth aspect of discernment focuses on the theme of illumination, McIntosh suggests that all five aspects can better be viewed as different moments or dimensions of discernment that recur throughout a person's life journey of growing toward God. Even as these moments sometimes overlap, McIntosh proposes a synthetic model to conceive these integrally related moments in an organic, sequential cycle of the discerning life, descending and ascending between the two modes of contemplation (ultimately the vision of the God of truth) and action (the practice of Christian living)[77]:

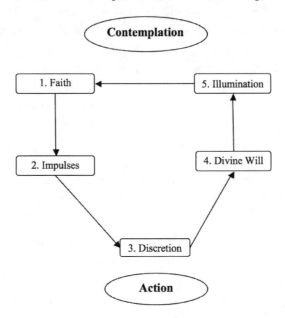

McIntosh especially highlights that every one of these discerning moments is built upon "the great prerequisite" of the transformation of the would-be discerners in their relationship of love with God and neighbor (8). Let us now look at McIntosh's probing of more biblical grounding of this link between transformation and discernment—between relationship of love and perception of truth—in each of the five aspects of the discerning life.

Loving Communion and Truthful Perception: Biblical Grounding

McIntosh notes that the first moment of discernment—discernment as faith—is grounded in one's loving trust in God. Noting that much Christian teaching on discernment has been focused on "the *objects* to be discerned," McIntosh points out that biblical authors (and important teachers of discernment in later centuries as well) have emphasized instead the priority of attending to "the discerning *subject*," as can be seen from Paul's admonition in Romans 12:2: "Do not be conformed to this world, but be transformed by the renewing of your minds, so that

77. Ibid., 5–7. The diagram is McIntosh's idea.

you may discern what is the will of God—what is good and acceptable and perfect" (ibid.). This focus on the knowing subject is different from, and even contrary to, the modern preoccupation for securing epistemic certainty (in such possession as a Cartesian ground or Kantian convictions), because it is precisely the fallen "habits of mind" that need to be renewed and transformed and "attuned to the realities" that only faith can perceive (ibid.). McIntosh declares: "Christian discernment begins with the confidence that human knowing can become enraptured by the very truth that creates and sustains it, that this truth is nothing less than the radiant logic of God's trinitarian life, and that this life re-creates humankind to become sharers in that ultimate knowing and loving which is God. Unless the discerning life is constantly nourished by the life of God, no growth in truer perception can occur" (ibid.).

McIntosh then attempts to show, from the Gospel of John (seen with the light of Thomas Traherne), why transformation of the knowers is the critical requirement for cultivating a discerning life. McIntosh sees that a major theme throughout John's gospel is that Jesus, the incarnation of the true light, is persistently being misperceived by a blind world. This blindness cannot perceive the true meaning of the (sacramental) signs represented by Jesus's speeches and acts, which are always "pointing to and sharing in a reality beyond," especially the infinite reality of the Father's abundance and mercy (10). Such analogical signs include Jesus's declaration that he is the true bread from heaven, the true vine, and the resurrection and the life, as well as all the signs Jesus performs such as the turning of water into wine at Cana, the feeding of the five thousand, and finally his own death and resurrection. By these signs, Jesus replaces "the world's economy of scarcity and necessity" with heaven's economy of unlimited abundance and grace (9). Such reality of divine abundance cannot be perceived by those whose minds and hearts are conformed to the world's mentality of "deprivation, suspicion, and scarcity" (10). This is why personal transformation is necessary for believers to attune to "that ever-sharing 'more' of divine life": "Believers must come to derive their whole existence no longer from their (literally minded) biological life, which ends, literally, with death, but from the ever-greater (analogically minded) infinite life of the Father in the Spirit—that is, life that never ends but always points beyond itself to another. Only then can believers finally come to know reality in truth" (9). Hence McIntosh points out that Christ's own death and resurrection is "the master key" to perceiving the reality of life abundant by undermining the "reduction of reality to scarcity and fear": "Jesus subverts this reduction by perceiving his death as in fact *more* than death, a going to the Father. . . ." (8–9).

Further, McIntosh suggests that there is a christological as well as trinitarian (or we could say pneumatological) structure embedded in both the (objective) reality and the (subjective) human knower. In John 14–17, Jesus is preparing the disciples to participate in the reality that "he has with the Father and the Spirit" through the paschal mystery, so that the disciples will receive the Spirit who will guide them into all truth (John 16:13) (10). Such perception of divine truth can happen only after the disciples have Jesus's dying and rising "worked within them" in some way—"beyond the dominion of death"—which means that they must come to share in the life of the infinite Spirit, and this was made possible by the resurrected Christ's breathing of the Holy Spirit upon the disciples (John 20:22) (10–11). McIntosh thus comments: "John's Gospel envisions this transformation of human consciousness in terms of the risen Christ communicating the Spirit of the Father with the disciples; Traherne echoes the Pentecost theme with his reference to the fire of the divine Love that begins to illuminate the world. . . ." (12). McIntosh thus underlines that true growth in discernment can occur only in this new life in the infinite Spirit that breaks loose the fears and bonds of the worldly mindset and transforms the heart through participating in the divine self-giving life of boundless love—revealed in the paschal mystery—by communion in love with God and people (11–13).

McIntosh notes that the second moment of discernment—distinguishing between good and evil impulses or voices that influence human desires—is a perennial issue dated all the way back to Adam and Eve, run through the Old Testament as the problem of distinguishing between true and false prophets, and persisted in the New Testament seen especially in the synoptics (to discern the nature of "the spirit that animates Jesus"), the first epistle of John (1 John 4:1), and Paul's letters (13–16). McIntosh points out that here again there is also an important relation between a grounding in God's self-sharing abundance of love and an ability for deeper discernment, and this link is made explicit by Paul in Philippians 1:9–10: "this is my prayer, that your love may overflow more and more with knowledge and full insight (*aisthesei*) to help you know what is best" (15–16). Moreover, McIntosh notes that while Paul identifies "the discernment of spirits" as one of the gifts of the Holy

Spirit (1 Cor 12:10), the apostle nonetheless proposes many criteria for the discernment of spirits—criteria that are far more communal than individualist—especially, "love and peaceful communion run through Paul's letters as the fundamental tests of healthy impulses" (15). And such communion of love and discernment of spirits are to be grounded in the humility and self-emptying love of Christ—"the humiliated and crucified one"—as described in Philippians 2 (16).

Even in the third moment of discernment—discretion and prudence—which seems most practical, McIntosh notes, there is imbedded within a profound loving anticipation for and availability to the call and will of Christ. McIntosh points out that the desire or yearning for and the actual pursuit of wisdom are required for obtaining the discerning practical wisdom, as the personified wisdom declares in Proverbs 8:17: "I love those who love me, and those who seek me diligently find me" (ibid.). This practical wisdom or discerning capacity comes partly as gift and partly by cultivation, observes McIntosh, for according to Mark's gospel, on the one hand we read, "do not worry beforehand about what you are to say; but say whatever is given you at that time" (13:11) and, on the other hand, we are to take heed to discern the signs of the time: "From the fig tree . . . you know that summer is near. So also, when you see these things taking place, you know that he is near" (Mark 13:28–29). The fact that human watchfulness and loving participation are required can also be seen in Matthew 25, wherein the five bridesmaids are wise precisely because they prepare well for the Bridegroom's coming in ways that the five foolish ones neglect (17). McIntosh thus suggests that various themes of this form of discretion or prudence might be summarized as "knowing how to be alert for Christ" (ibid.). Moreover, McIntosh notes how Jesus trains his disciples, namely, "training them in his own patterns of life, his own confidence in God, his own perception of God's call to him" in ordinary everyday existence (ibid.). McIntosh then points out that such discretion or practical wisdom is grounded not only in Jesus's own love and openness to his Abba's will and calling in each situation, but also in "the *practicing*" of that same availability by the community of his disciples (18). The relation of such practice of Christian disciples and acquiring practical discernment can be seen in Paul's injunctions in his Letter to the Ephesians: "Live as children of light—for the fruit of the light is found in all that is good and right and true. Try to find out what is pleasing to the Lord. . . . So do not be foolish, but understand what the will of the Lord is" (Eph 5:8–10, 17) (ibid.). Likewise, McIntosh notes that the Letter to the Hebrews also talks about training and practice that cultivate the discerning capacity of the mature disciples: "those whose faculties (*aisthētēria*) have been trained by practice to distinguish good from evil" (Heb 5:14) (ibid.). In short, there is an intimate connection between growth in discernment or discretion and growth in maturity of life through practicing Christ's own pattern of self-giving life that radically opens up to the Abba, the true source of all wisdom and light.

McIntosh then shows that the fourth moment of discernment—seeking and serving the truth of God's will—is grounded also in love, in Jesus's love for knowing the Father's intentions and for bringing them into fulfillment in the world, and in the Christian community's loving "participation in Jesus' relationship with the Father" (19–20). As John 5:19 reports that Jesus does nothing on his own but only what he sees the Father doing, McIntosh notes that the passage that follows suggests that what the Father does through Christ is chiefly the work of bestowing eternal life, and it is this eschatological truth of eternal life that lights up the present conditions of all created things as they move toward fulfilling their consummate truth as destined by God. McIntosh thus comments: "It is this eschatological truth, the deathless reality of God's infinitely self-sharing life, that environs all creation and reveals the true intention and goal inherent in every creature" (19). Further, as Jesus declares, "I know that his commandment is eternal life" (John 12:50), McIntosh points out that the truth of God's commandment for every creature is "purely and absolutely life" (ibid.). Thus discernment of truth here is not about a static kind of truth, but truth that is life eternal, or that is "the living reality of each creature *existing in communion with its Creator*" (19–20). Jesus can be seen as ushering in the inbreaking of this eternal life of love, as he leads his disciples to rediscover "*reality as participation in divine communion*" (20). Hence Jesus teaches that the Father's commandment is for the disciples to love one another as Christ has loved them, so that in this way they will become a visible sign to the world for the eternal communion of love (John 14). Thus such discernment of the divine truth or intension is to spring from the Christian community's participation in Jesus's loving relationship with the Father—with single-hearted desire to know and do the Father's will as well as wholehearted devotion to loving one another. This fourth moment of discernment, then, is intimately tied to loving communal involvement as well as the desire and effort to bring the divine intention of eternal loving communion with all things into "ever greater expression in the world" (19–20).

For the fifth moment of discernment—discernment as illumination or contemplative wisdom—McIntosh notes that the goal of the discerning life is identified here with the "delighted wonder" and loving gaze "upon the consummation of all creation in God"—upon eternal life as well as the infinite wisdom of God. While such beatific vision can only be realized eschatologically (in the new heaven and new earth), a glimpse of such light (however transiently) can nonetheless break into the present world—shattering its darkness and distortion of understanding, and setting the old pattern of human thinking "free from the constraints of fear and death" (21). Looking into the verses in Colossians 3:1–11, McIntosh points out that such illumination from the eschatological vision disposes believers to see the present estranged and divided world with "freedom, confidence, and hope"—to see the world with "that limitless life for which it was created," and the "infinitely self-sharing love to which all things are called" (21–22). Transformed by the power of the risen Christ into the new self that is "being renewed in knowledge according to the image of its creator" (Col 3:10), believers are to overcome the world's alienations and divisions with the "preliminary form" of the eternal life of divine communion (21). Thus the beatific vision and wonder for the glory of God transform the believers' present perception of reality and draws them onward to the "vision of truth which is the very life of heaven and a new earth's everlasting joy" (7).

In short, drawing from different scriptural witnesses, McIntosh suggests that all five moments of discernment are vitally related to personal transformation of the heart in love and communion, thus transformation of the human subject is the crucial prerequisite for discerning truth in all its dimensions. Let us now turn to some of McIntosh's understanding of how such transformation can be effected—based on his analysis of the history of Christian spiritual discernment.

Participating in the Paschal Mystery: Ascetical Noetic Transformation

McIntosh notes that the event of Christ's death and resurrection reveals the hidden reality of God's boundless mercy toward humanity as well as the infinite divine power over death. This Christ event, in St. Paul's view, begins a new era or the end time (the "eschaton"), and opens up a new order of reality which must now be understood in terms of an

"eschatological noetic" (140). To be able to thus discern "the eschatological significance" of the paschal mystery, a noetic transformation must
occur that is necessarily painful or ascetical, because, to the survival
instincts that are so accustomed "to think in very purposeful, utilitarian
ways about what surrounds us," the cross inevitably appears foolish or
"painfully enigmatic" (138). This noetic transformation must go through
a process of transition accompanied by all the unsettling and uncontrol-
lable feelings and states of mind. It is a phase in which one is caught in
the uncertainty of the in-between, because "the convenient older noetic
is no longer accessible, but a new vision is not yet at work either"; it is "an
epistemological crisis" resulting from the cross event (139). One may
well find this process particularly unsettling because the new vision that
is beginning to open up can no longer fit into one's own grasp or possession. McIntosh points out that this is precisely Paul's criticism of the
Corinthians' seeking of "a perfectly graspable, religious wisdom of their
own," rather than "abiding there with Christ on the cross, trusting in the
unimaginable hope of the Father's love" (ibid.).

Echoing 1 Corinthians chapter 1, McIntosh observes that this noetic transformation process requires a participation in the paschal mystery that includes suffering the loss of "all status, all claims to cultural,
biological, moral, or spiritual superiority" and resting one's "sole confidence in the resurrection of Jesus" (136–37). Following James Alison,
McIntosh sees that this scattering process is particularly painful because
"those who have begun to derive their self-worth from God will likely
not fit in well with the world's schemes of approval, and hence come to
seem to others and perhaps to themselves like dismal failures" (137).
Drawing from Alison's comments on John 5:41–44 ("I do not accept
glory from human beings. . . . How can you believe when you accept
glory from one another and do not seek the glory that comes from the
one who alone is God?"), McIntosh highlights that preoccupation with
spiritual achievement is contrary to the message of the cross, and such
preoccupation renders one blind to the reality of the glory of God (ibid.).
As Alison notes:

> In order to receive your reputation, your being noticed and rec-
> ognized, by God, you have to be prepared to lose the reputation
> which comes from the mutually reinforcing opinion and high
> regard of those who are bulwarks of public morality and good-
> ness. . . . The order of this world has its own glory, which depends

on mutually rivalistic imitation. . . . But those whose minds are fixed on the things that are above, that is, who have begun to receive their "I" from their non-rivalistic imitation of Jesus, already begin to derive their reputation from the Father and not from their peers.[78]

McIntosh notes that as the children and heirs of God, we must proceed by way of the cross of Christ, as Paul writes: "for you did not receive a spirit of slavery to fall back into fear, but you have received a spirit of adoption. When we cry, 'Abba! Father!' it is that very Spirit bearing witness with our spirit that we are children of God, and if children, then heirs, heirs of God and joint heirs with Christ—if, in fact, we suffer with him so that we may also be glorified with him" (Rom 8:15–17).[79]

McIntosh thus suggests that "the cross becomes the basis of discernment because it grounds the mind in reality free from the distortions of fear, envy, and anger—all of which have as their ultimate bogey-totem the shame and humiliation of death itself" (ibid). And because Christians believe that the whole personal identity of Jesus is encapsulated in his loving relationship with his Abba, participating in the paschal mystery results in a transformation of one's identity, one's perception of self-worth, and consequently one's relations with others— patterned after Jesus's relationship with the Father. In other words, the cross and resurrection of Jesus opens up a new way of seeing oneself and one another, bringing about a conversion from self-centered living to living for the love of God and for loving others out of God's love, as Paul writes in 2 Corinthians 5:14–15: "we are convinced that one has died for all; therefore all have died. And he died for all, so that those who live might live no longer for themselves, but for him who died and was raised for them" (140). Quoting Raymond Pickett, McIntosh sees that this new authentic way of knowing is granted "not to the natural person, but to those who are able to discern the eschatological significance of Christ's death and who view reality in terms of its consequences."[80]

Thus a painful noetic transformation needs to happen to change the mind from the old framework of thinking into a new one that can

78. Alison, *Raising Abel*, 181–82, as quoted in McIntosh, *Discernment and Truth*, 137.

79. Cf. McIntosh, *Discernment and Truth*, 136.

80. Pickett, *Cross in Corinth*, 155–56, as quoted in McIntosh, *Discernment and Truth*, 140.

perceive the reality of God's infinite love and power (revealed by the cross event). For instance, drawing from Diadochus's discussion on different stages of spiritual development, McIntosh notes that this noetic transformation involves a progression from an initial blindness to the injustice around oneself (due to self-preoccupied indifference), to an awakened righteous hatred and "self-approving indignation," and finally onto a compassionate and patient bearing of the world's brokenness. McIntosh especially underscores this second noetic transition, that is, from a "perception of injustice and consequent anger" for the world's wrongs, to a perception of "the plenitude of God's grace" for the brokenness and injustice of the world.[81] This transition, notes McIntosh, takes an "even more radical abandonment" of the self, an even more daring risk and trust in God's overwhelming mercy: "There is a noetic blindness caused by self-preoccupation, says Diadochus, but there is another more subtle form of mental constriction that can only be healed by an even more radical abandonment and handing over of all into the presence of God. It is relieved, says Diadochus, not by an impatient insistence on one's own rectitude of judgment but by a steady holding of all things up into the plenitude of God's grace" (ibid.). Deriving from Evagrius and Origen, McIntosh points out that to obtain this new noetic vision of reality takes an ascetical process of "self-stripping" or self-denial—which paradoxically liberates the self from its own constrictions and compulsions:

> Evagrius had prescribed for this period a time of patience, stillness, waiting, attention to the other—to use his term, *apatheia*. It is an ascetical process of self-stripping which, paradoxically, does not annihilate but rather liberates the self from its compulsions, from the "higher" temptation to attack violence with more violence, to combat injustice with an insidiously self-approving indignation. . . . The real may accost us only in an experience of futility and darkness. Origen had suggested that ascesis and moral discipline would lead one to a clearer vision in which we begin to sense the true heart of things in themselves (rather than as fantasized by us). But this clarity is a difficult vision in which most of the world of our striving appears as pointless, in vain . . . (ibid.)

---

81. McIntosh, *Discernment and Truth*, 138.

Moreover, McIntosh thinks that a characteristic feature of such a "eschatological noetic"—a new pattern of thinking or seeing for the new era—is a new way of interpreting and understanding the neighbor *vis-à-vis* the new reality opened up by Jesus's self-giving on the cross. Quoting J. Louis Martyn, McIntosh agrees that such knowing "is not in some ethereal sense a spiritual way of knowing. It is not effected in a mystic trance, as the pseudo-apostles had claimed, but rather right in the midst of rough-and-tumble life . . . life in the midst of the new-creation community, in which to know by the power of the cross is precisely to know and to serve the neighbor who is in need."[82] For instance, in contrast to those in the grip of vainglory who crave "to make their struggles known publicly, to hunt after the praise of men,"[83] McIntosh notes a story of a desert father who is free from such obsessions and is thus able to show forth the generosity of divine mercy. The story is about a monk and a virgin who visited an elder and during the night had sexual relations in the elder's cell. After they left the next day they were wondering how the old man could have said nothing to them the whole time. So they went back to the elder and learned that he had indeed been aware of everything. Upon being asked what he was thinking at that time, he answered: "At that time my thoughts were standing where Christ was crucified, and weeping." Profoundly shaken by his deep compassion and grief, the monk and the virgin were converted.[84] McIntosh comments thus: "The elder's mind, fixed on Christ crucified for sinners, is free from the need to assert his own virtue in an act of angry condemnation, free from the fear of losing his own reputation; the cross in this narrative represents God's powerful mercy breaking into the itching, pusillanimous needs of the fallen world, holding open the possibility of a wholly other disposition grounded in the generosity of divine action."[85] McIntosh therefore highlights that such a new way of seeing and relating to others explains the unusual and often thought-provoking humility and patience that

82. Martyn, "Epistemology," 109, as quoted in McIntosh, *Discernment and Truth,* 139.

83. Evagrius, *Praktikos and Chapters,* §13, 19, as quoted in McIntosh, *Discernment and Truth,* 134.

84. Greek Anonymous Series, *Apothegmata Patrum,* N 13, cited in McIntosh, *Discernment and Truth,* 135.

85. McIntosh, *Discernment and Truth,* 135.

the desert fathers exhibit "in the face of many faults and weaknesses."[86] McIntosh quotes Abba Poemen's comments regarding this: "'Greater love hath no man than this that a man lay down his life for his friends' (John 15:13). In truth if someone hears an evil saying, that is, one which harms him, and in his turn, he wants to repeat it, he must fight in order not to say it. Or if someone is taken advantage of and he bears it, without retaliating at all, then he is giving his life for his neighbor.'"[87]

McIntosh notes that the neighbor here is a test for one's spiritual maturity, a test "of the degree to which one is beginning to live into the new reality opened up by the cross."[88] The reason why in the face of injustice one no longer has the need to assert one's own rectitude, McIntosh believes, is because Jesus's death and resurrection ushers in a new order of reality "in which vindication and moral worth and righteousness are not achieved by blotting out the other but by resurrection, by the Father's infinite loving of the other into the new state of being. . . ." (140–41). In other words, the old order "marked by need, condemnation, and rapacity" is now being replaced by a new order of "endless resource" that is full of abundance, generosity, and forgiveness (141). Thus one needs to die to one's old way of thinking about and perceiving of everything and everyone around, in order to truthfully discern the reality that is newly revealed by the divine self-giving love on the cross.

The Mind of Christ: Noetic Significance of Relational Love

As this new order of reality is emerging, McIntosh asks, "what noetic shifts and epistemological possibilities begin to appear?" (ibid.). He then points out that in this transitory stage, one is likely not only to develop from the old mentality to a new one "marked by the paschal mystery," but also to have one's mind awakened by the Holy Spirit to the hidden divine presence (of profound depth and abundance) by participating in Christ's own thinking and knowing (ibid.). This, McIntosh argues, is precisely what it means to "have the mind of Christ" (1 Cor 2:16): "To 'have the mind of Christ' means, I will argue, to think within the framework of Jesus' own fidelity and joy with respect to the Father's abundant life; it

---

86. Ibid., 140.

87. *Sayings of the Desert Fathers*, 184, as quoted in McIntosh, *Discernment and Truth*, 140.

88. McIntosh, *Discernment and Truth*, 140.

also means, therefore, to be drawn into God's own humanly incarnate form of knowing" (142).

McIntosh highlights the vision of the loving divine generosity as "what most crucially marks the Spirit-filled mind of Christ" (ibid.). Noticing Paul's parallel use of *nous* in Philippians 2:5: "Let the same mind be in you that was in Christ Jesus," McIntosh sees that Paul is calling the Philippians, like the Corinthians, to share in the mind of Christ. In the Philippians passage McIntosh notes that a clear characteristic of the mind of Jesus is the freedom to give his own life away, which comes from his confidence in "the outpouring (Spirit) of" the divine resource—including the mercy of God and the power of resurrection (ibid.). Following Maximus, McIntosh suggests that to have the "mind of Christ" is not to lose the human mental power or to have it replaced by something else, but rather, it is by way of a mystical participation in Christ that the human mind "in all its human rationality" is healed and illuminated and energized so that it now learns "to think as Christ thinks" (128). Thus McIntosh reasons that the "mind of Christ," other than negating or replacing native human rationality, is itself "a pattern of rationality" that is "constantly held open by faith to the wideness of God's mercy" (142). In other words, the partaking or sharing in the mind of Christ disposes the mind to understand all things in a way of thinking that is similar to Christ's. Further, this particular pattern of rationality is more than pure reason or a type of individual rationality; rather it has an indispensable relational dimension orienting always toward loving communion. This relational dimension of the mind of Christ can be seen in Diadochus's view that while faith and hope help to free the soul from worldly compulsions and fears, it is love that finally unites the soul with God—the primary knower—making the knowledge of divine truth possible. McIntosh states: "The noetic significance of love cannot be overestimated here. . . . the knowledge that love makes possible is a discernment of the relational ground of all things, their existence in and through and for communion with God and by means of participation in God's triune life" (144). McIntosh thus suggests that a significant constitutive characteristic of the mind of Christ is its relationality of love.

Not only is the mind of Christ orienting toward communion and love, but one can share in the mind of Christ only through participating in loving activities in relation to others. McIntosh notes that for Diadochus, spiritual knowledge cannot be understood by those who do not love, especially those who do not humbly seek out loving reconciliation with people who are alienated from them: "For spiritual knowledge, consisting wholly of love, does not allow the mind (*nous*) to expand and embrace the vision of the divine, unless we first win back to love even one who has become angry with us for no reason."[89] Underlining the crucial role love plays in developing a discerning eye for true knowledge, McIntosh thus contends that access to the knowledge of reality is made possible only by love, because all things exist "in and through and for communion with God and by means of participation in God's triune life."[90]

McIntosh hastens to add that such knowledge—which is made possible by faith, hope, and love—however, is not a kind of purely spiritual knowledge nor is it limited to the religious sphere. First, McIntosh suggests that a "trinitarianly constituted" universe would "make possible a perception of reality in its truest depths" even in scientific investigation. Thus a Christian scientist, while also discovering (say) the same particles as quarks, "would discern such particles in their true identity as expressive events, outpourings, in the infinite exchange of love that is the divine life" (ibid.). Secondly, McIntosh sees that such knowledge has relevance for life beyond the ecclesial realm in the world, for he believes that the existence and the transformation of the church are not taking place in the world "instead of the rest of the universe," but "as a sign to the whole creation of what God has in store for everything" (ibid.).

Drawing again from Diadochus, McIntosh suggests that this relational framework for true knowledge is a result of the reception of God's love in the heart which expands one's whole being with an intense desire for divine truth. This is because the reception of divine love and the subsequent illumination of truth free one from self-preoccupation and the enmities toward others, now making the person available for loving their neighbor (145–46) as Diadochus writes:

> When a man begins to perceive the love of God in all its richness, he begins also to love his neighbour with spiritual perception. This is the love of which all the scriptures speak. Friendship after the flesh is very easily destroyed on some slight pretext. . . . But when a person is spiritually awakened, even if something irritates

89. Diadochus, *Spiritual Knowledge*, §92, 290, as quoted in McIntosh, *Discernment and Truth*, 143.

90. McIntosh, *Discernment and Truth*, 144.

him, the bond of love is not dissolved; rekindling himself with the warmth of the love of God, he quickly recovers himself and with great joy seeks his neighbour's love, even though he has been gravely wronged or insulted by him. For the sweetness of God completely consumes the bitterness of the quarrel.[91]

McIntosh comments that such divine love "inhabits the human relationship, making it possible, and bringing to light within it the amiable truth of the other which God alone (sometimes!) can know."[92] Such "feasting of the perception upon" the luminous love of God fills the mind with a "self-forgetting desire for the other" and prepares it "to risk the truth of the other, rather than merely the fantasized objectification of the other" (ibid.). Put another way, such reception of the generous self-giving divine love leads a person to seek the other's interest and edification—with "an acute insight into the shape of God's loving design for the other"—and to "embrace the destiny of oneself with another, by which to allow God's call to self and neighbor to take flesh and come to life in the world" (ibid.).

Further, McIntosh notes the crucial role that faith (especially faith in Christ's power over death) plays in sharing in the mind of Christ. Faith here is understood in the sense of "the ideas by which the mind knows and seeks to understand what God has accomplished in Christ" (148). McIntosh sees that such faith (or "ideas") "becomes a new cognitive framework by means of which the Holy Spirit 'will guide you into all truth' (John 16:13), re-structuring the mind and prying it open to the infinite, deathless reality of God. This sets the believing community free to enact a new pattern of relationship, free from the fear, envy, and enmity that are death's instruments in controlling the mind" (ibid.). Yet such "ideas" or "new cognitive framework" by virtue of which the mind knows the truth of divine reality are not merely or purely conceptual (while they do include conceptual contents), because the divine reality seems to make itself known through "primarily relational events, acts of mercy and love" (as exemplified by the Incarnation) (ibid.).

Such knowing in faith, then, is a sharing in "the trinitarian event of God's knowing and loving" through which the community, bringing everything in the world eucharistically into this communal event, finds

91. Diadochus, *Spiritual Knowledge*, §15, 256–57, as quoted in McIntosh, *Discernment and Truth*, 146.

92. McIntosh, *Discernment and Truth*, 146.

that "its thoughts are not solely its *own* at all, but God's" (ibid.). Put another way, as the divine and human exchange of love takes place, a new
act of knowing also emerges, a knowing that is "a being known" by the
divine Subject—by sharing in the trinitarian divine life "by which God
knows and loves God" (147). For Paul the church is to be built up as the
temple of the Holy Spirit (Eph 2:19–22), as the dwelling place of the God
of love. In McIntosh's words, the church is to be "the earthly locus and
form of the heavenly exchange of love that is God's life" (ibid.). McIntosh
thus states that his "most basic conviction" is that "sharing in Christ's
mind is knowing, in the provisional form possible in this life, something
of the glory of the Father's love," and such sharing in the mind of Christ
sets the community free to live for one another in a generous self-giving
love (ibid.).

In McIntosh's view, therefore, sharing in the mind of Christ has a
dual orientation or pattern simultaneously: paschal and relational, pre-
supposing both the cross event and a communal context. First, the cross
event reveals two basic truths about the creation: it is loved boundlessly
by God and it has the capacity to live beyond death. Secondly, because
Jesus has destroyed the power of death, now the believing community
can live no longer under the fear of death; this liberates the believers to
freely offer humble service and mutual love to one another. So knowing
with Christ's mind is not simply about acquisition of truths, but rather,
it is about the church's sharing in Christ's relationship with the Father
by loving one another as Christ has loved them (John 14:23; 15:12), and
bringing that eternal life of loving communion—"an expanding possession of the believer by the Father and the Son"—into the midst of the
world of survival and division.[93]

The Life of the Church: The Communal Structure for Knowing Truth

Knowledge of truth is possible only through communion with God,
whereby believers participate in God's own life (of knowing and loving
God). Yet such human participation in the divine life can only happen
through relationships in the communal life, as McIntosh comments:
"The ultimate state of knowing is one in which God is the primal knowing subject in whose act we participate, and that this divine act by which
God is God, knows and loves God, is an exchange of love which can

---

93. See McIntosh, *Discernment and Truth*, 148. The quote is from Alison, *Joy of
Being Wrong*, 189, as quoted in McIntosh here.

only take place in human terms by means of the loving interactions of communal life."[94] McIntosh suggests that such communal life for true knowing and loving can be realized in the common life of the church, because the church comprises "a new network of relations and practices" of believers who have encountered the risen Christ (250; cf. 255). Using the analogy of a poem, McIntosh shows that there is a difference of understanding between, on the one hand, the meaning of individual *words*, and on the other hand, the deeper meaning of the poem that can only be known through its "overall *structure* of meter, rhythm, and rhyme" (250). Yet this latter form of knowing is no less a kind of noetic activity, as McIntosh notes: "It is true that we can partially know the poem by knowing the definition of individual words, but there is another kind of knowing that takes place as we begin to sense the relations between the words. . . . We could say that this structural sensibility comes to inhabit our knowing minds, and it is undoubtedly noetically laden, not so much as a knowledge of objects 'out there' but as a way of thinking and sensing that permits us to apprehend the objects (the particular words) in a whole new horizon of significance" (ibid.). McIntosh thus suggests that it is precisely by means of the church's practices such as "prayer, sacramental life, forgiveness, repentance, and communion"—signs of "the eternal *relational patterns* of the trinitarian life"—that believers are able to realize "a churchly knowing" (of the true reality) that is otherwise unattainable (ibid.). McIntosh likens such churchly or liturgical knowing as "a more overtly communal form" of divine illumination, and such knowing is realized not by way of grasping "a series of truths" but by participating in "an intrinsically sharable reality" of the trinitarian life—through communal practices and activities of self-sharing love (ibid.). For McIntosh, then, "Whatever kind of knowing takes place in the act of being church, it is going to be a knowing that is eventful, that happens, that takes place in practice and activity, and yet for all that is a real form of knowledge" (ibid.). Drawing again from Maximus, McIntosh notes that such "ecclesial noetics" (251)—the organic process of communal knowing—is not merely notional, but involves "a painful yet joyful communal activity" of reconciliation patterned after the Word's own life (254), so much so that the church's knowing is "at the same time the church's life" (255).

Moreover, the church is called to exist as an icon for Jesus's loving relationship with his Abba, as a place to "reconfigure"—according

94. McIntosh, *Discernment and Truth*, 249.

to the divine pattern of love—"the distorted patterns of the world's life" (251). Drawing from Maximus, McIntosh notes that such "distorted patterns" include "painful divisions, rivalries, and mutual recriminations" that arise from people revolving around created things with possessive desires instead of enjoying all things with God as the center of their attention and desire (253). The result is that such people tend to perceive every other creature "as a destructive threat" to their own existence (ibid.). McIntosh observes that for Maximus, to overcome such distorted perceptions and life patterns, the church is called to be "the sign of God's reconciling love" in the world, to exemplify a divine life pattern characterized by unbounded abundance and compassionate relationality—by being first in relationship with the Creator of all things (251). In other words, the forming of such relationships in the Body of Christ—in which believers see each other no longer as enemies but as friends—is made possible by way of the believers' new identities coming from their mutual relationship with God: "this relationship of each creature to the other *by virtue of their mutual relationship to God* releases them from the lethally rivalrous relationships of each creature directly with others" (253). McIntosh also points out that such new relationship with God allows believers to participate in the unifying trinitarian life without canceling out their individual differences. This is possible for them because they can draw upon the divine "unifying power of freedom and love that permits true otherness to exist and fosters true unity without effacing difference" (252). McIntosh thus concludes that discerning truth is inevitably tied to the life of a worshipping community oriented toward the most loving divine Giver of life and everything:

> Spiritual discernment has arisen naturally and most necessarily for such a common life, because it reflects the pressure of a living truth—refusing partiality and bias, pushing beyond individual understanding, opening the discerning community to the creative, self-sharing life from which all truth springs. Discerning truth could never be a lonely form of life. The truth humanity hungers for seems far too large a feast for solitary diners. It requires a sharing far too joyful for any but the truly wise. For they alone discern the depth of thanks most justly due so great a giver. Knowing the giver in each gift, they are themselves set free from small desires and awake to God's desire in every thing; they discern its truth in praise. (255)

Not only does McIntosh understand community as the essential structure for knowing truth, but he also underscores a grander vision that not just human persons, but all things in creation are called to their consummate truth of communion with the divine, which in turn has profound implications for humanity's role in the journey toward truth for all creation—including human creatures themselves. Let us turn now to McIntosh's understanding of the divine destiny for all things in creation and the calling for humanity to assist all things in fulfilling their consummate truth in the divine design.

Fulfilling Destiny: Humanity's Call for Assisting All Things in the Journey of Truth

Noting that Augustine, Bonaventure, and Thomas Aquinas all agree that there is a particular calling or vocation for humanity in bringing out the realization of the destiny or full truth of the material creation (234), McIntosh especially looks to Thomas Traherne (ca. 1637–1674) for elucidating two crucial points. First, all created things—as resonance of the trinitarian communion or as "events of divine self-sharing communication"—are called to fellowship and especially to praise and worship their Creator. Secondly, human beings—endowed with the capacity to understand the Creator's intention in all things—are called to assist and participate in the creatures' truth-faring journey into their consummate reality (237). McIntosh notes that in Traherne's early childhood perception, the world is radiant with divine glory and God's love, and as a sign of God's love, every creature (especially every human being) is given to every other; there is an unending sharing of enjoyment or mutual rejoicing in all this: "the joy each soul delights in is precisely the happiness it is able to give to others" (239). McIntosh sees that this is a glimpse of the heavenly beatific vision (of the end of all things) which, for Traherne, sheds illuminative light in the present: both the calling of all things toward their consummate goal and the role of human beings in fulfilling the destiny for all things (239–40). Yet the blissful vision of Traherne's childhood was soon to be blown out by the "contrary winds" of the needy and grasping mentalities and actions of the adults around him. Oblivious to the gratuitous love and abundance poured out on every side, these "mature" people were busy for smaller possessions, setting their hearts on smaller desires and on whatever they perceived to be valuable for securing their survival and happiness. In effect the

adult mind is blinded or deluded by "the systemically functioning il-
lusion" that deflects its desire "from the vast and endless treasures of
God's giving to the small and artificial treasures of its own manufacture"
and by its "grasping more and more contentiously after less and less"
(241–42). So for Traherne, there is a vital connection between "our ability to receive life gratuitously" and our capacity to perceive the reality of
life truthfully (241).

How do we overcome such misperception of reality? Here Traherne
proposes an unusual solution that, in McIntosh's view, might be called
Traherne's "most characteristic insight" (242). For Traherne, the remedy
involves not abandoning or relinquishing the desires for smaller things,
but embracing or enlarging such desires infinitely to the divine source
of all true bounty and goodness. In other words, rather than the usual
course of rigorous self-denial or self-abnegation, Traherne moves toward "a growing reception of God's bounty, not the extinguishing of his
natural desire but the enlarging of it immeasurably" (ibid.). McIntosh
sees in this a "marvelous freedom to embrace all things as themselves,
each and every one uniquely, opportunities for communion with the divine Giver of all things" (238). Thus we need first to (re)learn to perceive
all things (including ourselves) in the light of the infinite self-sharing
generosity of our divine Giver in order to be able to perceive the truth
of reality alright. As McIntosh comments: "Unless the very principles of
God's life—the profligate extravagance and infinite self-sharing—have
become present in our minds, we do not in fact know how to think
about things at all" (241).

For Traherne, as we begin to see and think about things as God
does, that is, as we begin to be illuminated by God's intention and ideas
of things as well as by the divine bounty and goodness in all things, we
begin to be transformed from an anxious and fearful grasping of possessions to a more generous giving and sharing of all things, namely,
from the mentality of the slave of destitution to that of the son of abundance. McIntosh comments thus: "To do so is 'to imitate our Infinite and
Eternal Father,' who holds nothing back but pours out everything to the
Beloved Son, who likewise does not grasp after his equality with God
but empties himself again" (244). Indeed, notes McIntosh, it is a joy for
God to be good and generous and loving to each and every creature, and
it especially delights God when any of the creatures notices this divine

goodness and seeks to imitate it with a similar generous self-giving love for others (245).

Yet ignorant of such glorious divine goodness, human beings are trapped in "grudging envy and possessive strife," and this, for Traherne, is what the Incarnation and Passion of Jesus work to undo. Traherne understands that Jesus's death on the cross lets us see in a temporally or "historically visible" form God's self-outpouring love for humanity, and it also draws us up into its ground in the eternal loving of "the inner-trinitarian life of God" (246). Further, the resurrection and Pentecost recreate in us a new capacity for loving and knowing analogous to what takes place within the life of the Trinity. As McIntosh comments: "The Son's own capacity to know and love the Father becomes present by the Holy Spirit within us, and this makes possible our own new discernment of all reality; for animated by the same Love with which the Father and the Son know and love each other, we are imbued with their own understanding of all things" (ibid.).

McIntosh then highlights Traherne's understanding that creation is an expression of God's wisdom and order in such a way that other intelligent beings, especially human beings, can perceive in creation a definite meaning and truth, and can assist in the truth-faring journey of all things toward their divinely purported goal. This is because, Traherne believes, God designs the intelligent beings as being able to perceive the divine intention in the universe and to "draw order out of confusion."[95] McIntosh notices a distinction in Traherne that is very similar to that made by Augustine between things and signs (which point beyond themselves to the Creator), for Traherne sees that there is a difference between seeing things narrowly "as instrumental to our own purposes" and seeing them in the much larger picture "as a beautiful feature of a vast mosaic."[96] This larger vision, in Traherne's view, does not disallow our use and enjoyment of things, but rather points to "their value as signs, sacraments, messages to us from God"; in other words, "everything has a double availability for us, as meeting our present needs and as drawing us more and more into that heavenly communion that is the real goal of existence" (ibid.). McIntosh remarks on what such a more contemplative understanding of creation can bring about for appreciating the goodness of all things: "by understanding everything in this

---

95. Traherne, *Centuries*, 3.31, as quoted in McIntosh, *Discernment and Truth*, 244.
96. McIntosh, *Discernment and Truth*, 242.

more contemplative way . . . by feeding not only the body's hunger for food but the mind's keenness for truth and the spirit's yearning for communion, the greater goodness deep down within all things becomes all the more available" (243). Here McIntosh underlines God's designs and goals for all things—to come into communion with God—as the larger context that sheds light on seeing not only the sacramental truth of all things, but also humanity's capacity to know in all things their consummate truth: "Because God has created all things with a purposive intent, that is, to draw the universe into communion with God, all things are . . . marked and configured to be intelligible, readable, to other minds capable of grasping purpose and intention" (244).

With such a capacity to know the divine destiny for all things to come into communion with God, how can humanity foster the journey of all things progressing toward their perfect truth as designed by God? While we are used to thinking of things purely in their physical form, notes McIntosh, this is a reductive reading of things that is most peculiar to our modern mindset. Traherne, however, is concerned not so much with what our physical eyes see in things as with what the eyes of our mind perceive in them or what affections we have for esteeming them.[97] Just as the mind is capable of conceiving God's purposive design for many things, it is also capable of esteeming them in the imagination as well as praising God for them—"as signs of God's love and as gifts to rejoice the recipients and the giver too."[98] As the believer is thus appreciating these things and praising God for them, they are transmuted into their "highest form of existence"—lifted up into their "communion with God" (ibid.). In so doing, the believers, not just the things they praise God for, are fulfilling also the truths of their own creation for sharing in the fullness of divine joy and eternal pleasure (ibid.). McIntosh thus comments: "When believers learn to know things according to God's idea of them and to rejoice in the gift of them and to praise God for that gift, they are lifting up those existing things into the flowing of giving and receiving praise and delight, that is the life of God" (ibid.). As this happens, "Things are no longer things, but moments of relationship, events in the life of heaven begun on earth" (248). As we are receiving and rejoicing in these things as gifts from God, notes McIntosh, we come to "know the deepest truth of them" and to give delight to God

97. Traherne, *Centuries*, 3.68, as quoted in McIntosh, *Discernment and Truth*, 247.
98. McIntosh, *Discernment and Truth*, 247.

"who created them to be enjoyed" (ibid.). In Traherne's view, such know-ing of the deepest truth of creaturely things is by virtue of the mind's bringing down God's blessings on them—accomplished through praises which fosters the fulfillment of their divine destiny. In a world filled with such praises, "you see the Blessed Sight of all men's praises ascending, and of all God's blessings coming down upon them."[99] The mind's role in the journey of truth, therefore, lies in thanking and praising God for the created things—in so doing we come to know the truth of their reality and to fulfill the truth of ourselves as well as the created things.

While the foregoing themes in McIntosh might have concentrated on understanding how the human part can cooperate with divine grace in the divine-human process of transformation, McIntosh also high-lights an important theme in the spiritual traditions, namely, the role that the Holy Spirit plays in the transformational journey of the human person. It is to McIntosh's understanding of this significance of the Holy Spirit that we now turn.

The Holy Spirit: Divine Love for Transformation

McIntosh notes that for Evagrius the soul is to cultivate such virtues as justice, understanding, wisdom, prudence, courage, patience, con-tinence, temperance, and charity; and such cultivation and practice of virtue "directly promotes a crucial first step in discernment, namely an awareness of the true origin of one's impulses and urgencies."[100] The goal for this ascetical progress in virtue is charity, which, for Evagrius, is the "doorkeeper" to the house of knowledge. Diadochus, a generation after Evagrius, subsumes these various moral and intellectual virtues mainly under the first two theological virtues of faith and hope, but like Evagrius, he also regards love (*agape*) as the governing force for "the contemplative goal of a discerning life" (ibid.).

Yet Diadochus believes, notes McIntosh, that the Holy Spirit plays a significant role in this progress of virtue, for the virtues are "the shin-ing forth of the Spirit's transforming presence" (88). For Diadochus the mind is constantly diverted from reality for it is subjected to "the suasion of demonic fantasy, false promises" and illusionary pleasures as well as to anxieties, fears, and obsessions (87). The Spirit's intervention

---

99. Traherne, *Centuries*, 2.94, as quoted in McIntosh, *Discernment and Truth*, 248.
100. McIntosh, *Discernment and Truth*, 87.

is necessary for purifying the mind and freeing it from its captivity to the demonic passions, because it is the light of the Spirit that inflames in the soul, "the lamp of spiritual knowledge burning always within" that exposes "all the dark and bitter attacks of the demons."[101] This darkness and bitterness will be dispelled by the "communion of the Holy Spirit"— which illumines the heart so that it is able "to taste God's goodness."[102] McIntosh notes that this foretaste of divine goodness and unbounded love awakens the soul not only to a deep longing for God, but also to a new discerning perceptivity to view everything "in terms of their divine destiny"; so for Diadochus, love—especially, experiencing divine love engendered by the Holy Spirit—is the midwife of true knowledge.[103]

Several centuries later, observes McIntosh, Catherine of Siena "strongly confirms the synthetic role of love, desire, and the Holy Spirit in the progress toward a discerning mind" (89). Like Diadochus, while believing that practice of virtue is a prerequisite, Catherine sees that any real growth in discernment can occur only when the soul comes to feed upon the divine love poured out by the Spirit. For her the soul's eye is blinded by the dazzling glitter of the things in the world that appeal to the soul's appetite for goodness and loveliness; yet, as noted by McIntosh, the soul is "created for a far greater communion" and so it cannot be satisfied by the delusional effort for smaller loves (ibid.). For Catherine the soul's memory, understanding, and will have fallen sick through self-love, and their healing must take place through a reorientation to divine love and *by* divine love.

McIntosh notes that for Catherine the starting place for formation of a discerning mind is not self-awareness, but the restoration of the soul from its self-centered love through "its enlightenment by the vision of *God's* love for it" which "sets the mind free to discern truth" (90). This conversion to God's love occurs through repentance and purification just as Jesus's first disciples went through during the days between the resurrection and Pentecost: "they persevered in watching and constant humble prayer until they were filled with the Holy Spirit."[104] Yet such

101. Diadochus, *Spiritual Knowledge*, §28, as quoted in McIntosh, *Discernment and Truth*, 87.

102. Diadochus, *Spiritual Knowledge*, §29, as quoted in McIntosh, *Discernment and Truth*, 88.

103. McIntosh, *Discernment and Truth*, 88.

104. Catherine of Siena, *Dialogue*, §63, as quoted in McIntosh, *Discernment and Truth*, 90.

purification and formation for discernment, for Catherine, has nothing to do with "a self-preoccupied remorse," but rather, it is crucially linked to "a genuine lifting up of the heart to feast again upon the fullness of God's mercy and abundance."[105] McIntosh observes that Catherine carefully probes the "reciprocal influence of heart and mind, will and understanding," for in her view: "The blazing divine charity both enkindles and enlightens; perhaps we could even say that it reveals truth precisely because it transforms *human* loving into divine loving *in* humanity—and this loving as God loves makes possible a vision of reality as it is in truth" (90–91).

As this conversion to God's love for humanity is experienced in the historical context of God's mercy in Christ, McIntosh points out that far more than the previous desert traditions, Catherine explicitly roots "the whole formation process in a growing attunement to Christ" (91). Thus true discernment is, for Catherine, none other than to taste and see God's love and goodness in the Spirit—with the eyes of Christ (or to "have the mind of Christ" as Paul puts it): "Through the flesh of Christ crucified, we suck the milk of divine sweetness, sweet light where no shadows fall. . . . This is what our enlightened understanding sees and contemplates as it gazes steadily into the eye of God's divine charity and goodness."[106] Noting that this transformation of consciousness happens when the risen Christ "breathes the Holy Spirit upon the disciples" (John 20:22), McIntosh sees that this Pentecost theme is echoed by Thomas Traherne in his view that it is in the fire of the divine Love, the Holy Spirit, that one is illuminated to see and possess all the things in the universe.[107]

In sum, McIntosh contends that the habits of mind that are characterized by anxiety and fear are keeping company with folly—incapable of comprehending the truth of reality—and thus personal transformation of the would-be discerners is "the great prerequisite" for discerning divine truth (8). The path of transformation is pointed out by the cross of Christ which reveals the infinite mercy and overwhelming abundance of the Abba for humankind, as well as the triumph over the ultimate fear and enemy of humanity—death. To have the mind of Christ is to

105. McIntosh, *Discernment and Truth*, 90.

106. Catherine of Siena, *Letters*, 266, as quoted in McIntosh, *Discernment and Truth*, 91.

107. McIntosh, *Discernment and Truth*, 11–12.

be drawn into Jesus's relationship with the Father, and so become accustomed to think in terms of the Father's boundless love for both humanity and all other created things. Such a mind of Christ can be formed by an ascetical process of self-stripping, especially by dying to one's possessive desires and obsessive worries through participating in the communal life of loving self-giving to others, through thanking and praising God for the divine loving purposes in all created things, and through encountering God's love, revealed in Christ, poured out into the human heart by the Holy Spirit. With this understanding of McIntosh's views of the relationship between discernment and transformation, let us proceed to a mutual dialogue between McIntosh and Nee.

NEE AND MCINTOSH IN DIALOGUE

Both Nee and McIntosh are emphatic about the point that discerning the divine will is not so much a matter of technique, but of personal formation of the discerners in their relationships with God. This view especially finds its support in Augustine's understanding that the human capacity to know truth depends upon the individual's moral condition. According to Nash, Augustine maintains that the source of all knowledge is divine and the condition of all knowledge is revelation, yet humans have different capacity to know such revelation—to varying degrees—depending on their moral purity.[108] Augustine sees that sin keeps people from being aware of God in either the visible creation or in the invisible eternal kingdom. In other words, depending on the purity of the soul, there will be varying results in the human perceptions and conceptions of truth.[109] Just as only the pure in heart can truly see God, true divine wisdom also has the quality or effect of purity as James 3:17 describes: "But the wisdom from above is first pure, then peaceable, gentle, willing to yield, full of mercy and good fruits, without a trace of partiality or hypocrisy." In short, both Nee's and McIntosh's understandings that personal formation is a critical prerequisite for true discernment concur with Augustine's views that the different degrees of human knowledge of truth are determined by the extent to which the human subjects participate in the pure and truthful reality of God.

---

108. Nash, *Light of the Mind*, 123.

109. Ibid., 122–23.

Submitting to Circumstances: "New Asceticism" of Ordinary Living

While teaching that the means of grace includes scripture reading, prayer, fellowship, service, and other traditional practices, Nee stresses that the greatest means of grace is the everyday happenings in one's circumstance, as these are specially arranged by the Holy Spirit for one's best benefits. Yet whether one can effectively receive such grace depends on one's attitude: while a grumbling and complaining heart drives out divine grace, a yielding as well as praising and thankful heart opens one to receiving the grace of God. This explains why Nee often did not defend or explain himself when being opposed or misunderstood adversely, as he himself exhorts the believers to "be joyful always" and to "give thanks in all circumstances" (1 Thess 5:16, 18).[110]

This accent on accepting oppositions and adversities with submission and gratitude might sound off note to contemporary ears, yet it is a theme that appears repeatedly in the history of Christian spirituality. For instance, McIntosh notes that Abba Poemen in the desert says thus: "If someone is taken advantage of and he bears it, without retaliating at all, then he is giving his life for his neighbor."[111] McIntosh also points out that for Jonathan Edwards, authentic marks of growth in discernment include such signs as "genuine charity toward one's enemies, patience with the erring, and a ceaseless practice of forgiveness."[112] True discerning hearts, in Edwards's words, "are attended with the lamblike, dovelike spirit and temper of Jesus Christ, or in other words, they naturally beget and promote such a spirit of love, meekness, quietness, forgiveness and mercy, as appeared in Christ."[113]

Contemporary to Nee in the twentieth century, Simone Weil (1909–1943) and novelist Iris Murdoch both speak of not only the "mysterious beauty" embedded in the world, but also the painstaking process it usually takes in order to behold such beauty and in order for the beholder to be transformed. As McIntosh notes: "Iris Murdoch . . .

---

110. Nee, *Yao changchang xile* [Be joyful always], esp. 7, 10, 14–18, 39–41, 61–64; also see Nee, "Zanmei" [Praise], 285–304; S. C. T. Chan, *Wo de jiufu Ni Tuosheng* [My uncle, Watchman Nee], 51–52; and Y. D. Lin, *Shizijia* [Cross], esp. 9, 17.

111. *Sayings of the Desert Fathers*, 184, as quoted in McIntosh, *Discernment and Truth*, 140.

112. McIntosh, *Discernment and Truth*, 208, 112.

113. Edwards, *Religious Affections*, 344–45, as quoted in McIntosh, *Discernment and Truth*, 111.

portrayed mysterious moments of awakening and new discernment, usually the result of some crisis, in which reality inscribes its true form (often very harshly) upon the unwilling ego. Simone Weil often speaks of this 'affliction' that either destroys the soul or sets it free. It is a painful exposure to the waves of necessity and circumstance that gradually wash into the soul some recovering memory of a truth and reality quite beyond its own manufacture."[114]

Appealing to the analogy of a sculptor who must bear with his or her hands the pain of working on a precious piece of art, McIntosh explains the "necessity" of the painful, embodied process in coming to "know" any true beauty in the world: "There are some patterns of reality so deep and so ungraspable that they only become known to us, to begin with, by their gradual patterning of our own being, taking up residence within us like the painstaking acquisition of the skill of a sculptor. It is as if there were a secret to this beauty so profound it can only be known by the muscles and nerves of the hands that serve it, while it remains hidden from the mind that perhaps too easily suborns it to smaller self-gratifying ends."[115]

Expounding on Maximus, McIntosh writes: "This means that each gift of existence and deified existence bears within it the power and character of Christ's paschal mystery. So for example when Maximus talks of the soul passing from death to life in Christ, he is not using the resurrection of Christ as a metaphorical aid in describing deification; rather, he is saying that what deifies the believer is precisely a sharing in Christ's dying and rising."[116] Again, McIntosh states: "Maximus makes quite clear that the pilgrimage in Christ leads *through* the mystery of the Cross of the Sixth Day, not around it: 'Absolutely no heavenly or earthly power can know these days before experiencing the passion, only the blessed divinity which created them.'"[117] Also, as we have seen in this chapter, McIntosh's exposition on Traherne about humanity's role in assisting the creation toward their consummate journey of truth is not without echoes for Nee's emphasis on giving thanks and praises in all circumstances. For in Traherne's view, it is precisely through thanking and praising God for all created things, that both the created things

114. McIntosh, *Discernment and Truth*, 206–7.
115. Ibid., 207.
116. McIntosh, *Mystical Theology*, 58.
117. Ibid., 59. His quote is from Maximus, "Chapters on Knowledge," 138.

and human beings themselves are reaching toward fulfilling their God-designed truths. McIntosh thus comments: "This brings us to the idea of accomplishing the truth through praise, of thinking by thanking. For Traherne suggests that when the mind, imbued with trinitarian principles of understanding, begins to prize all creatures as they should be, then the mind in fact helps to accomplish the ultimate truth of all creatures by lifting them up into communion with God. . . . His concern is not so much what we see 'as with what eyes we behold them' . . . So the fulfillment of each thing can only be as it is esteemed as a gift from God, receive and delighted in . . ."[118] While Traherne here speaks mostly about praising and thanking God for the gift of all created things, it seems not too far a stretch to see such gift as encompassing life circumstances that inevitably play out with and in the creation, and so to praise and thank God for all the gifts of circumstances as well. At any rate, the tradition that McIntosh expounds on stands in good company with Nee for his conviction that the adverse circumstances in one's life, if responded to properly, are the grace-filled way of the cross that eventually leads to the presence of glory and joy.

While Nee's particular insights might well be the fruit of the "precious lessons" that he learned from Barber,[119] one could not help but notice the striking similarity between Nee's views of the "discipline of the Holy Spirit" as the greatest means of grace and the recommendation of John Wesley (one of Nee's sources of inspiration) to "cheerfully bear your cross" in his teaching of the "prudential" means of grace.[120] It may thus be helpful to take a closer look at Wesley's understanding in this matter.

Wesley is convinced that not just problems with people, but also suffering and losses of any kind, are to be seen as potential channels of receiving divine grace, because everything and every moment in life should be seen in relation to God.[121] Since God is present to us in every situation, our job is to "respond to the pushes and pulls of God" in our circumstances.[122] Wesley especially emphasizes the passive part we play in the midst of suffering: "We ought quietly to suffer whatever

118. McIntosh, *Discernment and Truth*, 247.

119. See chapter 1 of this book. See also Y. D. Lin, *Shizijia* [Cross], 17.

120. Wesley, "Several Conversations," 322–24.

121. Oden, *Wesley's Scriptural Christianity*, 312.

122. Moore, "Wesleyan Spirituality," 295.

befalls us, to bear the defects of others, and our own, to confess them to
God in secret prayer, . . .but never to speak a sharp or peevish word . . .
We are his lambs, and therefore ought to be ready to suffer, even to the
death, without complaining."[123] Further, suffering is to be recognized as
a special favor from God: "One of the greatest evidences of God's love to
those that love him is to send them afflictions with grace to bear them."[124]
Indeed, Wesley believes that one should receive suffering with a grateful
heart because suffering is the royal road leading to divine grace: "The
best helps to growth in grace are the ill usage, the affronts, and the losses
which befall us. We should receive them with all thankfulness, as prefer-
able to all others. . . ."[125]

Lying at the center of Wesley's prudential means of grace is the idea
of accepting whatever comes one's way as the will of God, or as channels to further receiving divine grace. The goal, then, is to reach, amidst
outward suffering, inward calmness and peace. Referring to the image of
the calmness in the bottom of the sea while its surface is stormy, Wesley
upholds that the inner soul should always remain in deep peace amidst
many outward troubles.[126] What is more, merely aiming at inner peace
of mind is not enough, but outwardly as well, one should also strive to
appear gentle and meek in front of others as a way of showing God's love
for them: "Why should not even your outward *appearance* and *manner* be soft? Remember the character of Lady Cutts: 'It was said of the
Roman Emperor, Titus, never anyone came displeased from him. But
it might be said of her, never anyone went displeased to her. So secure
were all of the kind and favorable reception which they would meet with
from her.'"[127] For Wesley, then, suffering and pain are the catalysts to
receive transformational grace,[128] and the bearing of them in peace is
the essence of Christian life: "The bearing men, and suffering evils in
meekness and silence, is the sum of a Christian life."[129]

123. Wesley, "Christian Perfection," 368.

124. Ibid.

125. Ibid.

126. Ibid.

127. Ibid., 366.

128. Joy, "Vocational Ideals in the Wesleyan Tradition," 302.

129. Wesley, "Christian Perfection," 369.

In short, Wesley's prudential means of grace prescribes a kind of "conscious involvement" in one's daily life.[130] The key is to recognize, in every situation of one's life, the "pushes and pulls" of the divine presence: the invitation to love one's neighbor—as both active service and patient forbearance—as well as the call to self-denial and submission to the will of God in suffering. Such means of grace is intended for ordinary believers who are "in the world," and what is said of Jesuit spirituality as being a form of "new asceticism" can be rightly said of Wesleyan spirituality as well: "a new asceticism begins to emerge that is not dependent for its practice on self-imposed austerities to curb one's own disordered tendencies, but on the rigors and hardship imposed by total dedication to an ideal of ministry in the world of ordinary people, with their often undisciplined needs and demands."[131] We can therefore see that Nee's emphasis on "the discipline of the Holy Spirit" in the circumstances of life has a great deal in common with this "new asceticism" of Wesleyan as well as Jesuit spirituality. This is so in their common conviction that all the contingencies and exigencies in our ordinary daily existence are to be viewed as divine providence for our good—as divinely measured graces for the growth of our perfection in love of God and neighbor, for the increase of our discerning capacity to "finding God in all things" and serving "the greater glory of God."[132]

Self-Will and Divine Will: Irresolvable Tension or Relational Identity?

A closely related issue in Nee's teaching is about surrendering the self-will in order to be available for the divine will. Lee Ken Ang suggests that Nee's theological system is too dualistic such that "the polar tension" between the will of a Christian and the will of God becomes irresolvable, "invariably escalated with great intensity, with no hope of relief."[133] This perception seems to be off focus especially in light of Nee's understanding of the life pattern of Jesus as well as similar spiritual writings in the Christian tradition.

130. See Schneiders, "Study of Christian Spirituality," 1, 3. Schneiders used the phrase in her definition of spirituality.

131. O'Malley, "Early Jesuit Spirituality," 8.

132. See O'Malley, "Early Jesuit Spirituality," 12, 18. "To find God in all things" is Ignatius of Loyola's customary exhortation to his followers, and "the greater glory of God" is also one of his favorite expressions.

133. K. Lee, "Watchman Nee," 180–81.

McIntosh notes that for Catherine of Siena "the governing polarity" in the spiritual life is "the struggle within the soul between self-will and the attractive power of the divine will."[134] Thus Catherine sees that discernment is not a matter of mere "judicious balance," but of "awakening love" for the goodness of God, especially for "the good that God longs to accomplish in the soul."[135] In other words, a truly discerning heart perceives everything "precisely in terms of God's will to bring the soul to blessedness."[136] Similarly, for Ignatius the spiritual life is "to discern and serve the divine will in all things," and so spiritual discernment is based on the reorientation of one's desire and the harmonious communion between the human will and the divine will.[137] Ignatius "subordinates everything, even one's own happiness, to the praise and service of God,"[138] and he encourages those seeking God to be saturated by the same Spirit "who animates Jesus' own desire to do the Father's will."[139] As Hans Urs von Balthasar comments, Ignatius sees that "human nature, even when it is elevated by grace, cannot act as the guide for man in his praise, reverence, and service of God; ultimately such guidance can only come from God and revelation of his will."[140]

Nee emphasizes the need to depend wholly on God and not on our own idea or will, because this is what the cross of Christ has modeled for us: "For only a thorough understanding of the Cross can bring us to that place of dependence which the Lord Jesus Himself voluntarily took when He said: 'I can of myself do nothing: as I hear, I judge: and my judgment is righteous; because I seek not mine own will, but the will of him that sent me'" (John 5:30).[141] Commenting on the same verse, McIntosh also notes that Christ's life is characterized by his "undivided pursuit of God's will."[142] Nee's understanding is also similar to that of Wesley. For Wesley, since every experience in life is to

134. McIntosh, *Discernment and Truth*, 54–55.

135. Ibid, 55.

136. Ibid., 56.

137. Ibid., 67, 72.

138. McIntosh, *Mystical Theology*, 106.

139. McIntosh, *Discernment and Truth*, 69.

140. Von Balthasar, *Thérèse of Lisieux*, 225–26, as quoted in McIntosh, *Mystical Theology*, 106.

141. Nee, *Normal Christian Life*, 164.

142. McIntosh, *Discernment and Truth*, 19.

be seen in relation to God, and since no human being would naturally will to suffer, suffering provides a special occasion to deny one's own will and to conform it to the will of God: "True *resignation* consists in a thorough conformity to the whole will of God, who wills and does all (excepting sin) which comes to pass in the world. In order to this we have only to embrace all events, good and bad, as his will."[143] Not only are we to see God's hand in every situation and embrace it cheerfully, but we are also to willingly endure suffering "as long as God pleases."[144] Here the notion of resignation, understood as not to resist the prompting of divine grace, seems to be the key to understand the outworking of grace in one's life, as David Lowes Watson comments: "The dynamic of this was a divine initiative which the human will was always able, with the freedom of prevenient grace, to resist. The path to perfection, therefore, was a growth in obedience to the divine initiative—a learning how not to resist the grace of God."[145] For Wesley such resignation on the part of Christ's disciples is a way to imitate the Master after his pattern of abandoning himself into the hand of God as well as bearing upon himself the infirmities of humankind.[146]

Likewise, McIntosh connects "the ultimate form of apophaticism"[147] of the paschal mystery with "the fact that to be human means to be crucified."[148] He regards the darkening moments of agonizing suffering (in terms of both knowing and being) that Jesus went through in the final hours before his death as the ultimate apophasis that is made necessary by the human limitations as a consequence of sin:

> As Jesus moves towards the Cross, his sense of identity as God's beloved becomes complicated, darkened. As he is drawn into further participation in the Father's will, so the infinity and absoluteness of the Father become overwhelming to him: to enact, to *be*, the Word of this One is necessarily to go beyond the perceived limits of human knowing and loving (precisely because our broken version of what it means to be human is cut short by sin). To speak this Word in a life lived out in the language of

---

143. Wesley, "Christian Perfection," 368.

144. Ibid.

145. Watson, "Methodist Spirituality," 224.

146. Wesley, "Christian Perfection," 368–69.

147. McIntosh, *Mystical Theology*, 100.

148. McCabe, *God Matters*, 93, as quoted in McIntosh, *Mystical Theology*, 133.

our world is to be reduced to silence. To interpret his identity as Word in the full depths of its mystery leads Jesus into the darkening apophasis of his final hours.[149]

Thus in the historical life, death, and resurrection of the Son, there can be seen a paradoxical pattern in the trinitarian dynamic, a pattern of self-loss and self-fulfillment at the same time: "a pattern inherently self-dispossessive and yet self-constitutive in its dispossession-for-the-other."[150]

McIntosh therefore points out that the loss of self in loving others is a necessary step in the realization of one's true selfhood as noted by various spiritual writers. For instance, Edith Stein sees that true personal freedom "can only be consummated by the soul's self-surrender to God,"[151] as McIntosh comments: "Stein certainly believed that she had found in her self-abandonment to God another self, a true self which lives not by fleeing from the suffering of others and herself but by weaving them into the eternal divine giving, the trinitarian abandonment of God to God."[152] Similarly, Simone Weil understands "the giving away of the self, even in suffering, as the constitution of the self—precisely in terms of the emplacement of the self within the intra-trinitarian self-giving."[153] McIntosh especially underlines this trinitarian understanding in Weil's view of the self: "The whole universe exists in this opening up of the divine being, in the risky stretching apart of the love between the First and Second Persons of the Trinity. The Spirit who sustains the bond between God and God is the love who sustains us also in our afflictions. So for the human subject 'our misery gives us the infinitely precious privilege of sharing in this distance placed between the Son and his Father.'"[154] A close parallel to this, according to McIntosh, is Eckhart's view that personal identity is consummated precisely "in breaking through to this paradoxical trinitarian life where one *is* only by being wholly for the other."[155]

This language of self-denial and self-abnegation might raise a concern in the mind of contemporary women that such calls have usually

149. McIntosh, *Mystical Theology*, 133.

150. Ibid., 135.

151. Ibid., 229.

152. Ibid., 232–33.

153. Ibid., 234.

154. Ibid. The quotation is from Weil, *Waiting for God*, 127.

155. McIntosh, *Mystical Theology*, 227.

been issued by men while "women were expected to heed."[156] McIntosh, however, points to the trinitarian language in both Edith Stein and Simone Weil that may extricate both women and men from such a predicament: "the trinitarian mutuality of self-dispossession is an eternally affirming, life-constituting reality. . . . No Person of the Trinity can *be* except by giving the whole divine essence to the others, yet that absolute—indeed infinite—kenosis is not the termination of the divine life but its very basis and meaning."[157] Commenting on John of the Cross, McIntosh notes that as the soul is increasingly participating in this trinitarian pattern of life, there emerges "a relational identity whose selfhood and agency is constituted by receiving all from and giving all freely to the other."[158] In John's exploration into the mysterious depth of the soul's gifted desire—given by the Holy Spirit—for union with her bridegroom, McIntosh observes that there is "the 'space,' the room for alterity and authentic human agency, even in that most intimate union of self-giving marked by sharing in the cross."[159] As John writes: "He will show her how to love Him as perfectly as she desires . . . As if he were to put an instrument in her hands and show her how it works by operating it jointly with her. He shows her how to love and gives her the ability to do so."[160]

Following Edith Wyschogrod, McIntosh notes that "while saintly life is characterized by renunciation and *loss* of self, the consequent action of the saint in respect of the other is an *empowerment*."[161] Drawing from both Rowan Williams and Denys Turner, McIntosh points out that in Augustine's view, selfhood is "something altogether more *relational*

---

156. Ibid., 235.

157. Ibid. For an insightful and nuanced analysis of, and response to, the feminist critiques of humility, see Ruddy, *Christological Approach to Virtue*, 33–46, 234–57.

158. McIntosh, "Trinitarian Perspectives," 183.

159. Ibid.

160. John of the Cross, *Spiritual Canticle*, 554, as quoted in McIntosh, "Trinitarian Perspectives," 183. For an insightful discussion on a feminist perspective regarding the issue of the Spirit and agency, McIntosh suggests to see Coakley, *Powers and Submissions*.

Another concern that might be raised here is the question of whether premature practice of self-denial is unhealthy for psychological development. This is a complex question that is beyond the scope of this book. For my own attempt to integrate some of the psychological and feminist concerns in the practice of Christian humility, see D. Wu, "Humility, Maturity, and Transformation."

161. McIntosh, *Mystical Theology*, 216–17, commenting on Wyschogrod, *Saints and Postmodernism*, 58.

than is usually supposed."[162] This relationality is seen first of all in one's relation with the divine Other. For Augustine, the Doctor of Grace, in our seeking to surrender to the divine call, "the self-in-relation to that Other" is not so much acting out of its own initiative, but only making itself available to be drawn into the activity of God, who is "the primary agent" that has been actively seeking all the time to bring each willful lost sheep to willingly come to the truly abundant life.[163] Such a view of relational selfhood is aptly pointed out by this contemporary semi-popular saying: personal identity is not so much about "*who* am I?" but "*whose* am I?" McIntosh therefore suggests that the basis of our human selfhood is constituted "in the infinite self-giving" of God's life, which is constantly seeking us out and beckoning us to give ourselves away in love for the other—by placing the "finite gifts of ourselves" ultimately "into the hands of *God*."[164] We can see, therefore, that Nee's teaching on surrendering the self-will resonates very well with some significant voices in the history of Christian spirituality, and so the fear for annihilation of the self-will that Nee's critics conceive is not warranted at all.

The Body of Christ: Communal Practices of Obedience and Love

Nee also points to the link between the denial of self-will and the relational identity of the self, especially as a member in the corporate Body of Christ. Nee notes that the event of Christ's death and resurrection issues forth a new creation—recreating each believer to become naturally gravitating toward the life of others in the Body of Christ: "Yes, the Cross must do its work here . . . in resurrection I have become not just an individual believer in Christ but a member of His Body. . . . The life of Christ in me will gravitate to the life of Christ in others. I can no longer take an individual line. Jealousy will go. Competition will go. Private work will go. My interests, my ambitions, my preferences, all will go. It will no longer matter which of us does the work. All that will matter will be that the Body grows."[165] Seeing each believer as a member of the body whose head is Christ, Nee insists on the paramount importance of not giving up on gathering together (as is exhorted in Hebrews 10:25). Nee thus

---

162. McIntosh, *Mystical Theology*, 220–21.

163. Ibid., 221–22.

164. Ibid., 239.

165. Nee, *Normal Christian Life*, 147–48.

adamantly advocates participating in the life of the church as a means of receiving surpassing "corporate grace" for both the individual and the church.[166] Nee's perspective, May notes, looks very much similar to his German contemporary Dietrich Bonhoeffer (1906–1945), who addresses the significance of Christian fellowship in his book *Life Together*.

Like Nee, McIntosh sees the supreme significance of the church's communal life, though emphasized mainly for the purposes of acquiring spiritual discernment and divine knowledge. For McIntosh, the Christian journey is accomplished through the ecclesial community after the paschal pattern of dying and rising—dying especially to narrow self-knowledge and self-identity, and rising with a truly free and joyful relational identity of ourselves as sons and daughters in the family of God. McIntosh understands that the community of the church is the basic structure for knowing truth and the dimension of love is an irreducible constitution of the mind of Christ. Drawing upon Robert Jewett's comments on Paul's use of *nous* in 1 Corinthians 2:16, McIntosh quotes: "If it [the mind of Christ] is the basis on which the church is to be united (1 Cor 1:10) . . . , then it must be more than an individual rational capacity. . . . I would say that *nous* is a complex of thoughts and assumptions which can make up the consciousness of a person. . . . It is a constellation of thoughts which is given in the gospel and as such it provides the basis for unity in the church."[167] McIntosh suggests that such a "constellation of thoughts" is "too large" to be thought by any individualistic effort, thus the communal life of the church is indispensable for any authentic knowledge of God.[168] Similarly, Stephen C. Barton emphasizes that true wisdom is "*mediated* wisdom" acquired in the company of those who embody it and in the context of "obedient discipleship" both within the church and in mission works: "the wisdom which Jesus teaches is a hidden, heavenly wisdom, not reducible to matters of empirical observation or existential need, but pointing instead to a transcendental reality discerned only by faith and in the context of obedient discipleship."[169]

Both Nee and McIntosh also appreciate the significance of the eucharistic communion for the spiritual journey. Parallel to Nee's

---

166. G. Y. May, "Breaking of Bread," 243–45.

167. Jewett, *Paul's Anthropological Terms*, 378, as quoted in McIntosh, *Discernment and Truth*, 143.

168. McIntosh, *Discernment and Truth*, 143.

169. Barton, "Gospel Wisdom," 109.

understanding that the bread-breaking communion enables believers and the church to remember and appropriate Christ's death and resurrection, McIntosh believes that Jesus, as the Word of God, not only spoke to us in his historical Incarnation in the first century, but also continues to speak to us today—expressed particularly in the eucharist of every Sunday, to bring the church more and more deeply into the paschal mystery of Christ: "Jesus' historical life is the embodiment of his identity as God's Word, but—and this is the crucial issue—his historical life is not the *limit* of his identity. For his identity and mission as God's Word is to pass into the very depths of human suffering and grief, into death itself, to pass into our lives and raise them up in him, weaving them into his joyous offering of himself to the Father."[170] McIntosh especially underlines "God's own self-giving way of life"—disclosed in the historical self-offering of Christ—as an invitation for believers "to risk living into that pattern of death and resurrection that marks the earthly form of God's life."[171] Akin to Nee's view that the Lord's Table bids believers to die to themselves and to live together in love and unity under Christ's headship, McIntosh sees that through the eucharist, Christ's Body—the church—is nourished and called to conform into the mind of Christ: "We see this happening every Sunday. All over the world the Holy Spirit calls Christ's people together, remembering his Body, nourishing it with word and sacraments, calling it back to conformity with the mind of Christ. In the eucharist we pray that God the Holy Spirit would bring our gifts of bread and wine, and our very selves, into the offering of Jesus."[172]

As Nee upholds the symbolic significance of the Supper for believers to dedicate their lives as offerings to God, McIntosh likewise sees the eucharist as representative of the critical—even the consummate—moment in our spiritual pilgrimage, the moment of self-offering as gift:

> Notice this two-beat pulse of the church's sacramental heart. There is the *baptismal moment* in which the creation is called, through participation in the dying and rising of Christ, into the freedom of new personhood. And there is the *eucharistic moment* when the church, now acting as the "personalized" face of creation, bears creation itself up into the self-offering of Christ, restoring the whole cosmos to a state of communion with God.

170. McIntosh, *Mysteries of Faith*, 82–83.

171. Ibid., 29.

172. Ibid., 83.

> So in our churchly pilgrimage from baptism to eucharist, we
> are constantly allowing the Spirit to transform our lives and our
> world from *possession* to *gift*, from something controlled and
> hoarded into something free and flowing.[173]

Yet there are some differences between Nee and McIntosh in their
understandings of the church as well as the divine-human relational
dynamics. For Nee the importance of the church is understood more in
Christo-centric terms[174] because the church is created for love and destined to be the Bride of the Son in eternity. For McIntosh it is conceived
in more theo-centric or trinitarian terms because the church is meant
to be "iconic of God's relational unity"[175] for bringing all created things
into their destiny of communion with the divine. Besides, while both
Nee and McIntosh view the divine-human relationship ultimately in the
context of love, they differ in their respective emphases. For McIntosh,
much stress is laid upon interpersonal love, particularly self-giving and
risk-taking interactions and encounters with others—both the human
others and the divine Others—which must first be practiced and learned
in the church's communal life. This emphasis on a life of self-giving does
seem to have its resonance in Nee's teaching about self-denial in inter-
personal interactions among brethren (out of the motivation for imitat-
ing Christ the Lamb). On the other hand, while Nee preaches on the
importance of being drawn into the inner chamber of divine love, his
accent seems to fall on attaining union with the Bridegroom's will.[176] So
in Nee's view, love for God is understood more in terms of obedience, for
he sees that obedience to God is a demonstration of one's love for God
(John 14:21, 23; 15:10; 1 John 5:2–3).[177] Nee's proclivity toward obedien-
tial terms could have been reinforced by his being brought up in a traditional Chinese family and society that were deeply imbedded with the
Confucian value of maintaining proper order among human relations
of all kinds. At any rate, in broad terms that risk over-generalization, we
might suggest that Nee underlines the dying (or denying) moment of the
cross whereas McIntosh underscores the rising (or affirming) moment
of the resurrection. Since the cross and resurrection necessarily impli-

173. Ibid., 163.
174. See Pamudji, "Little Flock Trilogy," 182.
175. McIntosh, *Discernment and Truth*, 254.
176. See esp. Nee, *Ge zhong de ge* [Song of Songs].
177. Nee, "Ai shen" [Loving God].

cate each other just as the dying and rising moments inevitably cycle round in the spiritual life journey, the different focuses in the views of Nee and McIntosh can be seen not as contradictory, but rather, as complementary. We will note more of this possibility of complementarity in the next, concluding chapter.

～

In this chapter, we have looked at the understandings of both Nee and McIntosh on the relation between receiving illumination or cultivating discernment on the one hand, and the formation or transformation of the would-be knowers or discerners on the other. The issues explored in this chapter can be understood as roughly corresponding to the *how* question underlying divine illumination: How can one facilitate a life of transformational growth toward God, so that one can be formed with a better capacity to hear the divine calling and to discern the divine desire in all things? After expounding on some related themes in both Nee and McIntosh, we have shown that there are substantial similarities between the two authors' views. We have suggested that Nee's idea of submitting oneself to one's life circumstances is in congruence with the world-affirming "new asceticism" of Jesuit and Wesleyan spiritualities as well as with other significant spiritual writings in the Christian history. For among them all, there is a shared understanding of self-surrender as participation in the paschal mystery of Christ—that leads eventually to the fulfillment of one's true personal identity. We have thus contended that the danger of eradication of self-will that Nee's critics worry about is in fact unwarranted. Further, we have also noted the basic complementarity between Nee's stress on obedience and McIntosh's emphasis on love as two moments in the paschal mystery. This chapter, then, constitutes the third and final of the three major building blocks toward substantiating the thesis of this book, namely, toward demonstrating that Nee's major theological convictions have strong parallels with related aspects in the Christian spiritual traditions as expounded by McIntosh, and that some major weaknesses in Nee's views perceived by his critics can be overcome or substantially ameliorated. We will now proceed to the conclusion and implications of this study.

Conclusion

THE PRECEDING CHAPTERS HAVE traversed through a range of topics revolving around the theme of spiritual knowledge—understood mainly in terms of revelation, illumination, and discernment—in the thoughts of Watchman Nee and Mark McIntosh. I have sketched the broad historical and theological contexts within which Nee's views emerge. I have investigated some important themes in Nee's spiritual theology, focusing my attention on the roles spiritual knowledge or spiritual knowing plays in the faith journey, especially with regard to receiving divine illumination, undertaking intellectual activity, and practicing the spiritual life. I have particularly explored a number of controversial issues in Nee's writings, mostly through a dialogue with McIntosh's studies on theology and the history of Christian spirituality. I have demonstrated that there are substantial similarities between the views of Nee and McIntosh on the concerned subjects, and that Nee's crucial theological convictions have strong parallels with related themes found in the treasures of the church's spiritual or mystical traditions. I have also thus contended that some major weaknesses Nee's critics perceive—such as Gnostic ambivalence, anti-intellectual tendency, and irresolvable loss of the human will—can be overcome or substantially ameliorated.

Since the topics dealt with in this study are quite pervasive and critical in Nee's spiritual theology, I would like to suggest that Nee's major theological convictions about the spiritual life are intelligible within the orthodox understanding of the Christian spiritual traditions. I would therefore also suggest that Nee's spiritual teachings are significant and relevant for the spiritual formation of contemporary believers. As to the "self-implicating" questions about spiritual knowing that I raise in the opening paragraph of this book, I believe that Nee's answers would be along the lines of these statements articulated by McIntosh: "there are many other ways of knowing what is real, living, and true. In these other ways of knowing, certainty is not something we exhaust ourselves to achieve, but something God provides. Revelation is not what we learn on our own about God, as though God were an especially complex lab specimen. Instead, revelation is the mystery of God 'undoing' us, taking our side against ourselves, and making us worthy to stand in divine fellowship."[1]

This book, however, is only a small step toward evaluating the legacy of Nee's theology. This is not only because Nee's writings are voluminous and complex, but also because any assessment itself is necessarily conditioned by the criteria of assessment being used. In the remainder of this concluding chapter, then, I would like to first note the kind of evaluating criteria envisioned by McIntosh, and then offer some of my reflections about the strengths and weaknesses of Nee's spiritual teachings.

McIntosh notes that since theology is concerned with the "meaningfulness of *truth*," there is therefore a need to explore at least briefly some possible ways for evaluating the truthfulness of any given spirituality. Since God, and the divine-human relationship, could never be a mere "object" for our study, McIntosh points out that "we cannot be assessing the truth of mystical speech and spiritual lives by criteria drawn from other modes of discourse, say, the biological sciences."[2] Drawing on both Paul Ricoeur's and David Tracy's proposals for the model of truth as "*manifestation* and *response*," McIntosh suggests that the truth of any particular spirituality can be evaluated in ways similar to appraising the value of art, namely, by assessing the meaning or beauty unveiled (and veiled) through the presentation, and the response that such manifestation evokes in the observer (143–44). In other words, "the truthfulness of a given spiritual stance" can be evaluated by "the kind of life it leads one to embrace, the kind of reality it leads one to encounter" (144). As an example of this approach, McIntosh refers to the critical measure adopted by von Balthasar drawing from Ignatian and other traditions of discernment.

According to McIntosh, possibly "the most central discriminating factor" proposed by von Balthasar is a given spirituality's "ecclesial

---

1. McIntosh, *Mysteries of Faith*, 76.

2. McIntosh, *Mystical Theology*, 143.

orientation" (ibid.). Contrary to popular concern for developmental stages and *"experiential signs"* of an individual's progress toward God, von Balthasar proposes to look at the *service* that a particular spirituality contributes to "the church's mission to embody Christ concretely in the world" (ibid.). Since "Jesus is the truth of God made flesh," for von Balthasar the test of truth is not the gift cherished by any self-preoccupied mystics, but whether such a gift is handed back freely to serve others in the church and in the world, "in obedience to the self-giving love of Christ" (ibid.). McIntosh thus suggests that one of the ways to discern the truthfulness of any spiritual text or saintly life is by observing whether its spiritual gravity is pulling toward the direction in the life pattern of Christ: "What kind of spiritual reality, in other words, would account for the particular shape of a given spirituality? If the pattern of Christ's life is an indication of the 'gravitational' pull that God exerts on human life, does a given spirituality seem to be in orbit around this centre or some other (ultimately idolatrous) reality?" (145). This way of evaluating a given spirituality, notes McIntosh, is only an example of what *kind* of critical tools we can adapt for such evaluation. This hints at the inevitable complexity involved in any attempt to assess the truthfulness of a particular spiritual stance.

The difficulty of this task of assessment, however, does not need to deter us from making some tentative judgments and evaluations, so long as we are clear about our own presuppositions and the critical criteria we are using, as well as being open to future revisions or corrections. I will therefore attempt to think along the particular line in von Balthasar's view as pointed out by McIntosh. Namely, I will ask this question: What have been some of the effects that Nee's spiritual teachings have had on the church? Such an inquiry, after all, is not unlike the biblical tradition of discerning by the fruits. While a thorough investigation of this matter would require at least another book, I would like to offer three brief observations on both the positive and negative influences that Nee's teachings have exerted. First, scholars have noted that Nee's teachings on the way of the cross and the church's eschatological glory have provided comfort and strength for many Christians amidst their sufferings in China's turbulent decades both before and after Nee's imprisonment.[3] As Grace May states: "In many ways, the Assembly was well suited for the hardships of the Cultural Revolution. Independent of

---

3. Lu, "Doctrine of the Church," 395–96; and G. Y. May, "Breaking of Bread," 231–36.

foreign support and denominational structures, accustomed to meeting informally in halls and homes, and aware of the terms of the Cross, many Assembly members adapted to years of underground worship, suffered for their faith, and endured persecutions. Furthermore, the training that Assembly members had received enabled brothers and sisters to witness wherever they went."[4] Liao Yuan-wei also notes that perhaps "Nee's message and ministry prepared some of the Chinese Christians to survive, at least in a certain degree, the severe persecutions in China especially during the 1950s and 1960s."[5]

Secondly, scholars have pointed out that the Local Church has exhibited a strong separatist tendency, especially in its attitude toward the denominations. Nee's views of the church have been a focus for several studies, which explore different themes such as the movement of the "Local Church," the priesthood of all believers, the communion practice of "breaking bread," and the glorious nature of the church.[6] Particularly, May suggests that Nee's rejection of, and lack of forgiveness for, the denominations of his day might have been not only because of the compromise and injustice in the institutional churches that Nee saw, but also due to his assumption of a perfectionist stance for a "high ecclesiology" that has its parallel in the late nineteenth-century Holiness view of entire sanctification for individuals. In other words, Nee insisted that perfection applies not merely to individuals, but to the corporate church as well.[7] May thus comments:

> Nee seemed uncomfortable with the ambiguity and mystery of God's incarnational work in the institutional church. Eager to acknowledge God's redeeming work in the individual, Nee was hesitant to acknowledge the same work of progressive sanctification in the church. Perhaps unconsciously he realized the implications of admitting to the church's need for sanctification. He would need to recognize that even though the Western church at times oppressed and exploited the Chinese church, he and they

4. G. Y. May, "Breaking of Bread," 344.

5. Liao, "Nee's Theology of Victory," 205.

6. G. Y. May, "Breaking of Bread," 240. Besides May's work, see notably Ng, "Priesthood of all Believers"; Lu, "Doctrine of the Church"; and C. Li , "Difang jiaohui yundong" [Local Church movement].

7. May, "Breaking of Bread," 261.

were members of the same church, which during her earthly so-
journ was capable of sin and error.[8]

While recognizing Nee's perfectionistic and radical tendencies in his
ecclesiology, Luke Lu, however, argues that Nee's ecclesiastic theory and
practice are innovative and—notably with its strong missionary or evangelistic emphasis—have contributed to "the well-being of the life and the
ministry of the church on earth."[9]

Thirdly, while Nee's focus on self-denial and submission was
timely for many Chinese Christians in their historical contexts, such
an emphasis is susceptible to misuse in other contexts. Particularly, an
over-emphasis on obedience and humility can potentially be abused
by both "the self-service of the powerless" and "the self-service of the
powerful."[10] It can be misused by the powerless as a way of spiritual
rationalization for not confronting obvious evils, which might have
partly contributed to the lack of social and cultural involvements by
Assembly members.[11] It can also be abused by the powerful as a way of
demanding blind submission as well as justifying sharp criticisms or
"rebukes." Thus while many of Nee's theological and pastoral teachings
are in congruence with scriptures and the church's spiritual traditions,
in actual practice one should always exercise caution and seek discerning wisdom from the Spirit as to when and how to appropriate Nee's
particular teachings for any concrete situations.

As we noted in chapter 5, Nee's focus on obedience emphasizes the
dying moment of the death-resurrection cycle, and this particular stress
can be complemented by McIntosh's attention to the overflowing life and
love of the divine Source. Especially, I would like to suggest that Nee's orientation toward self-denial and submission could be complemented by
McIntosh's grand vision of the limitless love and mercy of the One who
Jesus called Abba. Understanding spirituality as "the activity of being led
by the Spirit into Christ's relationship with the Father,"[12] McIntosh points
to the importance of conversion to the Father's love with a (Christlike)
fearless trust in the Abba's goodness toward sinners, as well as an un-

8. Ibid.

9. Lu, "Doctrine of the Church," 395–96, 1–2.

10. Ruddy, *Christological Approach to Virtue*, 47.

11. Lam notes that the passive attitude toward social and cultural involvement is
part of Nee's spirituality. See Lam *Shuling shenxue* [Spiritual theology], 285.

12. McIntosh, *Mystical Theology*, 152.

flinching confidence in the divine boundless abundance and its infinite power—especially over death. McIntosh highlights Traherne's attraction toward not "a rigorous course of self-denial," but an awakening to the "*true* bounty and goodness" of the divine.[13] This vision of God's infinite love and unconditional acceptance can be apprehended in terms of the "father heart" or "mother heart" of God, as shown in the story of the prodigal son in Luke 15.[14] Encountering such a loving divine heart grounds believers firmly in their identity as God's adopted sons and daughters, affording at the same time a new perspective for viewing the mistakes or immaturities of other children of God. As parents would automatically assume a sure hope for their children's future growth as well as delighting in the gifts of the children as they are at present, such a loving perspective would lead to a more affirmative and encouraging approach that can love the children into becoming who they are destined to be.

This perspective of parental love—which recognizes the intrinsic worth and the infinite value of the children—also has a close parallel with one's perception that is affected by divine love or influenced by human romance. While "love is blind" in the human setting usually refers (somewhat disapprovingly) to not seeing the romantic partner's negative traits, those who are drunk by the loving sweetness of the divine Spirit also usually perceive only their human neighbor's loveliness. Although such moments of intoxication by divine love are rare and usually brief, they are often regarded as illuminative glimpses or foretastes of the "face to face" beatific vision that no longer merely "sees through the glass dimly" (1 Cor 13:12). We could even possibly believe that the perception during intense romantic periods is actually a truer perception of the reality of the other person, for it is indeed closer to the divine loving perspective that is not bound by human or temporal limits. If this is the case, then, most of the time our perceptions of other persons are terribly distorted—skewing toward the negative side. The remedy to such noetic pathology and to become capable of discerning the truth in the other—to use McIntosh's suggestion—lies in a contemplative glimpse of the boundless divine love toward us, or we could say, in catching a vision of our being loved and enjoyed infinitely by God as God's beloved.

13. McIntosh, *Discernment and Truth*, 242.

14. Reflecting on Rembrandt's painting "The Return of the Prodigal Son," Henri Nouwen has written on the father figure in this parable as exhibiting the characteristics of both a father and a mother. See Nouwen, *Return of the Prodigal Son*, 98–102.

This perspective of love can perhaps provide a proper balance for avoiding some potential misapplications of Nee's accent on the cross and the Spirit's discipline. (One also needs to keep in mind here that the divine discipline that Nee so emphasizes is itself indispensable for expressing genuine parental love as shown in such scriptural passages as Hebrews 12:5–11 and various sayings in Proverbs.)

Besides these three brief observations for the effects or fruits of Nee's teachings on the church, it seems quite apparent that the overall strength and vigor displayed by different overseas communities sprung out from Nee's movement—as well as the many church leaders who would readily attribute Nee's life or writing as one of their major influences—also attest in Nee's favor. At any rate, this study of Nee's emphasis on discipline and the cross has been intentionally one of retrieval, driven by a concern about the neglect of some essential aspects in Christian life and discipleship. As J. Louis Martyn points out, the current eschatological age (which is ushered in by "the apocalyptic event" of Christ's death and resurrection) is an age of "in-between," characterized by the constant tension between the already and the not yet.[15] Thus any "knowing by the Spirit" in the present era can occur only as a knowing by "the Spirit of the Crucified Christ," or as a knowing "by the power of the cross."[16] This paradoxical tension and mutual implication of death and resurrection for earthly pilgrims are well noted by McIntosh in the concluding statements of his book *Mystical Theology*: "being human means being drawn into that endless resource and generativity which may lead one in love for the other beyond what seem like the very bounds of human existence into the death of self. But that same giving life leads thereby, Christians believe, to the death of death, to that ultimate creation of the human being which we call resurrection and which has irreversibly begun in the resurrection and ascension of Jesus Christ."[17] Not surprisingly, this theme of dying and rising after the paschal pattern of Christ was also sung over repeatedly by Nee and the Local Church members, as shown by the following lyrics taken from different hymns in the hymnody complied by Nee and his colleagues:

15. Martyn, "Epistemology," 95, 107.
16. Ibid., 107–8.
17. McIntosh, *Mystical Theology*, 239.

O, Cross of Christ, I take thee
    Into this heart of mine,
That I to my own self may die
    And rise to thy life Divine.[18]

'Tis the plan of life, for you die to live,
    One with Jesus crucified;
With the life alone to be lived through you,
    Of the Risen, the Glorified.[19]

Oh! it is so sweet to die with Christ,
    To the world, and self, and sin;
Oh! it is so sweet to live with Christ,
    As He lives and reigns within.[20]

Then the Cross! for via Calvary
    Every royal soul must go;
Here we draw the veil, for Jesus
    Only can the pathway show;
"If we suffer with Him," listen,
    Just a little, little while,
And the memory will have faded
    In the glory of His smile![21]

18. Nee, *Song of Songs and Hymns*, Hymn no. 45 (Hymns, no. 477).

19. Ibid., Hymn no. 42 (Hymns, no. 630).

20. Ibid., Hymn no. 47 (Hymns, no. 482).

21. Ibid., Hymn no. 131 (Hymns, no. 628).

Glossary

Anhui 安徽

bobing 擘餅

Chen Chonggui (Marcus Cheng) 陳崇桂

CPC (Communist Party of China) 中國共產黨

Dao (Tao) 道

Fan Zimei (Fan Tzu-mei) 范子美

Fujian (Fukien) 福建

Fuzhou (Foochow) 福州

Guangdong 廣東

gui 鬼

Guomindang 國民黨

He Shouen (Margaret E. Barber) 和受恩

Jia Yuming 賈玉銘

Jiang Jieshi (Chiang Kai-shek) 蔣介石

Katheryn Leung 梁潔瓊

Lam Wing-hung 林榮洪

Leung Ka-lun 梁家麟

Li Yuanru (Li Yuenju, Ruth Lee) 李淵如

Liao Yuan-wei 廖元威

Lin Heping (Lin Huo-ping) 林和平

Mao Zedong (Mao Tse-tung) 毛澤東

Nanjing (Nanking) 南京

Shantou 汕頭

Song Meiling 宋美齡

Song Shangjie (John Sung) 宋尚節

Sun Yat-sen (Sun Zhongshan) 孫中山

Tianjin (Tientsin) 天津

Wang Mingdao (Wang Ming-tao) 王明道

Wang Zai (Wang Tsai, Leland Wang) 王載

Wei Zhuomin (Wei Cho-min, Francis Wei) 韋卓民

Witness Lee 李常受

Wu Leichuan (Wu Lei-ch'uan) 吳雷川

Wu Yaozong (Y. T. Wu) 吳耀宗

Yantai 煙台

Yenching University 燕京大學

Yu Chenghua (C. H. Yu) 俞成華

Yu Cidu (Dora Yu) 余慈度

Zhang Pinhui (Charity Zhang) 張品蕙

Zhang Yijing (Chang I-ching) 張亦鏡

Zhao Zichen (Chao Tzu-ch'en, T. C. Chao) 趙紫宸

Bibliography

Abraham, William J. "The Epistemological Significance of the Inner Witness of the Holy Spirit." *Faith and Philosophy* 7 (Oct 1990) 434–50.

Achtemeier, Paul J., et al. *The New Testament: Its Literature and Theology*. Grand Rapids, MI: Eerdmans, 2001.

Acworth, Richard, SJ. "God and Human Knowledge in St Augustine." *The Downside Review* 75 (Jan 1957) 207–21.

Alison, James. *The Joy of Being Wrong: Original Sin Through Easter Eyes*. New York: Crossroad Herder, 1998.

———. *Raising Abel: The Recovery of the Eschatological Imagination*. New York: Crossroad, 1996.

Allen, Diogenes. *Spiritual Theology: The Theology of Yesterday for Spiritual Help Today*. Boston, MA: Cowley, 1997.

Anderson, Ray S. "Christian Anthropology." In *The Blackwell Encyclopedia of Modern Christian Thought*, ed. Alister E. McGrath, 5–9. Oxford: Blackwell, 1993.

———. "On Being Human: The Spiritual Saga of a Creaturely Soul." In *Whatever Happened to the Soul? Scientific and Theological Portraits of Human Nature*, ed. Warren S. Brown, Nancey Murphy, and H. Newton Malony, 175–94. Minneapolis, MN: Fortress, 1998.

Athanasius. *The Life of St Antony and the Letter to Marcellinus*. Translated and Introduction by Robert C. Gregg. Preface by William A. Clebsch. Classics of Western Spirituality. Mahwah, NJ: Paulist, 1980.

Augustine of Hippo. *De civitate Dei*. Translated by D. B. Zema and G. G. Walsh. Writings of St. Augustine, Fathers of the Church. New York: CIMA Publishing, 1950.

———. *Selected Writings*. Translation and Introduction by Mary T. Clark. Preface by Goulven Madec. Classics of Western Spirituality. Mahwah, NJ: Paulist, 1984.

———. *The Trinity*. Translated by Edmund Hill. Brooklyn, NY: New City, 1991.

Barry, William A. "Discernment of Spirits: A Response to the Spiritual Crisis of Our Age." *Review for Religious* 50 (Jan–Feb 1991) 103–9.

Barton, Stephen C. "Gospel Wisdom." In *Where Shall Wisdom be Found? Wisdom in the Bible, the Church and the Contemporary World*, ed. Stephen C. Barton, 93–110. Edinburgh: T & T Clark, 1999.

Barabas, S. "Keswick Convention." In *Evangelical Dictionary of Theology*, 2d ed., ed. Walter A. Elwell, 654. Grand Rapids, MI: Baker Academic, 2001.

Bass, Clarence. *Backgrounds to Dispensationalism*. Grand Rapids, MI: Baker, 1960.

Bassett, William C. "The Foundation of a Basis for Counseling From a Christian Theory of Personality as Presented by C. S. Lewis and Watchman Nee." PhD diss., University of Arkansas, 1976.

Bates, M. Searle. "China." In *The Prospects of Christianity throughout the World*, ed. M. Searle Bates and Wilhelm Pauck, 211–26. New York: Scribner, 1964.

Bays, Daniel H, ed. *Christianity in China: From the Eighteenth Century to the Present.* Stanford, CA: Stanford University Press, 1996.

———. "Indigenous Protestant Churches in China, 1900–1937: A Pentecostal Case Study." In *Indigenous Responses to Western Christianity*, ed. Steven Kaplan, 124–41. New York: New York University Press, 1995.

———. "The Growth of Independent Christianity in China, 1900–1937." In *Christianity in China: From the Eighteenth Century to the Present*, 307–16. Stanford, CA: Stanford University Press, 1996.

Bede. *Bede: On the Tabernacle.* Translated with Notes and Introduction by Arthur G. Holder. Vol. 18 of Translated Texts for Historians. Liverpool: Liverpool University Press, 1994.

Benedict. *The Rule of Saint Benedict.* Edited by Timothy Fry, OSB. Vintage Spiritual Classics. New York: Vintage Books, 1998.

Bernard of Clairvaux. *Selected Works.* Translated and Foreword by G. R. Evans. Introduction by Jean Leclercq, OSB. Preface by Ewert H. Cousins. Classics of Western Spirituality. New York: Paulist, 1987.

Blaising, C. "Dispensation, Dispensationalism." In *Evangelical Dictionary of Theology*, 2d ed., ed. Walter A. Elwell, 343–45. Grand Rapids, MI: Baker Academic, 2001.

Blumhofer, Edith L., and Randall Balmer, eds. *Modern Christian Revivals.* Urbana: University of Illinois Press, 1993.

Bonaventure. *The Soul's Journey into God, The Tree of Life, The Life of St. Francis.* Translated and Introduction by Ewert Cousins. Preface by Ignatius Brady, OFM. Classics of Western Spirituality. Mahwah, NJ: Paulist, 1978.

Bondi, Roberta C. *To Love as God Loves: Conversations with the Early Church.* Philadelphia, PA: Fortress, 1987.

Brook, Timothy. "Toward Independence: Christianity in China Under the Japanese Occupation, 1937–1945." In *Christianity in China: From the Eighteenth Century to the Present*, ed. Daniel H. Bays, 317–37. Stanford, CA: Stanford University Press, 1996.

Brother Lawrence of the Resurrection. *The Practice of the Presence of God.* Translated by Salvatore Sciurba, OCD. Washington, DC: ICS, 1994.

Brown, Alexandra R. *The Cross and Human Transformation: Paul's Apocalyptic Word in 1 Corinthians.* Minneapolis, MN: Fortress, 1995.

Browning, Don S. "Exploring Practical Wisdom and Understanding." In *A Fundamental Practical Theology*, 34–54. Minneapolis, MN: Fortress, 1991.

Buckley, Michael J. "The Structure of the Rules for Discernment." In *The Way of Ignatius Loyola: Contemporary Approaches to the Spiritual Exercises*, ed. Philip Sheldrake, 219–37. London: SPCK, 1991.

Bundy, David D. "Keswick and the Experience of Evangelical Piety." In *Modern Christian Revivals*, ed. Edith L. Blumhofer and Randall Balmer, 118–44. Urbana: University of Illinois Press, 1993.

———. "Keswick Higher Life Movement." In *The New International Dictionary of Pentecostal and Charismatic Movements*, ed. Stanley M. Burgess et al., 820–21. Grand Rapids, MI: Zondervan, 2002.

Bunyan, John. *The Pilgrim's Progress*. Edited by N. H. Keeble. Oxford World Classics. Oxford: Oxford University Press, 1998.

Burton-Christie, Douglas. *The Word in the Desert*. New York: Oxford University Press, 1993.

Callahan, James Patrick. *Primitivist Piety: The Ecclesiology of the Early Plymouth Brethren*. Lanham, MD: Scarecrow, 1996.

Callen, Barry. *Authentic Spirituality: Moving Beyond Mere Religion*. Grand Rapids, MI: Baker Academic, 2001.

Calvin, John. *Institutes of the Christian Religion*. Edited by J. T. McNeill. Translated by F. L. Battles. Vol. 1. Philadelphia, PA: Westminster, 1960.

Casey, Michael, OCSO. *Truthful Living: Saint Benedict's Teaching on Humility*. Leominster, UK: Gracewing, 2001.

Cassian, John. *The Conferences*. Translated by Boniface Ramsey, OP. Ancient Christian Writers. New York: Paulist, 1997.

Catherine of Siena. *The Dialogue*. Translated and Introduction by Suzanne Noffke, OP. Preface by Giuliana Cavallini. Classics of Western Spirituality. Mahwah, NJ: Paulist, 1980.

———. *The Letters of Catherine of Siena*. Translated by Suzanne Noffke, OP. Vol. 1. Tempe, AZ: Arizona Center for Medieval and Renaissance Studies, 2000.

Cha, James Shih-Chieh [查時傑]. "Ni Tuosheng" [倪柝聲, Watchman Nee]. In *Zhongguo jidujiao renwu xiaozhuan* [中國基督教人物小傳, Concise biographies of important Chinese Christians], 305–40. Taipei: China Evangelical Seminary Press, 1983.

Chadwick, Owen. Introduction to *Conferences*, by John Cassian, 1–36. Translated and Preface by Colm Luibheid. Classics of Western Spirituality. Mahwah, NJ: Paulist, 1985.

Chan, Simon. *Spiritual Theology: A Systematic Study of the Christian Life*. Downers Grove, IL: InterVarsity, 1998.

Chan, Stephen C. T. [陳終道]. *Wo de jiufu Ni Tuosheng* [我的舅父倪柝聲, My uncle, Watchman Nee]. 4th ed. Hong Kong: Golden Lampstand Publishing, 1999.

Chao, Jonathan. *The China Mission Handbook: A Portrait of China and Its Church*. Hong Kong: Chinese Church Research Center, 1989.

Chase, Steven. *Contemplation and Compassion: The Victorine Tradition*. Traditions of Christian Spirituality, edited by Philip Sheldrake. Maryknoll, NY: Orbis, 2003.

Chen, Fu-zhong [陳福中]. *Ni Tuosheng zhuan* [倪柝聲傳, The biography of Watchman Nee]. Hong Kong: Christian Publishers, 2004.

Chen, James [陳則信]. *Ni Tuosheng dixiong jianshi* [倪柝聲弟兄簡史, Meet brother Nee]. 4th ed. Hong Kong: Christian Publishers, 1997.

Chen, Xi-zeng [陳希曾]. "Paomao yu wuxian—He Shou-en" [拋錨於無限—和受恩, Anchoring on eternity—M. E. Barber]. No pages. Online: http://www.bodani.cn/article/?bk=100001&v=19#100001.

Chow Tse-tsung. *The May Fourth Movement: Intellectual Revolution in Modern China*. Cambridge, MA: Harvard University Press, 1960.

Christensen, Michael J. "Theosis and Sanctification: John Wesley's Reformulation of a Patristic Doctrine." *Wesleyan Theological Journal* 31 (Fall 1996) 71–94.

Cliff, Norman Howard. "The Life and Theology of Watchman Nee, Including a Study of the Little Flock Movement which He Founded." MPhil diss., Open University, UK, 1983.

―――. "Watchman Nee—Church Planter and Preacher of Holiness." *Evangelical Review of Theology* 8 no. 2 (Oct 1984) 289–97.

Climacus, John. *The Ladder of Divine Ascent.* Translated by Colm Luibheid and Norman Russell. Introduction by Kallistos Ware. Preface by Colm Luibheid. Classics of Western Spirituality. Mahwah, NJ: Paulist, 1982.

Cloud of Unknowing, The. Edited with an Introduction by James Walsh, SJ. Preface by Simon Tugwell, OP. Classics of Western Spirituality. Mahwah, NJ: Paulist, 1981.

Coad, F. Roy. *A History of the Brethren Movement.* 2d ed. Grand Rapids, MI: Eerdmans, 1976.

Coakley, S. *Powers and Submissions: Spirituality, Philosophy, and Gender.* Oxford: Blackwell, 2002.

Cohen, Paul. "Christian Missions and their Impact to 1900." In *Late Ch'ing: 1800–1911.* Vol. 10 of *The Cambridge History of China,* ed. John K. Fairbank, 543–90. Cambridge, MA: Cambridge University Press, 1978.

Collins, Kenneth J. *Exploring Christian Spirituality: An Ecumenical Reader.* Grand Rapids, MI: Baker, 2000.

Cooper, John W. *Body, Soul, and Life Everlasting: Biblical Anthropology and the Monism-Dualism Debate.* Grand Rapids, MI: Eerdmans, 1989.

Cortright, Brant. *Psychotherapy and Spirit: Theory and Practice in Transpersonal Psychotherapy.* SUNY Series in the Philosophy of Psychology, edited by Michael Washburn. Albany: State University of New York Press, 1997.

Cousins, Ewert. "The Humanity and the Passion of Christ." In *Christian Spirituality II: High Middle Ages and Reformation,* ed. Jill Raitt, in collaboration with Bernard McGinn and John Meyendorff, 375–91. New York: Crossroad, 1987.

Covell, Ralph R. *Confucius, The Buddha, and Christ: A History of the Gospel in Chinese.* American Society of Missiology, no. 11. Maryknoll, NY: Orbis, 1986.

Csikszentmihalyi, Mark, and Philip J. Ivanhoe, eds. *Religious and Philosophical Aspects of the Laozi.* SUNY Series in Chinese Philosophy and Culture, ed. David L. Hall and Roger T. Ames. Albany: State University of New York Press, 1999.

Cunningham, Lawrence S., and Keith J. Egan. *Christian Spirituality: Themes from the Tradition.* New York: Paulist, 1996.

Davies, R. E. "Revival, Spiritual." In *Evangelical Dictionary of Theology,* 2d ed., ed. Walter A. Elwell, 1025–28. Grand Rapids, MI: Baker Academic, 2001.

De Sales, Francis, and Jane de Chantal. *Francis de Sales, Jane de Chantal: Letters of Spiritual Direction.* Edited by Wendy M. Wright and Joseph F. Power, OSFS. Classics of Western Spirituality. Mahwah, NJ: Paulist, 1988.

De Wit, Han F. *Contemplative Psychology.* Translated by Marie Louise Baird. Pittsburgh, PA: Duquesne University Press, 1991.

Diadochus of Photiki. *On Spiritual Knowledge and Discrimination.* Vol. 1 of *The Philokalia.* Translated by G. E. H. Palmer, Philip Sherrard, and Kallistos Ware. London: Faber and Faber, 1983.

Dieter, Melvin E. "The Development of Holiness Theology in the Nineteenth Century." *Wesleyan Theological Journal* 20 (Spring 1985) 61–77.

―――. *The Holiness Revival of the Nineteenth Century.* Lanham, MD: Scarecrow, 1996.

―――, ed. *The 19th-Century Holiness Movement.* Kansas City, MO: Beacon Hill, 1998.

———. "Revivalism." In *Evangelical Dictionary of Theology*, 2d ed., ed. Walter A. Elwell, 1028–31. Grand Rapids, MI: Baker Academic, 2001.

Donovan, Mary Ann, SC. "Dancing Before the Lord: Theological Anthropology and Christian Spirituality as Graceful Partners." In *Proceedings of the Fifty-third Annual Convention of the Catholic Theological Society of America Held in Ottawa 11–14 June 1998*, ed. Michael Downey, 73–87. Camarillo, CA: Catholic Theological Society of America, 1998.

Driskill, Joseph D. *Protestant Spiritual Exercises: Theology, History, and Practice.* Harrisburg, PA: Morehouse Publishing, 1999.

Downey, Michael. *Understanding Christian Spirituality.* New York: Paulist, 1997.

Drobner, Hubertus R. "Studying Augustine: An Overview of Recent Research." In *Augustine and His Critics*, ed. Robert Dodaro and George Lawless, 18–34. London: Routledge, 2000.

Duffy, Stephen J. *The Dynamics of Grace: Perspectives in Theological Anthropology.* New Theology Studies 3, edited by Peter C. Phan. Collegeville, MN: Liturgical, 1993.

Dunch, Ryan. *Fuzhou Protestants and the Making of a Modern China, 1857–1927.* New Haven, CT: Yale University Press, 2001.

Dupré, Louis. "Jansenism and Quietism." In *Christian Spirituality III: Post-Reformation and Modern*, ed. Louis Dupré and Don E. Saliers, in collaboration with John Meyendorff, 121–42. New York: Crossroad, 1989.

Dupré, Louis, and Don E. Saliers, eds. *Christian Spirituality III: Post-Reformation and Modern.* In collaboration with John Meyendorff. Vol. 18 of World Spirituality: An Encyclopedic History of the Religious Quest. New York: Crossroad, 1989.

Dupré, Louis, and James A. Wiseman, OSB, eds. *Light from Light: An Anthology of Christian Mysticism.* New York: Paulist, 1988.

Durham University. "Staff Profile: Prof Mark McIntosh." No pages. Online: http://www.dur.ac.uk/theology.religion/staff/profile/?id=7617.

Edwards, Jonathan. *The Great Awakening.* Edited by C. C. Goen. New Haven, CT: Yale University Press, 1972.

———. *A Treatise Concerning Religious Affections.* Edited by John E. Smith. The Works of Jonathan Edwards, vol. 2. New Haven, CT: Yale University Press, 1959.

Erb, Peter C., ed. *Pietists: Selected Writings.* Edited and Introduction by Peter C. Erb. Preface by F. Ernest Stoeffler. Classics of Western Spirituality. Mahwah, NJ: Paulist, 1983.

Evagrius Ponticus. *The Praktikos and Chapters on Prayer.* Translated by John Eudes Bamberger. Cistercian Studies Series 4. Kalamazoo, MI: Cistercian Publications, 1981.

Fairbank, John King. *The Great Chinese Revolution: 1800–1985.* New York: Harper & Row, 1986.

Fee, Gordon. *1 Corinthians.* Grand Rapids, MI: Eerdmans, 1987.

Ferrer, Jorge N. *Revisioning Transpersonal Theory: A Participatory Vision of Human Spirituality.* Foreword by Richard Tarnas. SUNY Series in Transpersonal and Humanistic Psychology, edited by Richard D. Mann. Albany: State University of New York Press, 2002.

Figgis, J. B. *Keswick From Within.* New York: Garland Publishing, 1985.

Fowler, James W. *Becoming Adult, Becoming Christian: Adult Development and Christian Faith.* San Francisco: Jossey-Bass, 2000.

Forman, Robert K. "Mysticism, Constructivism, and Forgetting." In *The Problem of Pure Consciousness: Mysticism and Philosophy*, ed. Robert K. Forman, 3–49. New York: Oxford University Press, 1990.

Foster, Richard, and James Bryan Smith, eds. *Devotional Classics: Selected Readings for Individuals and Groups*. New York: HarperCollins, 1993.

Francis and Clare of Assisi. *Francis and Clare: The Complete Works*. Classics of Western Spirituality. Mahwah, NJ: Paulist, 1986.

Frohlich, Mary. "Spiritual Discipline, Discipline of Spirituality: Revisiting Questions of Definition and Method." *Spiritus* 1, no. 1 (Spring 2001) 65–78.

Fung, Yu-lan. *A Short History of Chinese Philosophy*. Edited by Derk Bodde. New York: Free Press, 1966.

Funk, Mary Margaret, OSB. *Thoughts Matters: The Practice of the Spiritual Life*. New York: Continuum, 1998.

Gaffin, Richard B., Jr. "Some Epistemological Reflections on 1 Cor 2:6–16." *Westminster Theological Journal* 57 (1995) 103–24.

Ganss, George E. Introduction to *Ignatius of Loyola: Spiritual Exercises and Selected Works*, ed. George E. Ganss, SJ, in collaboration with Parmananda R. Divarkar, SJ, et al., 9–63. Classics of Western Spirituality. Mahwah, NJ: Paulist, 1991.

Gao, Wangzhi. "Y. T. Wu: A Christian Leader Under Communism." In *Christianity in China: From the Eighteenth Century to the Present*, ed. Daniel H. Bays, 338–52. Stanford, CA: Stanford University Press, 1996.

Geivett, R. Douglas, and Brendan Sweetman, eds. *Contemporary Perspectives on Religious Epistemology*. New York: Oxford University Press, 1992.

George, Timothy. "The Spirituality of the Radical Reformation." In *Christian Spirituality II: High Middle Ages and Reformation*, ed. Jill Raitt, in collaboration with Bernard McGinn and John Meyendorff, 334–71. New York: Crossroad, 1987.

Gerrish, B. A. *Grace and Gratitude: The Eucharistic Theology of John Calvin*. Minneapolis, MN: Augsburg Fortress, 1992.

Gerson, Jean. "On Distinguishing True from False Revelations." In *Jean Gerson: Early Works*, trans. Brian Patrick McGuire, 334–64. Classics of Western Spirituality. New York: Paulist, 1998.

Gooch, Paul W. *Partial Knowledge: Philosophical Studies in Paul*. Notre Dame, IN: University of Notre Dame Press, 1987.

Grant, Robert M. "Gnostic Spirituality." In *Christian Spirituality I: Origins to the Twelfth Century*, ed. Bernard McGinn, John Meyendorff, and Jean Leclercq, 44–60. New York: Crossroad, 1985.

Green, Joel B. "'Bodies—That Is, Human Lives': A Re-Examination of Human Nature in the Bible." In *Whatever Happened to the Soul? Scientific and Theological Portraits of Human Nature*, ed. Warren S. Brown, Nancey Murphy, and H. Newton Malony, 149–74. Minneapolis, MN: Fortress, 1998.

GTU Doctoral Program Handbook. 10th ed. Graduate Theological Union, Berkeley, CA. Unpublished, Spring 2002.

Guyon, Madame Jeanne. *Autobiography*. No pages. Online: http:ccel.wheaton.edu.

———. *Experiencing the Depths of Jesus Christ*. Library of Spiritual Classics, vol. 2. Sargent, GA: SeedSowers, 1975.

Hadot, Pierre. *Philosophy as a Way of Life: Spiritual Exercises from Socrates to Foucault*. Edited by I. Davidson Arnold. Translated by Michael Chase. Oxford: Blackwell, 1995.

Hardy, Julia M. "Influential Western Interpretations of the *Tao-te-ching*." In *Lao-tzu and the Tao-te-ching*, ed. Livia Kohn and Michael LaFargue, 165–88. Albany: State University of New York Press, 1998.

Hays, Richard B. "Wisdom According to Paul." In *Where Shall Wisdom be Found? Wisdom in the Bible, the Church and the Contemporary World*, ed. Stephen C. Barton, 111–24. Edinburgh: T & T Clark, 1999.

Heard, J. B. *The Tripartite Nature of Man: Spirit, Soul, and Body*. 3d ed. Edinburgh: T & T Clark, 1870.

Henry, Carl F. H. "Footnotes: Sharper Focus on Watchman Nee." *Christianity Today* 19 (May 9, 1975) 31–32.

Hessel-Robinson, Timothy. "'Be Thou My Onely Well Belov'd': Exegesis and the Spirituality of Desire in Edward Taylor's 'Preparatory Meditations' on the Song of Songs." PhD diss., Graduate Theological Union, 2006.

Hinson, E. Glenn. "The Progression of Grace: A Re-Reading of the *Pilgrim's Progress*." *Spiritus* 3, no. 2 (Fall 2003) 251–62.

Hoffecker, W. A. "Darby, John Nelson." In *Evangelical Dictionary of Theology*, 2d ed., ed. Walter A. Elwell, 317–18. Grand Rapids, MI: Baker Academic, 2001.

Holder, Arthur, ed. *The Blackwell Companion to Christian Spirituality*. Oxford: Blackwell, 2005.

Hsu, Immanuel C. Y. *The Rise of Modern China*. 5th ed. New York: Oxford University Press, 1995.

Hunter, Alan. "Continuities in Chinese Protestantism 1920–1990." *China Study Journal* 6.3 (Dec 1991) 5–12.

Ignatius of Loyola. *Spiritual Exercises and Selected Works*. Edited by George E. Ganss, SJ, in collaboration with Parmananda R. Divarkar, SJ, Edward J. Malatesta, SJ, and Martin E. Palmer, SJ. Preface by John W. Padberg, SJ. Classics of Western Spirituality. Mahwah, NJ: Paulist, 1991.

Jewett, Robert. *Paul's Anthropological Terms: A Study of Their Use in Conflict Settings*. Leiden, Netherlands: E. J. Brill, 1971.

Johann Arndt. *Johann Arndt: True Christianity*. Translated and Introduction by Peter Erb. Classics of Western Spirituality. Mahwah, NJ: Paulist, 1979.

John of the Cross. *Selected Writings*. Edited and Introduction by Kieran Kavanaugh, OCD. Preface by Ernest E. Larkin, OCarm. Classics of Western Spirituality. Mahwah, NJ: Paulist, 1987.

———. "The Spiritual Canticle." In *The Collected Works of St John of the Cross*, trans. K. Kavanaugh and O. Rodriguez, 459–630. Washington, DC: Institute of Carmelite Studies, 1979.

Johnson, Stephen C. "The Spirituality of Watchman Nee, Its Sources and Its Influences." Paper Presented at the 39th Annual Meeting of the Evangelical Theological Society, South Hamilton, MA, Dec. 3, 1987.

Jones, C. E. "Holiness Movement." In *The New International Dictionary of Pentecostal and Charismatic Movements*, ed. Stanley M. Burgess et al., 726–29. Grand Rapids, MI: Zondervan, 2002.

Joy, Donald M. "Some Biblical Foundations and Metaphors of Vocational Ideals in the Wesleyan Tradition." In *Wesleyan Theology Today: A Bicentennial Theological Consultation*, ed. Theodore Runyon, 299–305. Nashville, TN: Kingswood Books, 1985.

Julian of Norwich. *Showings*. Translated and Introduction by Edmund Colledge, OSA, and James Walsh, SJ. Preface by Jean Leclercq, OSB. Classics of Western Spirituality. Mahwah, NJ: Paulist, 1978.

Katz, Steven T, ed. *Mysticism and Philosophical Analysis*. New York: Oxford University Press, 1978.

Kinnear, Angus. *Against the Tide: The Story of Watchman Nee*. Fort Washington, PA: CLC Publications, 2004.

Knox, Ronald A. *Enthusiasm: A Chapter in the History of Religion*. Notre Dame, IN: University of Notre Dame Press, 1994.

Kostlevy, William C. Introduction to *Historical Dictionary of the Holiness Movement*, ed. William C. Kostlevy and Gari-Anne Patzwald, 1–5. Lanham, MD: Scarecrow, 2001.

Ladd, G. E. *Theology of the New Testament*. Grand Rapids, MI: Eerdmans, 1975.

Lam, Wing-hung [林榮洪]. *Chinese Theology in Construction*. Pasadena, CA: William Carey Library, 1983.

———. *Shuling shenxue: Ni Tuosheng sixiang de yanjiu* [屬靈神學: 倪柝聲思想的研究, The spiritual theology of Watchman Nee]. Hong Kong: China Alliance Press, 2003.

———. "Huaren shenxue san da luxian" [華人神學三大路線, Three great streams in Chinese theology]. In *Jidujiao yu Zhongguo wenhua de xiangyu* [基督教與中國文化的相遇, Encounter between Christianity and Chinese culture], ed. Lung-kwong Lo, 1–104. Hong Kong: Chung Chi College, Chinese University of Hong Kong, 2001.

Land, Steven J. "Pentecostal Spirituality: Living in the Spirit." In *Christian Spirituality: Post Reformation and Modern*, ed. Louis Dupré and Don E. Saliers, in collaboration with John Meyendorff, 479–99. New York: Crossroad, 1989.

Lane, Belden C. "Galesville and Sinai: The Researcher as Participant in the Study of Spirituality." *Christian Spirituality Bulletin* 2 (Spring 1994) 18–20.

Latourette, Kenneth Scott. *A History of Christian Missions in China*. New York: Russell & Russell, 1967.

Lauder, Robert E. "Augustine: Illumination, Mysticism, and Person." In *Augustine: Mystic and Mystagogue (Collectanea Augustiniana)*, ed. Frederick Van Fleteren, Joseph C. Schnaubelt, OSA, and Joseph Reino, 177–205. New York: Peter Lang, 1994.

Lee, Joseph Tse-Hei. "Watchman Nee and the Little Flock Movement in Maoist China." *Church History* 74, no. 1 (March 2005) 68–96.

Lee, Ken Ang. "Watchman Nee: A Study of His Major Theological Themes." PhD diss., Westminster Theological Seminary, 1989.

Lee, Samuel Mau-Cheng. "A Comparative Study of Leadership Selection Processes Among Four Chinese Leaders." DMiss diss., Fuller Theological Seminary, 1985.

Lee, Witness [李常受]. *The Baptism in the Holy Spirit*. No pages. Online: http://www.ministrybooks.org/books.cfm?id=%23%28N%2F%5D%0A.

———. *Ni Tuosheng: jin shidai shensheng qishi de xianjian* [倪柝聲—今時代神聖啟示的先見, Watchman Nee: A seer of the divine revelation in the present age]. Translated by editors of Taiwan Gospel Book House. Taipei: Taiwan Gospel Book House, 1999.

———. *Watchman Nee: A Seer of the Divine Revelation in the Present Age*. Anaheim, CA: Living Stream Ministry, 1991. No pages. Online: http://www.ministrybooks.org/witness-lee-books.cfm.

Leung, Ka-lun [梁家麟]. "Cong fenxing yundong dao shenmi zhuyi—Binluyi shimu de shuling shenxue sixiang" [從奮興運動到神秘主義—賓路易師母的屬靈神

學思想, From revivalism to mysticism—Mrs. Penn-Lewis's thought on spiritual theology]. In *Ni Tuosheng zaonian de shengping yu sixiang* [倪柝聲早年的生平與思想, Watchman Nee: his early life and thought], 2–56. Hong Kong: Graceful House, 2005.

———. *Fu lin zhonghua—Zhongguo jindai jiaohui shi shijiang* [福臨中華—中國近代教會史十講, Blessing upon China—ten talks on the contemporary church history of China]. Hong Kong: Tien Dao, 1988.

———. "Huaren nuosidi zhuyi de shuling guan—Ni Tuosheng *ren de posui yu ling de chulai* yandu" [華人諾斯底主義的屬靈觀—倪柝聲《人的破碎與靈的出來》研讀, The spiritual perspective of Chinese Gnosticism—studies on Watchman Nee's *The Breaking of the Outer Man and the Release of the Spirit*]. In *Watchman Nee: His Glory and Dishonor*, 185–275. Rev. and enl. ed. Hong Kong: Graceful House, 2004.

———. *Ni Tuosheng de rongru shengchu* [倪柝聲的榮辱升黜, Watchman Nee: his glory and dishonor]. Rev. and enl. ed. Hong Kong: Graceful House, 2004.

———. *Ni Tuosheng zaonian de shengping yu sixiang* [倪柝聲早年的生平與思想, Watchman Nee: his early life and thought]. Hong Kong: Graceful House, 2005.

———. "*Shuling ren* yu Ni Tuosheng de sanyuan renlun" [《屬靈人》與倪柝聲的三元人論, Trichotomistic anthropology of Watchman Nee in his *The Spiritual Man*]. *Jian Dao* no. 13 (Dec 1999) 183–232.

Leung, Katheryn [梁潔瓊]. "Ping Nixi de *ge zhong de ge* yu yuyifa jiejing" [評倪氏的《歌中的歌》與寓意法解經, On Ni's Song of Songs and allegorical interpretation of scripture]. In *Shuling shiji de zhuixun: cong shengjing, lishi, shenxue kan Ni Tuosheng de sixiang* [屬靈實際的追尋: 從聖經, 歷史, 神學看倪柝聲的思想, Seeking for spiritual reality: viewing Watchman Nee's thought from the biblical, historical, and theological perspectives], ed. Hong-du Xu, 21–48. Taipei: China Evangelical Seminary, 2003.

Li, Chia-fu [李佳福]. "Ni Tuosheng yu Zhongguo difang jiaohui yundong" [倪柝聲與中國地方教會運動, Watchman Nee and the Local Church movement in China]. MA thesis, Taipei: Guo Li Taiwan Shi Fan Da Xue Li Shi Yan Jiu Suo, 2001.

Li, Kan [李侃], et al. *Zhongguo jindai shi* [中國近代史, The modern history of China]. 4th ed. Beijing: China Publishing, 1994.

Li, Yading [李亞丁]. *Huaren jidujiaoshi renwu cidian* [華人基督教史人物辭典, Biographical dictionary of Chinese Christianity]. No pages. Online: http://www.bdcconline.net/zh-hant/stories/by-person/y/yu-chenghua.php.

Liao, Yuan-wei [廖元威]. "Ni Tuosheng sanyuan renlun guan" [倪柝聲三元人論觀, The tripartite anthropology of Watchman Nee]. In *Shuling shiji de zhuixun: cong shengjing, lishi, shenxue kan Ni Tuosheng de sixiang* [Searching for the spiritual reality: viewing Watchman Nee from the biblical, historical, and theological perspectives], ed. Xu Hong-du, 91–104. Taipei: China Evangelical Seminary, 2003.

———. "Pingjie jiben Ni Tuosheng de zhuanji" [評介幾本倪柝聲的傳記, On several biographies of Watchman Nee]. In *Shuling shiji de zhuixun: cong shengjing, lishi, shenxue kan Ni Tuosheng de sixiang* [Searching for the spiritual reality: viewing Watchman Nee from the biblical, historical, and theological perspectives], ed. Xu Hong-du, 279–91. Taipei: China Evangelical Seminary, 2003.

———. "Watchman Nee's Theology of Victory: An Examination and Critique from a Lutheran Perspective." ThD diss., Luther Seminary, 1997.

Liebert, Elizabeth. "The Role of Practice in the Study of Christian Spirituality." *Spiritus* 2, no. 1 (Spring 2002) 30–49.

Lin, Yuan-du [林元度]. *Ni Tuosheng dixiong de shizijia* [倪柝聲弟兄的十字架, Brother Ni Tuosheng's cross]. Lin Yuandu, 1995.

Lin, Yutang. *The Wisdom of China and India*. New York: Modern Library, 1942.

Lindbeck, George A. *The Nature of Doctrine: Religion and Theology in a Postliberal Age*. Louisville, KY: Westminster John Knox, 1984.

Livingstone, E. A. "Fundamentalism." In *The Concise Oxford Dictionary of the Christian Church*. Oxford: Oxford University Press, 2000. No pages. Online: http://o-www.oxfordreference.com.grace.gtu.edu:80/views/ENTRY.html?subview=Main&entry=t95.e2261.

Lossky, Vladimir. *The Mystical Theology of the Eastern Church*. Crestwood, NY: St. Vladimir's Seminary Press, 2002.

Loughlin, Gerard. "See-Saying/Say-Seeing." *Theology* 91 (May 1988) 201–8.

Louth, Andrew. *Discerning the Mystery: An Essay on the Nature of Theology*. New York: Oxford University Press, 1983.

———. *The Origins of the Christian Mystical Tradition: From Plato to Denys*. Oxford: Clarendon, 1981.

Lu, Luke Pei-Yuan. "Watchman Nee's Doctrine of the Church with Special Reference to Its Contribution to the Local Church Movement." PhD diss., Westminster Theological Seminary, 1992.

Lund, Eric, and Albert C. Outler. "Protestant Spirituality: Orthodoxy and Piety in Modernity." In *Christian Spirituality III: Post-Reformation and Modern*, ed. Louis Dupré and Don E. Saliers, in collaboration with John Meyendorff, 213–56. New York: Crossroad, 1989.

Lutz, Jessie. *Chinese Politics and Christian Missions: The Anti-Christian Movements of 1920–1928*. Notre Dame, IN: Cross Roads, 1988.

Lyall, Leslie T. *Three of China's Mighty Men*. London: Hodder and Stoughton, 1980.

Marsden, George M. *Fundamentalism and American Culture: The Shaping of Twentieth-Century Evangelicalism: 1870–1925*. New York: Oxford University Press, 1980.

———. *Understanding Fundamentalism and Evangelicalism*. Grand Rapids, MI: Eerdmans, 1991.

Martin, D. D. "Mysticism." In *Evangelical Dictionary of Theology*, 2d ed., ed. Walter A. Elwell, 806–9. Grand Rapids, MI: Baker Academic, 2001.

Martyn, J. Louis. "Epistemology at the Turn of the Ages." In *Theological Issues in the Letters of Paul*, 89–110. Edinburgh: T & T Clark, 1997.

Maximus the Confessor. "Chapters on Knowledge." In *Maximus Confessor: Selected Writings*, trans. George C. Berthold, 127–80. Classics of Western Spirituality. New York: Paulist, 1985.

———. "The Four Hundred Chapters on Love." In *Maximus Confessor: Selected Writings*, trans. George C. Berthold, 33–98. Classics of Western Spirituality. New York: Paulist, 1985.

May, Gerald G. *Will and Spirit: A Contemplative Psychology*. New York: HarperCollins, 1982.

May, Grace Y. "Watchman Nee and the Breaking of Bread." ThD diss., Boston University, 2000.

McCabe, Herbert, OP. *God Matters*. London: Geoffrey Chapman, 1987.

McClendon, James Wm., Jr. *Witness: Systematic Theology*, vol. 3. Nashville, TN: Abingdon, 2000.

McDermott, Gerald, R. *Seeing God: Jonathan Edwards and Spiritual Discernment.* Vancouver: Regent College Publishing, 2000.

McGinn, Bernard. *The Foundations of Mysticism: Origins to the Fifth Century.* Vol. 1 of The Presence of God: A History of Western Christian Mysticism. New York: Crossroad, 1991.

———. *The Growth of Mysticism: Gregory the Great through the 12th Century.* Vol. 2 of The Presence of God: A History of Western Christian Mysticism. New York: Crossroad, 1994.

———. "The Language of Inner Experience in Christian Mysticism." *Spiritus* 1, no. 2 (Fall 2001) 156–71.

———. "Love, Knowledge, and *Unio Mystica* in the Western Christian Tradition." In *Mystical Union and Monotheistic Faith: Mystical Union in Judaism, Christianity, and Islam*, 59–86. New York: Continuum, 1996.

McGinn, Bernard, John Meyendorff, and Jean Leclercq, eds. *Christian Spirituality I: Origins to the Twelfth Century.* Vol. 16 of World Spirituality: An Encyclopedic History of the Religious Quest. New York: Crossroad, 1985.

McGrath, Alister E. *Christian Spirituality: An Introduction.* Oxford: Blackwell, 1999.

McGrath, Joanna, and Alister McGrath. *Self-Esteem: The Cross and Christian Confidence.* Wheaton, IL: Crossway, 2002.

McIntosh, Mark A. *Discernment and Truth: The Spirituality and Theology of Knowledge.* New York: Crossroad, 2004.

———. *Mysteries of Faith.* The New Church Teaching Series. Boston, MA: Cowley, 2000.

———. *Mystical Theology: The Integrity of Spirituality and Theology.* Challenges in Contemporary Theology, ed. Lewis Ayres and Gareth Jones. Oxford: Blackwell, 1998.

———. "Trinitarian Perspectives on Christian Spirituality." In *The Blackwell Companion to Christian Spirituality*, ed. Arthur Holder, 177–89. Oxford: Blackwell, 2005.

Mead, Frank S., and Samuel S. Hill. *Handbook of Denominations in the United States.* 10th ed. Nashville, TN: Abingdon, 1995.

Meister Eckhart. *The Essential Sermons, Commentaries, Treatises, and Defense.* Translated and Introduction by Edmund Colledge, OSA, and Bernard McGinn. Preface by Huston Smith. Classics of Western Spirituality. Mahwah, NJ: Paulist, 1981.

Meyendorff, John. "Theosis in the Eastern Christian Tradition." In *Christian Spirituality III: Post-Reformation and Modern*, ed. Louis Dupré and Don E. Saliers, in collaboration with John Meyendorff, 470–76. New York: Crossroad, 1989.

Moore, Mary Elizabeth. "Wesleyan Spirituality: Meeting Contemporary Movements." In *Wesleyan Theology Today: A Bicentennial Theological Consultation*, ed. Theodore Runyon, 291–98. Nashville, TN: Kingswood Books, 1985.

Murphy, Nancey. "Human Nature: Historical, Scientific, and Religious Issues." In *Whatever Happened to the Soul? Scientific and Theological Portraits of Human Nature*, ed. Warren S. Brown, Nancey Murphy, and H. Newton Malony, 1–29. Minneapolis, MN: Fortress, 1998.

Nash, Ronald H. *The Light of the Mind: St. Augustine's Theory of Knowledge.* Lexington, KY: The University Press of Kentucky, 1969.

Nee, Watchman [倪柝聲, Ni, Tuosheng]. "Ai shen" [愛神, Loving God]. In *Ni Tuosheng zhushu quanji* [The complete works of Watchman Nee], vol. 24 [CD-ROM]. Hong Kong: Manna, n.d.

———. "The Anointing of the Body." In *Conferences, Messages, and Fellowship*. Vol. 44 of *The Collected Works of Watchman Nee*. Anaheim, CA: Living Stream Ministry, 1993. No pages. Online: http://www.ministrybooks.org/collected-works.cfm.

———. "Appendix—Ancient Writings of the Church Concerning the Lord's Day." In *Messages for Building Up New Believers*. Vol. 48 of *The Collected Works of Watchman Nee*. Anaheim, CA: Living Stream Ministry, 1993. No pages. Online: http://www.ministrybooks.org/collected-works.cfm.

———. "Bobing" [擘餅, Bread-breaking]. In *Xintu zaojiu* [信徒造就, Building Christian virtues], 305–22. Hong Kong: Christian Publishers, 1999.

———. "Bread-Breaking." In *Messages for Building Up New Believers (1)*. Vol. 48 of *The Collected Works of Watchman Nee*. Anaheim, CA: Living Stream Ministry, 1993. No pages. Online: http://www.ministrybooks.org/collected-works.cfm.

———. *The Breaking of the Outer Man and the Release of the Spirit*. Anaheim, CA: Living Stream Ministry, 1997.

———. *The Collected Works of Watchman Nee*. 62 vols. (sets 1 to 3). Anaheim, CA: Living Stream Ministry, 1993. No pages. Online: http://www.ministrybooks.org/collected-works.cfm.

———. *The Finest of the Wheat*, vol. 1. New York: Christian Fellowship Publishers, 1993.

———. "The First Testimony—Salvation and Calling," Chap. 7 of *Collection of Newsletters (2) and Watchman Nee's Testimony*. Vol. 26 of *The Collected Works of Watchman Nee*. Anaheim, CA: Living Stream Ministry, 1993. No pages. Online: http://www.ministrybooks.org/collected-works.cfm.

———. *Ge zhong de ge* [歌中的歌, The Song of Songs]. Hong Kong: Christian Publishers, 2002.

———. "A Glorious Church." In *What Shall This Man Do?* Vol. 40 of *The Collected Works of Watchman Nee*. Anaheim, CA: Living Stream Ministry, 1993. No pages. Online: http://www.ministrybooks.org/collected-works.cfm.

———. *The Glorious Church*. Vol. 34 of *The Collected Works of Watchman Nee*. Anaheim, CA: Living Stream Ministry, 1993. No pages. Online: http://www.ministrybooks.org/collected-works.cfm.

———. *Hymnary* [Shige, 詩歌]. Translated by Testimony of Christ Mission from Works of Watchman Nee and Others. Culver City, CA: Testimony Bookroom, 1980.

———. *Jiaohui de zhengtong* [教會的正統, The orthodoxy of the Church]. Taipei: Taiwan Gospel Book House, 1967.

———. *Messages for Building Up New Believers*. Vol. 48 of *The Collected Works of Watchman Nee*. Anaheim, CA: Living Stream Ministry, 1993.

———. *The Ministries*, No. 2. Vol. 55 of *The Collected Works of Watchman Nee*. Anaheim, CA: Living Stream Ministry, 1993.

———. *Ni Tuosheng shuxin ji* [倪柝聲書信集, Letters of Watchman Nee]. Hong Kong: Christian Publishers, 1997.

———. *Ni Tuosheng wenji* [倪柝聲文集, The collected works of Watchman Nee]. 62 vols. (sets 1 to 3). Taipei: Taiwan Gospel Book House, 1992–1993. No pages. Online: http://www.lsmchinese.org/big5/07online_reading/nee/index.htm.

———. *Ni Tuosheng zhushu quanji* [倪柝聲著述全集, The complete works of Watchman Nee] [CD-ROM]. Hong Kong: Manna, n.d.

————. *The Normal Christian Life*. Fort Washington, PA: Christian Literature Crusade, 1969.

————. *The Orthodoxy of the Church*. Los Angeles: The Stream Publishers, 1970.

————. *The Present Testimony (1)*. Vol. 8 of *The Collected Works of Watchman Nee*. Anaheim, CA: Living Stream Ministry, 1993.

————. *The Present Testimony (4)*. Vol. 11 of *The Collected Works of Watchman Nee*. Anaheim, CA: Living Stream Ministry, 1993. No pages. Online: http://www.ministrybooks.org/collected-works.cfm.

————. "The Protection, Limitation, and Ministry of the Body." In *Conferences, Messages, and Fellowship*. Vol. 44 of *The Collected Works of Watchman Nee*. Anaheim, CA: Living Stream Ministry, 1993. No pages. Online: http://www.ministrybooks.org/collected-works.cfm.

————. *Ren de posui yu ling de chulai* [人的破碎與靈的出來, The release of the Spirit]. Hong Kong: Christian Publishers, 1996.

————. "The Second Testimony," Chap. 8 of *Collection of Newsletters (2) and Watchman Nee's Testimony*. Vol. 26 of *The Collected Works of Watchman Nee*. Anaheim, CA: Living Stream Ministry, 1993. No pages. Online: http://www.ministrybooks.org/collected-works.cfm.

————. *Sit, Walk, Stand*. Wheaton, IL: Tyndale, 1977.

————. *Shuling ren* [屬靈人, The spiritual man]. Hong Kong: Christian Publishers, 2000.

————. *Shuling ren* [屬靈人, Spiritual man], vol. 1. Taipei: Taiwan Gospel Book House, 1992.

————. *The Song of Songs and Hymns*. Vol. 23 of *The Collected Works of Watchman Nee*. Anaheim, CA: Living Stream Ministry, 1993. No pages. Online: http://www.ministrybooks.org/books.cfm?id=%23%2B0OJ%0A.

————. *The Spiritual Man*. 3 vols. Anaheim, CA: Living Stream Ministry, 1998.

————. *Spiritual Man*, vol. 1. New York: Christian Fellowship Publishers, 1977.

————. "The Third Testimony," Chap. 9 of *Collection of Newsletters (2) and Watchman Nee's Testimony*. Vol. 26 of *The Collected Works of Watchman Nee*. Anaheim, CA: Living Stream Ministry, 1993. No pages. Online: http://www.ministrybooks.org/collected-works.cfm.

————. *Wuxing de gengxin* [悟性的更新, Renewal of your mind]. Hong Kong: Christian Publishers, 2001.

————. *Xintu zaojiu* [信徒造就, Building Christian virtues]. 2 vols. Hong Kong: Christian Publishers, 1999. [English Translation as *Messages for Building Up New Believers*. Vols. 48–50 of *The Collected Works of Watchman Nee*. Anaheim. CA: Living Stream Ministry, 1993.]

————. *Yao changchang xile* [要常常喜樂, Be joyful always]. Hong Kong: Christian Publishers, 2002.

————. "Zanmei" [讚美, Praise]. In *Xintu zaojiu* [信徒造就, Building Christian virtues], 285–304. Hong Kong: Christian Publishers, 1999.

————. *Zhengchang de jidutu shenghuo* [正常的基督徒生活, The normal Christian life]. Vol. 17 of *Ni Tuosheng zhushu quanji* [The complete works of Watchman Nee] [CD-ROM]. Hong Kong: Manna, n.d.

————. *Zhuo jianzheng* [作見證, Testimonies]. Vol. 33 of *Ni Tuosheng zhushu quanji* [The complete works of Watchman Nee]. Hong Kong: Manna, 1995.

Newman, John Henry. "The Humiliation of the Eternal Son." In *Parochial and Plain Sermons*, vol. 3., 581–93. San Francisco: Ignatius press, 1987.

Ng, Wai Man. "Watchman Nee and the Priesthood of All Believers." ThD diss., Concordia Seminary, 1985.

Ni Tuosheng shengping yantao hui [倪柝聲生平研討會, Seminar on the life of Watchman Nee] [CD-ROM]. Hong Kong: Truth Publishing, n.d. [ca. 2003].

Noll, Mark A. *The Scandal of the Evangelical Mind.* Grand Rapids, MI: Eerdmans, 1994.

Nouwen, Henri J. M. *The Return of the Prodigal Son: A Story of Homecoming.* New York: Image, 1992.

———. *The Wounded Healer.* New York: Image, 1990.

O'Malley, John. "Early Jesuit Spirituality: Spain and Italy." In *Christian Spirituality: Post Reformation and Modern*, ed. Louis Dupré and Don E. Saliers, in collaboration with John Meyendorff, 3–27. New York: Crossroad, 1989.

Oden, Thomas C. *John Wesley's Scriptural Christianity: A Plain Exposition of His Teaching on Christian Doctrine.* Grand Rapids, MI: Zondervan, 1994.

Origen. *An Exhortation to Martyrdom, First Principles: Book IV, Prologue to the Commentary on the Song of Songs, Homily XXVII on Numbers.* Translated by Rowan A. Greer. Classics of Western Spirituality. Mahwah, NJ: Paulist, 1979.

———. *On First Principles.* Translated by G. W. Butterworth. Gloucester, MA: Peter Smith, 1973.

Pamudji, Peterus. "Little Flock Trilogy: A Critique of Watchman Nee's Principal Thought on Christ, Man, and the Church." PhD diss., Drew University, 1985.

Pasnau, Robert. "Divine Illumination." In *Stanford Encyclopedia of Philosophy.* No pages. Online: http:plato.stanford.edu/entries/illumination.

Penn-Lewis, Jessie. *Much Fruit: The Story of a Grain of Wheat.* 4th ed. Bournemouth, England: The Overcomer Book Room, n.d.

Perkins, Pheme. *Gnosticism and the New Testament.* Minneapolis, MN: Fortress, 1993.

Pickett, Raymond. *The Cross in Corinth: The Social Significance of the Death of Jesus.* Sheffield: Sheffield Academic Press, 1997.

Pierard, R. V. "Holiness Movement, American." In *Evangelical Dictionary of Theology*, 2d ed., ed. Walter A. Elwell, 564–65. Grand Rapids, MI: Baker Academic, 2001.

Principe, Walter H., CSB. "Broadening the Focus: Context as a Corrective Lens in Reading Historical Works in Spirituality." *Christian Spirituality Bulletin* 2 (Spring 1994) 1, 3–5.

Pseudo-Dionysius. *The Complete Works.* Translated by Colm Luibheid. Foreword, Notes, and Translation in collaboration with Paul Rorem. Preface by Rene Roques. Introductions by Jaroslav Pelikan, Jean Leclercq, and Karlfried Froehlich. Classics of Western Spirituality. Mahwah, NJ: Paulist, 1987.

Raitt, Jill, ed. *Christian Spirituality II: High Middle Ages and Reformation.* Vol. 17 of World Spirituality: An Encyclopedic History of the Religious Quest. In collaboration with Bernard McGinn and John Meyendorff. New York: Crossroad, 1987.

———. "Saints and Sinners: Roman Catholic and Protestant Spirituality in the Sixteenth Century." In *Christian Spirituality II: High Middle Ages and Reformation*, ed. Jill Raitt, in collaboration with Bernard McGinn and John Meyendorff, 454–63. New York: Crossroad, 1987.

Raser, H. E. "Holiness Movement." In *Dictionary of Christianity in America*, ed. Daniel G. Reid et al., 543–47. Downers Grove, IL: InterVarsity, 1990.

Reetzke, James, ed. *M. E. Barber*. Chicago: Chicago Bibles and Books, 2000. No pages. Online: http://www.jesusloversincleveland.org/English/biographies/mebarber/me1lvprt.htm.

Roberts, Dana. *Secrets of Watchman Nee*. Gainesville, FL: Bridge-Logos, 2005.

Rothberg, Donald. "Contemporary Epistemology and the Study of Mysticism." In *The Problem of Pure Consciousness: Mysticism and Philosophy*, ed. Robert K. Forman, 163–210. New York: Oxford University Press, 1990.

Ruddy, Deborah Wallace. *A Christological Approach to Virtue: Augustine and Humility*. PhD diss., Boston College, 2001.

Ruusbroec, John. *The Spiritual Espousals and Other Works*. Translated and Introduction by James A. Wiseman, OSB. Preface by Louis Dupré. Classics of Western Spirituality. Mahwah, NJ: Paulist, 1985.

The Sayings of the Desert Fathers: The Alphabetical Collection. Translated by Benedicta Ward. Rev. ed. Kalamazoo, MI: Cistercian Publications, 1984.

Schiefelbein, Dennis. "A Lutheran Confessional Critique of the Function of the Union with Christ in the Theology of Watchman Nee." STM thesis, Concordia Seminary, 1979.

Schneiders, Sandra M. "A Hermeneutical Approach to the Study of Christian Spirituality." *Christian Spirituality Bulletin* 2 (Spring 1994) 9–14.

———. "Scripture and Spirituality." In *Christian Spirituality I: Origins to the Twelfth Century*, ed. Bernard McGinn, John Meyendorff, and Jean Leclercq, 1–20. New York: Crossroad, 1985.

———. "The Study of Christian Spirituality: Contours and Dynamics of a Discipline." *Christian Spirituality Bulletin* 6 (Spring 1998) 1–12.

Schweizer, E. "Pneuma." In *Theological Dictionary of the New Testament*, ed. G. Friedrich, trans. G. W. Bromiley, vol. 6, 332–455. Grand Rapids, MI: Eerdmans, 1968.

Scofield, C. I. *Rightly Dividing the Word of Truth*. Grand Rapids, MI: Zondervan, 1965.

Scroggs, Robin. "New Being: Renewed Mind: New Perception." In *The Text and the Times: New Testament Essays for Today*, ed. Robin Scroggs, 167–83. Minneapolis, MN: Fortress, 1993.

Sell, Phillip W. "A Theological Critique of the Spiritual Life Teaching of Watchman Nee." ThM thesis, Dallas Theological Seminary, 1979.

Senn, Frank C., ed. *Protestant Spiritual Traditions*. New York: Paulist, 1986.

Sheldrake, Philip, SJ. *Spirituality and History: Questions of Interpretation and Method*. Rev. ed. Maryknoll, NY: Orbis, 1995.

———. *Spirituality and Theology: Christian Living and the Doctrine of God*. Maryknoll, NY: Orbis, 1998.

Shelley, B. L. "Keswick Movement." In *Dictionary of Christianity in America*, ed. Daniel G. Reid et al., 612–13. Downers Grove, IL: InterVarsity, 1990.

Siu, Paul. "The Doctrine of Man in the Theology of Watchman Nee." ThM thesis, Bethel Theological Seminary, 1979.

Spohn, William C., SJ. *Go and Do Likewise: Jesus and Ethics*. New York: Continuum, 2003.

———. "Pragmatism and the Glory of God: An American Reading of Ignatian Discernment." In *The Labor of God: An Ignatian View of Church and Culture*, ed. William J. O'Brien, 23–44. Washington, DC: Georgetown University Press, 1991.

Stackhouse, J. G. "Plymouth (Christian) Brethren." In *Dictionary of Christianity in America*, ed. Daniel G. Reid et al., 914. Downers Grove, IL: InterVarsity, 1990.

Stowers, Stanley K. "Paul on the Use and Abuse of Reason." In *Greeks, Romans, and Christians: Essays in Honor of Abraham J. Malherbe*, ed. David L. Balch et al., 253–86. Minneapolis, MN: Fortress, 1990.

Sumiko, Yamamoto. *History of Protestantism in China: The Indigenization of Christianity.* Tokyo: Toho Gakkai, 2000.

Sze, Newman [史伯誠]. *Ni Tuosheng xundao shi* [倪柝聲殉道史, The martyrdom of Watchman Nee]. Culver City, CA: Testimony Publications, 1995.

Teresa of Avila. *The Interior Castle.* Translated by J. Venard. Sydney: E. J. Dwyer, 1980.

Thomas àKempis. *The Imitation of Christ.* In *Christian Classics: The Confessions of Saint Augustine, The Imitation of Christ, Pilgrim's Progress.* London: Hodder & Stoughton, 1997.

Thunberg, Lars, and Bernard McGinn. "The Human Person as Image of God." In *Christian Spirituality I: Origins to the Twelfth Century*, ed. Bernard McGinn, John Meyendorff, and Jean Leclercq, 291–330. New York: Crossroad, 1985.

Toner, Jules, SJ. "Discernment in the Spiritual Exercises." In *A New Introduction to the Spiritual Exercises of St. Ignatius*, ed. John E. Dister, 63–72. Collegeville, MN: Liturgical, 1993.

Tracy, David. "Part I." In *Blessed Rage for Order: The New Pluralism in Theology*, 3–87. New York: Seabury, 1975.

Traherne, Thomas. *Centuries.* Oxford: A. R. Mowbray, 1985.

Travis, W. G. "Revivalism, Protestant." In *Dictionary of Christianity in America*, ed. Daniel G. Reid et al., 1012–15. Downers Grove, IL: InterVarsity, 1990.

Tung, Siu Kwan. "The Waves of the 'Local Church,' I, II." *Bridge* 56 (Nov–Dec 1992) 2–23.

———. "The Waves of the 'Local Church,' III, IV." *Bridge* 57 (Jan–Feb 1993) 2–23.

Turner, Denys. "Apophaticism, Idolatry and the Claims of Reason." In *Silence and the Word: Negative Theology and Incarnation*, ed. Oliver Davies and Denys Turner, 11–34. Cambridge: Cambridge University Press, 2002.

Tyson, John R, ed. *Invitation to Christian Spirituality: An Ecumenical Anthology.* New York: Oxford University Press, 1999.

Underhill, Evelyn. *Evelyn Underhill: Modern Guide to the Ancient Quest for the Holy.* Edited by Dana Greene. Albany: State University of New York Press, 1988.

———. *The Ways of the Spirit.* Edited by Grace Adolphsen Brame. New York: Crossroad, 1997.

Varg, Paul A. *Missionaries, Chinese and Diplomats: The American Protestant Missionary Movement in China, 1890–1952.* Princeton, NJ: Princeton University Press, 1958.

Vine, W. E., et al. *Vine's Complete Expository Dictionary of Old and New Testament Words with Topical Index.* Nashville, TN: Thomas Nelson, 1996.

Von Balthasar, Hans Urs. *Thérèse of Lisieux: The Story of a Mission.* Translated by Donald Nichol. New York: Sheed and Ward, 1954.

Waaijman, Kees. "Discernment: Its History and Meaning." *Studies in Spirituality* 7 (1997) 5–41.

———. *Spirituality: Forms, Foundations, Methods.* Translated by John Vriend. Studies in Spirituality Supplement 8. Leuven: Peeters, 2002.

———. "The Soul as Spiritual Core Concept: A Scriptural Viewpoint." *Studies in Spirituality* 6 (1996) 5–19.

———. "Transformation: A Key Word in Spirituality." *Studies in Spirituality* 8 (1998) 5–37.

Wan, Milton Wai-yiu [溫偉耀]. "Jidujiao de zongjiao jingyan: ren yu shen 'you qingyi de xiangyu'" [基督教的宗教經驗：人與神「有情意的相遇」, The religious experience in Christianity: the personal encounter between human and God).] Chapter 4 of *Jidujiao yu Zhongguo de xiandaihua* [基督教與中國的現代化, Christianity and the modernization of China]. Vol. 1 of *Christian Faith in Chinese Perspective*, 77–148. Hong Kong: Christian Excellent Mission, 2001.

———. "Lun jidujiao yu Zhongguo xinyang zhong de chaoyue tiyan" [論基督教與中國信仰中的超越體驗, Two models of transcendence: towards a Christian reconsideration of Chinese philosophic experience of self-transcendence]. In *Jidujiao yu Zhongguo wenhua de xiangyu* [基督教與中國文化的相遇, Encounter between Christianity and Chinese culture], ed. Lung-kwong Lo, 105–220. Hong Kong: Chung Chi College, Chinese University of Hong Kong, 2001.

Wan, Xiaoling [萬小玲]. "Wan Xiaoling de jianzheng" [萬小玲的見證, The testimony of Wan Xiaoling]. In *Dui zai pidou Ni Tuosheng de pingyi* [對再批鬥倪柝聲的平議, Countering the new censure on Watchman Nee], ed. James Yu et al., 56–60. Hong Kong: Golden Lampstand, 2004.

Wang, Weifan [汪維藩]. *Zhongguo shenxue ji qi wenhua yuanyuan* [中國神學及其文化淵源, Chinese theology and its cultural sources]. Nanjing: Jin Ling Xie He Shen Xue Yuan, 1997.

Wang, Zhixin [王治心]. *Zhongguo jidujiao shigang* [中國基督教史綱, A concise history of Christianity in China). Introduction by Xu Yihua. Shanghai: Shanghai Gu Ji Chu Ban She, 2004.

Watson, David Lowes. "Methodist Spirituality." In *Protestant Spiritual Traditions*, ed. Frank C. Senn, 217–73. New York: Paulist, 1986.

Weil, Simone. *Waiting for God*. Translated by Emma Craufurd. New York: Harper & Row, 1973.

Wesley, John. "A Plain Account of Christian Perfection." In *John and Charles Wesley: Selected Prayers, Hymns, Journal Notes, Sermons, Letters and Treatises*, ed. and Introduction by Frank Whaling, 297–377. Classics of Western Spirituality. New York: Paulist, 1981.

———. "Minutes of Several Conversations between the Rev. Mr. Wesley and Others from the Year 1744, to the Year 1789." In *The Works of John Wesley*, vol. 8, 299–338. Grand Rapids, MI: Zondervan, 1958.

Westphal, Merold. "A Reader's Guide to Reformed Epistemology." *Religious and Theological Studies Fellowship Bulletin* 10 (Jan–Feb 1996) 11–14.

Wetmore, Robert K. "An Analysis of Nee's Doctrine of Dying and Rising with Christ as It Relates to Sanctification." ThM thesis, Trinity Evangelical Divinity School, 1983.

Wickeri, Philip L. "Making Connections: Christianity and Culture in the Sino-American Dialogue." *Chinese Theological Review* 11 (1997) 54–70.

———. *Seeking the Common Ground: Protestant Christianity, the Three-Self Movement, and China's United Front*. Maryknoll, NY: Orbis, 1988.

Willard, Dallas. *Hearing God: Developing a Conversational Relationship with God*. Downers Grove, IL: InterVarsity Press, 1999.

———. *The Spirit of the Disciplines: Understanding How God Changes Lives*. New York: HarperCollins, 1990.

Williams, Rowan. "Teaching the Truth." In *Living Tradition: Affirming Catholicism in the Anglican Church*, ed. Jeffrey John, 29–43. Cambridge, MA: Cowley, 1992.

———. *The Wound of Knowledge: Christian Spirituality from the New Testament to St. John of the Cross.* 2d ed. Cambridge, MA: Cowley, 1991.

Wu, Dongsheng John. "Humility, Maturity, and Transformation: Theological, Feminist, and Psychological Dialogue on RB 7." *American Benedictine Review* 58:2 (June 2007) 182–208.

Wu, Kuang-ming. "Chinese Mysticism." In *Mysticism and the Mystical Experience: East and West*, ed. Donald H. Bishop, 230–59. Selinsgrove, PA: Susquehanna University Press, 1995.

Wu, Silas [吳秀良]. *Po ke feiteng—Ni Tuosheng de beiqiu yu tuibian* [破殼飛騰—倪柝聲的被囚與蛻變, Breaking out and flying—the imprisonment and transformation of Watchman Nee]. Boston, MA: Pishon River, 2004.

Wu, Zhuguang [吳主光]. "Yong aixin shuo chengshi hua" [用愛心説誠實話, Speaking the truth in love]. In *Dui zai pidou Ni Tuosheng de pingyi* [對再批鬥倪柝聲的平議, Countering the new censure on Watchman Nee], ed. James Yu et al., 83–89. Hong Kong: Golden Lampstand, 2004.

Wyschogrod, Edith. *Saints and Postmodernism: Revisioning Moral Philosophy.* Chicago: University of Chicago Press, 1990.

Xu, Hong-du [許宏度], ed. *Shuling shiji de zhuixun: cong shengjing, lishi, shenxue kan Ni Tuosheng de sixiang* [屬靈實際的追尋: 從聖經, 歷史, 神學看倪柝聲的思想, Seeking for spiritual reality: viewing Watchman Nee's thought from the biblical, historical, and theological perspectives]. Taipei: China Evangelical Seminary, 2003.

Yates, John. "How Does God Speak To Us Today: Biblical Anthropology and the Witness of the Holy Spirit." *Churchman* 107, no. 2 (1993) 102–29.

Ying, Fuk-tsang [邢福增]. *Fandi, aiguo, Shuling Ren—Ni Tuosheng yu jidutu juhuichu yanjiu* [反帝 ·愛國 ·屬靈人—倪柝聲與基督徒聚會處研究, Anti-imperialism, patriotism and the Spiritual Man: a study on Watchman Nee and the "Little Flock"]. Hong Kong: Christian Study Centre on Chinese Religion and Culture, 2005.

Yip, Ka-che. *Religion, Nationalism and Chinese Students: The Anti-Christian Movement of 1922–1927.* Bellingham, WA: Western Washington University, 1980.

Yu, James [于中旻] et al. *Dui zai pidou Ni Tuosheng de pingyi* [對再批鬥倪柝聲的平議, Countering the new censure on Watchman Nee]. Hong Kong: Golden Lampstand, 2004.

Yuan, Simon [元西門]. *Zhongguo jiaohui shi* [中國教會史, Chinese church history]. Lomita, CA: Overseas Campus Magazine, 1999.

Zhuang, Bai-yi [莊百億]. "Ni Tuosheng shengping yanjiu" [倪柝聲生平研究, A study of Watchman Nee's life]. MDiv thesis, Taipei: China Evangelical Seminary, 1985.